Dedicated to God

Dedicated to God

An Oral History of Cloistered Nuns

ABBIE REESE

OXFORD
UNIVERSITY PRESS

OXFORD
UNIVERSITY PRESS

Oxford University Press is a department of the University of Oxford.
It furthers the University's objective of excellence in research, scholarship,
and education by publishing worldwide.

Oxford   New York
Auckland   Cape Town   Dar es Salaam   Hong Kong   Karachi
Kuala Lumpur   Madrid   Melbourne   Mexico City   Nairobi
New Delhi   Shanghai   Taipei   Toronto

With offices in
Argentina   Austria   Brazil   Chile   Czech Republic   France   Greece
Guatemala   Hungary   Italy   Japan   Poland   Portugal   Singapore
South Korea   Switzerland   Thailand   Turkey   Ukraine   Vietnam

Published in the United States of America by
Oxford University Press
198 Madison Avenue, New York, NY 10016

ISBN 978-0-19-994793-5

9 8 7 6 5 4 3 2 1
Printed in the United States of America
on acid-free paper

For Evan, Gabriel, and Eve

Contents

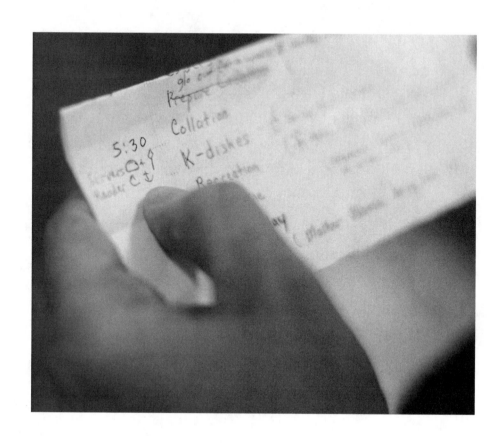

Preface

I really think the presence of God would be the sense that you have. I think that's the sense that the people have when they come here; they can tell this is a place of God. And that's a special and wonderful thing, to have a place that's dedicated to God. If I'm meant to be dedicated to God as His spouse, I need to be in a place like this. This is the certain monastery that He decided, in His wisdom, that I belong here, and that this is the place that is the best for me.

Sister Mary Monica of the Holy Eucharist

A South African friend once described the documentation of others' stories by way of biblical tradition; he referred to God's instructions to the Israelites, to set up memorial stones as visual memories that would call to mind oral histories of the hardships, triumphs, and God's miraculous interventions.

Oral history still yields these markers. The stories can serve as pillars and reminders for present and future generations. As I worked on this book about the Poor Clare Colettine Order in Rockford, Illinois, the community's newest and youngest member, Sister Maria Benedicta, said to me, "I'm sure anyone who falls in love, they look back and say, 'Oh, remember how we met? Or how he showed his love?' It's the same, how God has shown His personal love. I think it's a joy to look back."

I was drawn to the cloistered monastery, something of a cultural time capsule, in part because the nuns do not "need" to be seen. At the outset, I probably had the incomplete sense that cloistered monastic nuns are not keen on public performance because they are hidden from public view. I assumed that the nuns perform their idealized selves, that they marry their ideal spouse, that they inhabit a societal role that represents an ideal. I expected more uniformity of belief than I encountered: It takes years for members to be socialized into a cloistered subculture, where communication is abbreviated and silence is observed. One nun's great-niece, when she was four years old, described her visits to the monastery as trips to "the Jesus cage." The nuns, who find the description amusing, make this distinction: The enclosure, rather than restricting them, offers freedom; the grille keeps the world out. The nuns revealed themselves, in one-on-one interviews, as self-deprecating and humorous, with a diversity of beliefs—opinions they did not know they did not share with one another because they observed monastic silence and did not have occasion to discuss matters they shared with me. Removing themselves from a visible, wider audience still impacts the congruity of their performances; there are high stakes in becoming absent from the world in order to enact one's beliefs for God. The rest of the community bears witness within the highly ritualized space that oscillates between the concrete and physical (demanding manual labor), and the intangible and virtual (prayers).

When I have talked about this oral history and photography project (and more recently, my filmmaking work with the community of cloistered monastic nuns), the most consistent, often pressing question is as predictable as the Liturgy of the Hours: How did I gain access? The short answer might seem evasive. Like any practice built on social contracts and long-term relationships, access is a matter of trust and negotiation. The fuller answer to this question of access begins with the recognition that any form of ethnographic work is a complicated endeavor; representing others and representing otherness are problematic territories, following an imperialistic tradition of exploiting native resources. The truth is, too, that it is difficult to dissect the evolution of a relationship or to unravel a process that unfolds fluidly. This work has probably sustained my intense focus because I find it challenging and nuanced.

My engagement with this community was predicated by variables that I could not have fully understood at the outset: the peculiar insider-outsider dynamic; a subculture facing an uncertain future (their possible extinction due to dwindling numbers); questions of power relations within the monastic hierarchy; and the contradictory nature inherent in a project that asks members of an insulated community (who seek anonymity, have limited contact with their closest loved ones, and observe monastic silence) to talk about themselves.

I began this project with a question: What compels a woman in this era of overexposure—at a time with the technological means to reach a global audience—to make a drastic, lifelong, countercultural decision for her life, in favor of obscurity? My assumption was that it would be of value to learn about the motivations and the lives of women who make vows of poverty, chastity, obedience, and enclosure. Cloistered monastic nuns mediate on behalf of humanity, believing that their prayers and penances can change the course of history.

I am not Catholic. During my first visit to the Corpus Christi Monastery, I explained that to the Mother Abbess. I said that I wanted to undertake a project about the lives of cloistered monastic nuns ever since I read an article about a trend, in Italy, of young women joining religious orders and wanting, in my recollection, a return to the habit. The way I remember the article, some of the women were the daughters of fashion designers. I told Mother Miryam that I did not know yet what form the project would take but that I wanted to work long-term with the community.

I acknowledged in our first meeting my awareness that monasteries were closing and that the number of women seeking religious life in the States was dwindling. She agreed; with changes following Vatican II, she said that nuns wearing habits are not as prevalent in mainstream culture's visual vocabulary. She said that nuns had been "erased from the landscape." Mother Miryam told me she would take my request under advisement and consult with the Vicaress, the other members of the elected council, and the rest of the community. A few weeks later, the answer was "yes"; I know now that the answer was "yes," by increments.

I was new, then, to the practice of oral history. As a teenager studying toward an undergraduate degree in history, I was prejudiced to be wary of traditional historical accounts, which have often privileged stories told from the perspective of the powerful, the victors in war, rather than the individuals and subcultures living on the fringe of the mainstream—those who are not compelled to add to the historical record with their own narratives. Having worked as a journalist and questioned some of that field's premises and practices, particularly interrogating distinctions between private performances and public lives, I took to the discipline of oral history when I first encountered it; I appreciated the pioneering figure of Alessandro Portelli, who called attention to the fact that memory, including collective memory, is faulty. When I first heard an elder in the field of oral history, perhaps when I was a fellow at Columbia University's Oral History Research Office Summer Institute in 2008, summarize a philosophy of oral history as advocating coauthorship and shared authority, this resonated with me.[1] A few years later, when I presented this work-in-progress at the Oral History in the Mid-Atlantic Region's annual conference, I was struck by another speaker's comments; Patrick Hurley, a political ecologist, said that whereas history can collapse identity, oral history features a multiplicity of identities.[2] I believe that we create stories to lend meaning, to call attention to themes, to explain our experiences. These stories reveal emotional and transcendent truths. As the South African journalist and poet Antjie Krog wrote of her homeland's struggle to reconcile after the horrors of apartheid: "We tell stories not to die of life."[3]

In working with the nuns, I demonstrated my rigor, my sincerity, my earnestness. I demonstrated, too, that I did not know enough of the culture. I think now that it took too long to realize that the nuns stand up as a sign of respect when the Mother Abbess walks into the room. (The first half-dozen times I visited with the Mother Abbess, though, I had a private audience; it was only when another nun was sitting and talking to me and the Mother Abbess walked into the room that I saw the nun stand. I then learned of the practice.) Only after I had extended my hand through holes in the metal grille in greeting the nuns did I realize that they do not, as a rule, touch even their loved ones; however, they will not refuse a hand that is extended to them. I course-corrected. The interviews continued. I was invited into the enclosure to make photographs. I respected their values and I picked up, probably intuitively and subconsciously at first, and then echoed their indirect style of communication. In retrospect, I understand that patience underscored this process. I made various requests; I waited. The nuns were gracious as I learned their culture. At times, I inadvertently tested the limits and was met with none-too-subtle jesting. During one of my first visits, in 2005, I asked the Mother Abbess if I could be "a fly on the wall" during one young woman's upcoming visit, when the two would discuss her interest in becoming a Poor Clare nun. My request was granted. Maybe thirty minutes into their conversation, I asked a question. The Mother Abbess glanced at me. "A fly, eh?" she said. "I wish I had a swatter!" I laughed nervously. She looked at me sternly, then smiled.

In tracing the lineage of this project, it seems constructive to describe my methodology by way of analogy. One day, while interviewing Sister Mary

Monica, I asked if she could talk about her notions of or experiences with mysticism. She mentioned a movie about Saint Faustina—"a true mystic," Sister Mary Monica said, "in that she gave up everything to be united with Christ." She continued: "So there it is. A true mystic is someone who gives up everything to be united with Christ, and so in that way we all can be mystics." She told me that in the monastery I should not expect to hear a lot of stories about mystical "experiences," that if anyone did have those experiences, she probably would not want to advertise it. Referring to Saint Teresa of Avila, who is said to have searched for God in her daily routines (in the "pots and pans"), Sister Mary Monica said, "I have to say I'm really plain Jane. I think that God speaks to me in the pots and pans. I think God is training me through the everyday life. I just need to be faithful where I am."

In a similar way, I think that the practice of oral history can be described as tending to the everyday, the "pots and pans." Other practitioners in the field of oral history have advised: *Consider the silences, the voices seldom heard in popular culture.* Cloistered nuns pursue anonymity and hiddenness; their tombstones do not document their birth names or birth dates. To respect the nuns' value of hiddenness and their desire for anonymity, we agreed that each would choose a pseudonym; their actual religious names would not be used. (At the Corpus Christi Monastery, the Mother Abbess assigns each woman her religious name; a postulant can submit three suggestions, and she is renamed during the Clothing Ceremony, when she progresses from postulant to novice.) The Vicaress chose the name Sister Maria Deo Gratias, Latin for "thanks be to God," because, she said, "If you're asking me about my vocation, that name depicts it. It's 'thanks be to God,' because it's all God's doing." The nuns also selected pseudonyms for their childhood names, for their lives before they were given religious names. One chose a pseudonym that was her actual childhood nickname; another chose the name of her niece.

After Mother Miryam and the community agreed to this project, each member decided whether or not she wanted to participate. One of the nuns explained her hesitancy to be interviewed but how she was compelled to take part. "Mother Abbess asked me," Sister Sarah Marie said. "I was like, 'Oh!' Just from the depths of me, 'Oh, Mother, no. What does she want to talk to me for?'" Mother Miryam told Sister Sarah Marie that I had seen the vase of roses on the ledge of the grille and had learned that when Sister Sarah Marie's mother died, in that same town, her body had been brought

into the parlor for one final goodbye. "I was moaning and groaning," Sister
Sarah Marie said. "So I said, 'You pray about it, Mother Abbess, and whatever you want me to do, I'll do. If you want me to talk to Abbie, I'll do it.
But if you don't want me to talk to Abbie, I won't. You know my gut feeling
is I'd rather not. But the only way I'm going to know God's will on this is
through you, so you let me know.' So she told me, 'I think you should talk
to her. I think maybe she'll understand our life a little bit more.' See this is
what's wonderful about these superiors." Sister Sarah Marie then said that
she teased the Mother Abbess that "God's going to get you." "But it was up to
her to decide," Sister Sarah Marie said. "She knew my feeling, my gut feeling;
I'd prefer not to because we live a hidden life. This is so precious to us. But
Mother Abbess can see an insight into this, sees something more than I can
see. She has a bit more direct contact with God than I do. Fine."

If Mother Miryam convinced Sister Sarah Marie to participate, Sister Sarah
Marie then encouraged others to take part in the oral history interviews.
Often, by way of introduction, the nuns would greet me for the first time
and say that they heard I was not what one expects of a journalist or reporter
or interviewer. One nun described herself as "social" and told me, "I love
to talk"; she seemed especially gratified by the connection afforded by this
project and she arranged, within the constraints of her community, more
visits (telling Mother Miryam and me that she would be happy to meet with
me again, if I would like).

Once, Sister Mary Nicolette broached me with a dilemma. I knew by then
that the nuns relied on a number of individuals for daily provisions, such
as a weekly donation of milk, an occasional box of fish, and help driving to
appointments. Sister Mary Nicolette had asked permission from the Mother
Abbess to share with me that in the past the nuns hand-poured candles to
sell in their gift shop; they needed a precise thickness of wick and had lost
their old connection. I told Sister Mary Nicolette that I could research this on
the Internet and bring her the results. She hesitated, not wanting to impose
on my time. I assured her it was no trouble. I found a supplier, purchased
the wick online for less than $20, and had it shipped to the monastery.
When I visited again, I declined the nuns' offers for reimbursement. I did
this without hesitation or much reflection at the time. I believe in retrospect
that this gesture impacted the dynamics of trust. This may have been, in
anthropological terms, my contribution toward a gift exchange.

The nuns refer to themselves as "mothers of souls." As counterintuitive as it might seem, at first blush, that cloistered nuns would choose to participate in a project that brings attention to themselves, they voiced many times the possibility that young women might learn about the cloistered monastic vocation, which could lead to prospective members of their community. Another factor influenced their involvement. Saint Clare, the founder of their order, is the Patron Saint of Television. The nuns express a feeling of responsibility for the world beyond their enclosure, the hope that sharing their own life stories might further their mission as hidden witnesses.

Dedicated to God

Introduction

Left to the human condition, we fail. But when we have a structure and we have God calling us, for instance to poverty, chastity, and obedience, then it's like a gift. It's a way of providing us to respond to God more fully. Those are all gifts that we give to God. And in giving those gifts, definitely we receive from Him. He's not God way out there and He doesn't care. There's a personal relationship. So then I say, "I take you Lord for my all," and I know that God is my enough. I don't need to give myself in marriage, beautiful as it is.

Sister Maria Deo Gratias of the Most Blessed Sacrament

Like a crack magician, she pulls a photograph from a pocket hidden within the folds of her uniform. She shows no irony and does not register my surprise. She is presenting me a gift, showing me what she looked like before she came here a quarter century ago. She holds up the photo, and then slides it under the metal bars for closer inspection. I see an attractive twentysomething with teased hair and a revealing top.

She places a few more photographs on the ledge in front of me. She is smiling in each, caught midlaugh. She appears to be the center of attention, comfortable in her assigned or assumed role of entertainer. She claims she played the part well: the extrovert who knew how to have a good time.

Sister Sarah Marie, whom I have come to know as direct and self-deprecating—"Italian" is the word she thinks best captures her personality—wants me to study one of the photos and note the difference between her small nose in the picture and the big nose before me now. The reality of her improved features in the photograph is an illusion, she says; she wore makeup back then and knew how to apply it.

Maybe I did not seem convinced before today when we talked about her life on the outside. If the photos do not make the point clear enough, she states it bluntly: Sister Sarah Marie was "normal" before she entered. This information—not the tangible object before me—is the gift. She wants me to know that she and the other women who joined this cloistered monastery, who made the three universal vows marking all men and women in religious life—vows of poverty, chastity, and obedience—along with a fourth vow of enclosure, were once quite average.

In her twenties, when she was known as Tiffany, she intended to get married. "I always got along with men," she says. "I never had a problem with them. I never had that feminist problem when they opened the door for me. I always enjoyed their company. I always had guys as just friends. It was just natural. There it is."

Before embracing anonymity, before surrendering her name and shoes and freedom of movement for a demanding life in one of the strictest orders, she and the other members of this community dressed up and went on dates. One wanted to be a "cowboy."

I have interacted with Sister Sarah Marie on occasion since 2005, as I have worked on an oral history and photography project with her community of cloistered monastic nuns at the Corpus Christi Monastery in Rockford, Illinois. Members of the eight-hundred-year-old Poor Clare Colettine Order seek anonymity and observe monastic silence. A metal grille separates the nuns' enclosure from the outside world. Family members are allowed a limited number of visits each year, always separated by the metal grille.

The calling to cloistered monastic life took many of the Rockford Poor Clares by surprise. It defied their God-given temperament. It violated dreams. It dashed plans for marriage and children. It meant their world would shrink, temporally, to a fourteen-acre campus, so that their minds could dwell on God.

Several nuns volunteered, in the course of the oral history interviews, that outsiders label their life as a form of escapism. They took pains to point out that religious life is not a rejection of the world or its inhabitants; the enclosure is instead a means for embracing humanity, a calling to, not a running from. This is not a place for the faint of heart or for women who could not survive elsewhere in the world. Mother Miryam says life in an enclosure is easier if a woman is functional, or "whole," and that members should strive for wholeness, as humans, and for holiness.

"You know what you expect?" Sister Sarah Marie asks. " 'Yes, Abbie, that's true, I am in this life and it is beautiful.' Quiet. Never says a word. Shy. Withdrawn. You expect most women that would come here are introverted, withdrawn; maybe somebody should interview us that is majoring in abnormal psychology. But you have to be normal to live this life, Abbie. You have to be real normal. You have to date, go to parties. Because I think when you enter an enclosure, if you're abnormal, it's going to come out—if there's something wrong. In the active world, you can keep it under for a little bit, if you've got a little psychological disorder. Not here, Abbie. Not here. That's why, I mean, when they think, 'They must be a little bit dingy to be back there', it's just the opposite."

According to the treatise *Verbi Sponsa: Instruction on the Contemplative Life and on the Enclosure of Nuns*, a publication that is given to all Poor Clare postulants when they enter the Corpus Christi Monastery as part of their formation, a cloistered contemplative yearns for "fulfillment in God, in an uninterrupted nostalgia of the heart," and with a "monastic recollection" that enables a constant focus on the presence of God, her "journey slows down and the final destination disappears from view."[1]

Pope John Paul II described the institutes whose members are completely devoted to contemplation as "for the Church a reason for pride and a source of heavenly graces. By their lives and mission, the members of these Institutes imitate Christ in His prayer on the mountain, bear witness to God's lordship over history and anticipate the glory which is to come."[2]

A daily schedule alternates prayer and manual labor. In the Corpus Christi Monastery, the Blessed Sacrament is not exposed perpetually, twenty-four hours a day, seven days a week; that would require constant shifts, one member of the community always absent to be with the Blessed Sacrament in prayer and adoration. The community values togetherness, and so the Rockford Poor Clares observe a prolonged exposition of the Blessed Sacrament, with one nun in the presence of the Blessed Sacrament during the day, and often through the night.

The nuns make altar breads that are shipped off to different churches. They tend their gardens, growing many of the vegetables they eat and solving bug troubles by slipping nylon stockings over the cabbage heads. They repair benches in their woodshop, fully equipped after one woman entered decades ago and had her tools delivered to the monastery. A small gift shop sits at the entrance of the monastery, where the Poor Clares sell Communion veils that a few of them sew, cards that others make with pressed flowers, and rosaries they bead using Job's Tears grown on their property. They pray, while working on these items, for the person who will come into possession of them. The nuns see the shop as a form more of outreach than of revenue; they depend on benefactors for food and monetary donations. Through the benefactors, their trust in God is realized.

Here, the cloistered nun becomes anonymous to the world. She is hidden from view. Each follows her convictions at incredible personal cost. A few describe that when they first felt called to religious life, it seemed "too radical." Some families were so adamantly against monastic life, which appeared so restrictive to them, that they ended all contact after their daughter or sister became a Poor Clare Colettine. For others, the decision to enter a contemplative order could not have been more natural.

Sister Maria Deo Gratias recalls the moment she was called. She was in her sixth-grade classroom when she heard a directive to go to the chapel after school. Before the Blessed Sacrament, she says, "I knew I would be His the moment I knelt down." Although she was not yet familiar with the terminology for giving her life totally to the unseen entity she believed spoke directly to her heart, she told God, "I will marry you."

"From the experience I had," she says, "I never doubted ever my vocation from that moment on. I was His." Since then, she has accepted each degree of commitment that has opened before her, from the aspirature (a boarding school for girls interested in pursuing religious life), to the active order of nuns where she worked first as a gym teacher and later on at a hospital psychiatric ward (having trained in pastoral care), to her life now at the Corpus Christi Monastery.

To her, the challenge is basic: Become a saint.

Others in her community are less stoical. They share their doubts and struggles. In pursuit of perfection, they list the practical challenges, chief among them, twenty women sharing a kitchen. Each sleeps on a carpet-stuffed mattress; the older generations remember stuffing their pillows and mattresses with straw. They rise at midnight, four hours after retiring for sleep, to pray at the first of seven scheduled prayers in the Divine Office.

Sister Joan Marie, who has lived here longer than any other member, is not sure if, in more than sixty years as a cloistered monastic nun, she has ever adapted. "When things got hard, I got sick," she says. "So I escaped that way."

Mother Miryam was the youngest of twelve siblings, born to parents who modeled a beautiful marriage. "It's hard to give up marriage," she says. "It's hard to give up that type of love. It's hard to give up children." She was moved by her parents' intimacy: "They just worked for each other. You could tell they were very close. Every evening for as long as I could remember, when we were doing the dishes, they would go and sit down. Dad would sit in the big chair and Mom would sit in his lap. Always. Always. Always. There was just always a lot of love and care there."

When she felt called to religious life, she was stymied, intellectually. She thought, "How can I deny life to all the children I could have had? How can I ever do that? It's not right." "Of course," she says now, "it's very simple. It took me a while until it dawned on me: 'Well, if God didn't want you to marry, He never wanted those children to exist.' So that was fine. But it really was a struggle until it finally hit me. 'Don't be so stupid! You could have maybe had ten, twelve children, but God never wanted them to exist if He wanted you to be a religious.'"

Poor Clare nuns devote their lives to prayer and penance and sacrifice; this is what they call their charism—the special spirit and focus of their community. Sister Mary Nicolette describes their charism as "living a life for others. We withdraw from the world into an environment that enables us to make those sacrifices, to call down graces and to obtain graces for people. So it's a willing penance and a loving sacrifice." A select few nuns are assigned the duty of answering phone calls from the outside to a prayer hotline at the monastery and they all pray, seven times a day during the Divine Office, for personal and catastrophic events around the globe. In one of the paradoxes of this life, they believe that in removing themselves from the world and embracing a life of anonymity, unseen and unknown to the world at large, by undertaking lives of self-sacrifice and prayer behind the scenes, they have a greater impact on mankind than if they maintained direct contact with strangers and loved ones. Each member of this community believes that there is power, along with challenges, in this life.

Poor Clare Colettine nuns give up their birth names, as well as all material possessions, as concrete, external signs of their vows. They walk barefoot indoors as a sign of the poverty they embrace. (An exception is that the nuns are permitted to wear shoes as they age.) Just as their lives are anonymous, they are not memorialized in death. Burial takes place in a small cemetery on the property, with a stone marker at the gravesite revealing only the woman's religious name and death date, not her birth name or birth date, to signify the start of her life in eternity.

The nuns operate, although they might not use this term, as agents of change. They intervene in the course of history, believing that their prayers and penances for strangers and family can alter outcomes. At the ceremony when a nun makes final, permanent vows, she hugs her family members for one final time. This sacrifice serves a purpose: The material world is not the end, and their sufferings and martyrdoms allow God's will to become manifest in the world.

Members of this unique subculture live as intermediaries to another realm, and for the afterlife. Cloistered contemplatives "embody the exodus from the world in order to encounter God in the solitude of the 'cloistered desert,' a desert that includes inner solitude, the trials of the spirit and the daily toil of life in community," according to *Verbi Sponsa*.[3]

Expatriates of mainstream culture, the cloistered nuns work to adapt to an ancient religious rule, an enclosed culture loaded with visual imagery and symbolic identifiers. They learn to tie the prayer cord, worn around their waists, with four knots, which represent their four vows. In this highly selective and self-selected subculture, the women choose to enter this place and the community decides whether to receive or reject them when they are eligible to become novices, make temporary vows, and make their final solemn vows, through voting and anonymous ballots.

The nuns observe monastic silence, a custom to preserve their spirit of recollection, speaking only what is necessary in order to complete a task. Even written communication is abbreviated;[4] each nun is assigned a mark when she enters the Corpus Christi Monastery as her identification. The mark—a chalice or crown of thorns or wild rose—is used when the nuns write notes to one another. This symbol is stitched or written with permanent ink on the items the woman is assigned for her use. (She does not own the items, since each gives up her worldly possessions when she joins the community.) The Mother Abbess might assign a mark that corresponds with the Feast Day a woman enters the monastery, or she might be inspired by what she gleans of the woman's spirituality. A former Mother Abbess often assigned new entrants a mark that was one letter from the name Jesus, Joseph, Mary, Francis, Clare, or Colette.

In a place imbued with ritual, where members do not explain every custom, the cloister can be a mystery to its residents. Sister Joan Marie, the community's eldest nun by what the nuns term her rank (of longevity), having joined the monastery before any of the other current members, says, "It seemed very mysterious to me when I first entered, I guess, because I just never knew what was going to happen next. Pretty soon I got onto the rhythm, to the schedule. And now it even seems tighter because I can't make it. I can't run fast enough. But then I was able to keep up."

The cloistered life is one of paradox. The nuns live in the tension of certainty and uncertainty, maintaining deep belief and embodying their convictions in total commitment, yet are aware that they will not experience resolution—or know the results in this lifetime—of their lives of dedication and sacrifice. They are comfortable with the uncertainty.

Six decades after joining the enclosure, Sister Joan Marie can still view monastic life (and convey it) through the eyes of an outsider. She follows the order's strict rules, not knowing the fruits of her life of penance. The nuns perceive that others, even family, even Catholics, do not understand their decision to enter the order. Loved ones have expressed their disdain for their vocation. Some deem their life as irrelevant. Or crazy. Or different, hard to decipher.

A metal grille makes tangible the signature vow—enclosure—of this otherworldly realm, a cultural time capsule. The concrete and symbolic demarcation sets the nuns apart from the world. Even during visits with family (they are allowed up to four visits a year), a nun sits on one side of the grille, inside the enclosure, and she visits with her relatives—out in the world—on the other side of the grille. While the nun and her family could reach through the five-inch square gaps in the seventy-inch-wide by forty-five-inch-high metal grille to holds hands, they are not supposed to touch.

One nun tells an anecdote of an outsider's impressions of the cloister. Sister Sarah Marie's four-year-old great-niece had visited the monastery several times before, when her mother announced another visit. The child had replied, "'Oh, yes, Mommy, that's the one that's in the cage.' And her mom says, 'Caylee!' And she says, 'Yes, Mommy, a Jesus cage.'"

The girl's mother prodded, and the girl described the "bars" she had seen—a zoo-like association with the place where religious women are kept and sometimes seen. Sister Sarah Marie believes the childlike understanding of her life is both profound and humorous. Sister Sarah Marie says it is an apt description of their physical space and their spiritual lives. "A Jesus cage,"

Sister Sarah Marie says. "A little four-year-old. She knew this looked like a little cage at a zoo or something, but she knew it was much deeper than that. This connected Jesus. I thought that was pretty profound. I told the sisters and we all kind of laughed. We laughed and said, 'Yes, the cage.' We laughed and laughed."

The nuns are lighthearted. They laugh at themselves and each other. Sister Maria Deo Gratias commends the nuns charged with maintaining the gardens; if it were her job to tend to the plants, she says, the monastery would host "ever-browns." Their childlike amusement says more about them and their outlook than it reveals of the strict demands of their vows to their order—a religious order the cardinals in Rome were reluctant to approve eight hundred years ago because they said it seemed impossible to live out Saint Clare's high ideals. Sister Mary Nicolette, who is translating from Italian to English a compilation of Poor Clare writings throughout the ages, recently translated this poignant sentence, by the Venerable Mary of Jesus of Agreda (1602–1665): "One of the lofty purposes of Christ coming into the world was to raise up poverty and to teach it to mortals who are horrified by it."

While others struggle to understand the nuns, they consider themselves chosen. They are the brides of Christ. Sister Maria Deo Gratias says,

A person can be very prayerful, and live her life on her own and consecrate herself privately to God; that's a private consecration. But if you want a public consecration, there has to be that acceptance. And then the Church accepts that and then in that acceptance of the superior, you pronounce the three vows. In the very beginning of the Church, that was lived but it wasn't specified in the terms that we say it now.

There was always what we called the Consecration of Virgins; there were some women who would give themselves to God—very early, even in the very beginnings of the Church in the 100s. In the very, very beginning of the Church there were people who set themselves apart to give themselves to God. They lived in chastity, they practiced poverty, and they certainly had obedience, to a limited degree, in the very beginning. Those individuals who were separate formed a community, and they had a superior that they could obey. You still had those who chose to be hermits on their own, just like we have today. We have hermits and consecrated virgins in the world, and then we have those that choose—and it's really a choice because of a divine inspiration that that person feels—that they're called by God to live in a community, so they join a community. And in joining that community, they freely give themselves to God by following the rule and the superior of that community.

The founding of the Poor Clare Colettine Order harkens back to 1212, when Clare Offreduccio, a young woman of noble birth whose parents planned to marry her off to a rich man, slipped away from home on the night of Palm Sunday to follow Saint Francis of Assisi, the founder of three Roman Catholic Franciscan orders: the Friars Minor (the Grey Friars), the Poor Clares (which began when he handed Clare her new garb), and the Third Order (laity who live in the world as Franciscans and who can marry).

Saint Clare, like Saint Francis, was born an aristocrat. Both embraced high ideals to live in absolute poverty and abandon material possessions—to the extent that Saint Francis initially restricted his disciples to one woolen coat and forbade them from wearing shoes. Pope Benedict XVI, in a biographical sketch of Saint Clare of Assisi, refers to her as "one of the best loved saints" whose "testimony shows us how indebted the Church is to courageous women, full of faith like her, who can give a crucial impetus to the Church's renewal."[5]

Saint Francis turned over the Church of San Damiano to Saint Clare for her new order to use as a convent.[6] The first woman to write a rule for a monastic community, Saint Clare met with resistance to her "Privilege of Poverty" from church authorities. Based on Saint Francis's ideal of utter poverty, the rule established that members of the community would not own any possessions, even the building they inhabited; this was deemed too extreme and impractical, impossible to live by. But at last, in 1253 Saint Clare's rule was approved.

Saint Clare's biological sister Agnes, her mother, an aunt, and a niece joined her community of Poor Ladies. In the 1300s, when the Poor Clare Order became lax in enforcing its original rule of possessing nothing in order to depend solely on God's provisions, Pope Benedict XIII nominated Colette of Corbie (a French hermit) to reform the order. The existing monasteries and new foundations that followed the reformed Holy Rule became known as Poor Clare Colettines.

The Poor Clare Colettines arrived in the United States with Mother Mary von Elmendorff of Dusseldorf, Germany, to found a new community in

Cleveland, Ohio. In 1916, following repeated requests by the Rockford, Illinois, diocese, nuns from the Cleveland community arrived in Rockford to start a new foundation.[7] In 1966, Reverend Loras T. Lane, the bishop of Rockford, wrote to the Rockford Poor Clare Colettines, "It is truly significant that the Bishops of Rockford, whose duty is to sustain and strengthen the faith of those entrusted for their care, have always maintained special interest in, and concern for, the welfare and success of your Monastery, wherein a small number of God's beloved souls have been called to serve Him in the cloistered atmosphere of prayer and meditation, of penance and sacrifice."[8]

For four years, the cloistered nuns occupied a Victorian home as their temporary monastery. In 1920, the bishop purchased a former sanitarium for the growing community. The building provided ample space but needed extensive remodeling. When the 1934 improvements were finally paid for, another bishop "encouraged the sisters to begin saving for a new monastery, as he considered the old building a real firetrap," the nuns wrote in their own historical account. "Due to the great increase in the cost of labor and building supplies, many years passed before there was any hope of replacing the temporary buildings in use since 1920."[9] In 1962, the Poor Clare Colettines moved into the newly constructed Corpus Christi Monastery.

"Poor Clare nuns live in utter freedom and simplicity," reads their brochure, entitled *Come Follow Me*.[10] It refers to a 1996 address by Pope John Paul II, in which he stated, "We come to understand the identity of the consecrated person, beginning with his or her complete self-offering, as being comparable to a genuine holocaust." The brochure explains the four vows:

By her vow of poverty the Poor Clare frees herself of all temporal concerns and puts in check the innate desire of man to acquire and possess. She, instead, understands herself to be a steward rather than an owner of God's manifold gifts. By the vow of chastity the Poor Clare expresses the yearning of a heart unsatisfied by any finite love. She proclaims to the whole world that God is enough by freeing her heart of any single human attachment in order to love God alone and all His creatures in Him. By her vow of obedience the Poor Clare freely renounces her own will, which is the most thorough sacrifice the human heart can make. She makes a holocaust of the very center of her being in order to conform her whole heart and will to that of her Beloved Spouse. By the vow of enclosure the Poor Clare leaves behind life in the world and

lives in imitation of Christ's hidden life at Nazareth. Within the enclosure she is free to listen to the voice of the Bridegroom and offer herself
as a victim with Jesus for the salvation of the world.[11]

The Franciscan friar Benet Fonck of the Order of Friars Minor (OFM) has
interacted with the Poor Clare Colettine Order since he joined the Franciscan
Order in 1965. Author of *To Cling with All Her Heart to Him: The Spirituality
of Saint Clare*, Friar Fonck writes that Poor Clares heed Christ's command to
Saint Francis to rebuild the Church and through their "poverty and prayer
and simple proclamation fulfill this mandate in an especially effective and
fruitful way."[12] Many women find contemplative cloistered life attractive,
Friar Fonck writes, "because many of the monasteries are more conservative with full habits and a strict life-style; a good number of contemporary
women seem to find a need satisfied with this kind of order and stability. The generation before them were accustomed to a more free-flowing
and unstructured way of being a member of the Church. As the pendulum
swings, their children have a longing and a need for something more conservative, more structured, and more tradition to satisfy their spiritual needs."[13]
The Corpus Christi Monastery in Rockford is the type of conservative monastery that Friar Fonck describes: The nuns wear the full habit and they adhere
to a strict lifestyle.

In 2012, the Poor Clare Colettine Order celebrated the eight hundredth
anniversary of its founding. But at the same time, the population of religious communities is declining. Over the past four decades, the number
of religious sisters in the United States dropped significantly—69 percent;
from 179,954 in 1965 to 54,018 in 2012—even as the Catholic population
in the country rose. From 1970 to 2010, there was a drop worldwide in
the total number of women religious, from 1,004,304 to 721,935, according to the Georgetown University affiliated Center for Applied Research in
the Apostolate, which conducts social scientific studies about the Catholic
Church.[14] As of 2010, there were twelve Poor Clare Colettine monasteries
in the United States, with a total membership of fewer than two hundred
cloistered nuns. Twenty nuns currently reside within the Corpus Christi
Monastery in Rockford, Illinois.

Sister Maria Deo Gratias says that when young women inquire about
joining the Corpus Christi Monastery, and ask if they can bring a computer
or cell phone into the monastery, she teases them by saying they will have a

cell, but it is not the technology they might be thinking of; they would retire at night to a spartan room.

Until recently, Sister Maria Benedicta was the community's youngest member, a thirtysomething former college softball pitcher who grew up in Kansas and did not see a religious sister in person or in a movie until the fourth grade. Sister Maria Benedicta has embraced the hidden life. She is "good," the older nuns say; she is suited to this life. Sister Maria Benedicta is in the midst of a series of transitions, a process of detoxification from the world and integration into community that takes six years before she commits herself to this space for the rest of her life by professing final, solemn vows of poverty, chastity, obedience, and enclosure.

One afternoon, Sister Maria Benedicta sits and sews with the Mother Abbess. She has completed one year as a postulant and two years as a novice. She hopes to make first vows, a temporary three-year term. The community is scheduled to vote the following day in a yes-no ballot to allow or deny her passage to the next phase. Each member of the community will receive a piece of paper with the word "yes" typed on one side and the word "no" typed on the other; they will circle one word. (In the past, the nuns voted with beans—a white bean indicating "yes" and a dark bean meaning "no"; the new system was put into place to make it easier for the older nuns.)

Sister Maria Benedicta and Mother Miryam spar, verbally. Sister Maria Benedicta mentions the Mother Abbess's recent message to the religious sisters that they are to be a "yes" community. Sister Maria Benedicta coyly seeks reassurance that she will be accepted by consensus. Mother Miryam demurs, saying something about the virtue of patience and not knowing for certain just yet. In truth, there is little doubt that Sister Maria Benedicta will be accepted by the community. She must know this, and so she turns and addresses me, a mostly silent but conspicuous presence. Sister Maria Benedicta counters the wait-and-see approach and jokingly provokes: Do I have extra space in my house?

I say that I do, indeed, have a spare room and could definitely arrange chores for someone with her carpentry skills. At this point, Mother Miryam tells Sister Maria Benedicta that making backup plans could be construed as less than the requisite seriousness needed to join the community. Both women are still teasing. Still, Sister Maria Benedicta blushes and her tone turns solemn. They discuss the demands and the joys of the cloistered monastic life. Sister Maria Benedicta makes clear she really does want this life, within these walls.

She, like the nineteen other women in the Corpus Christi Monastery, wants to become a Poor Clare to devote her life to prayer, to intercede on behalf of humanity. She has left the world because of her devotion to it.

Sister Maria Benedicta continues the detailed work of affixing beads to a veil for her biological sister's upcoming wedding, a ceremony that Sister Maria Benedicta will not attend because she cannot leave the monastery. She falls back on what seems to be second nature; her cheeky analysis amuses Mother Miryam, who is sewing a baptismal gown and bonnet to sell in the gift shop. Sister Maria Benedicta tells Mother Miryam about a conversation that also took place in my presence with her Novice Mistress, Sister Mary Nicolette, earlier that same day in the woodshop. Sister Mary Nicolette, elected by the community to the post, oversees Sister Maria Benedicta's instruction and guides her toward the Poor Clare ideals. While the two stood near a window, sending a plank through the teeth of a table saw, the afternoon sunlight refracted particles of sawdust, which appeared to glow around Sister Mary Nicolette. I photographed the pair and commented on the beautiful imagery. Then I opened myself up to their teasing by saying, earnestly, that the scene looked almost "mystical" or "magical." Both Sister Maria Benedicta and Sister Mary Nicolette laughed. They joked that it was "holy dust," or "mystical dust."

Sister Maria Benedicta suggested that Sister Mary Nicolette should be canonized because the glow proved she is a saint. At this point in Sister Maria Benedicta's retelling, Mother Miryam quips that it is a good thing a photograph documented the event, as that might be the closest Sister Mary Nicolette gets to becoming a saint. Sister Maria Benedicta laughs.

Cloistered monastic nuns submit to a radical life, a hard life, but they rarely allow themselves—or anyone else who enters these walls—to be too pleased with herself or her own progress.

Here, Sister Maria Benedicta is striving for perfection. Here, women who have departed contemporary American culture at various stages over the last century move together in a routine yet timeless space, focused on eternity as they synchronize to the cycle of prayers, manual labor, prayers, sleep, prayers.

They pull weeds and sew veils. This work frees their minds to contemplate God and pray for others.

One day after sewing with Mother Miryam, Sister Maria Benedicta learns that she has, indeed, been accepted by the community and can thus advance and make temporary vows as a Poor Clare Colettine nun. She and her community will continue to discern for the next three years until she can make final vows whether she truly is called to this vocation, in this place.

In a somber, reflective moment, during a one-on-one interview, Sister Maria Benedicta shares her most basic desire. "It's not just that I want to get to heaven," she says. "I want everyone else to get there, too. And it is very urgent. It's life or death, for eternity."

In this pursuit, she wants nothing less than to change the world, anonymously, by living virtue.

Called

Sister Mary Monica
of the Holy Eucharist

I started when I entered: I was counting the first week and I was making percentages. My nickname was Sister Calculata because I was counting and counting and counting. I didn't do this out in the world; I never had something to look forward to as much as this, or something that I thought was really important.

It has been a drain for me, for fifteen years to desire to be our Lord's spouse and to not be able to do so, to long so much for this and to have the longing unfulfilled. Finally, by the Church, I am His spouse and that's a wonderful thing.

When I was real little, I thought about having the call to be a nun. And I decided against it because I really was more interested in the things of the world. I really think it was a call inside from God. I had this feeling that I was never meant to marry—a man anyway. I had this conviction that I was not meant to marry. And it was very strong. I think God was trying to tell me, but I did shut the door. I shut the door. I will admit I really deeply regret that. I really do because I really feel like I said "no" to God. I trust that He makes good out of that, but I will admit that I admire the sisters here that were courageous enough, and self-giving and selfless enough, to give themselves to Jesus right away and not get caught up in what they wanted and the things of the world. I very much admire the sisters here who did that and anyone who did that. But I didn't. And I ended up forgetting about it. I don't think that I ever told anybody about it, but there was one day where I decided no. I was particularly fond of horses. We had a horse farm and the reason we had it was because of me.

I was on our farm and there was one day I was in the barn, and I was just having this real strong feeling inside to be a nun. And, at that point,

I actually reversed the decision. I was cleaning the barn, and I had that feeling about being a nun and I just said, "Okay, Lord, I will give up everything," and I meant it. Even when I was a child, I knew. I knew that if you were asked to give up everything, at that time you should say, "Yes, alright, Lord, I'll give up everything."

I was twenty-six or twenty-seven years old. I made the choice at that time that I would give up everything. I didn't understand the spiritual part, but the material part, I understood what it meant. It meant giving up the farm and the horses and the dogs and everything else. So I made the promise. And I really knew very little, very little, about my faith, to speak of. I'd been working on it, I think, at that time, but I didn't know that much. I hadn't seen that much of sisters, and I didn't know properly what a nun is because sisters are the ones outside that are active, and nuns are usually the ones in the cloister.

We had quite a few horses, and so it really ended up being five years before I got off the farm after I told my parents that I needed to be a nun. I said, "I need to be a nun and I can't wait two years." Oh, that was good! It was five years before I could finish with the farm.

I read *Diary of Saint Maria Faustina Kowalska*. She wasn't a saint at that time; she wasn't even blessed at that time. There was a community that she felt our Lord was asking her to start. It was a cloistered community. The order that Saint Faustina was asked to found, our Lord said, "Your purpose, and that of your companions, is to unite yourselves as closely as possible. Through love, you will reconcile earth with heaven and soften the just anger of God." I liked that idea. I thought that sounded great—a great purpose! I tried to find out if the Divine Mercy movement existed; it didn't exist. I got into contact with some other girls that were interested in starting the community mentioned in the diary, but we went through years and years of seeing if it would work. We would get together and there would be times where some of us would live together for a while, but it never worked out. We found we didn't really seem to have the same call.

But I still felt called, and I had spiritual directors that thought I really was called to do this. I really needed authentic religious training. I was reading this book, *The Spiritual Legacy of Sister Mary of the Holy Trinity*, about a Poor Clare. In the front and back of the book, there were pictures of *this* monastery with little description of the life. I said, "Gee, that really sounds like Saint Faustina's way of life." I thought it would be a very good place to go for training. It was funny. In about six weeks, I was here. I came here for a visit for a week. I couldn't go in the cloister, but I got to pray the Divine Office. I was in the sacristy and they were in the choir, and I heard that Divine Office being sung and I wanted to get through that grate and get in there and I couldn't! It was the chanting of the Divine Office. I just wanted to get in there and pray with them! I think there were other things, too. I had been feeling in my heart, before I came, a drive to be with community. I really needed to be with community. I couldn't be living alone anymore. I went away for two weeks to think about it, and I was so completely miserable. All I wanted to do was get back here.

I went to another place, a religious-oriented place. I thought maybe I'm called to be there for a while. But it wasn't centered around the Divine Office. I needed my life centered around the Divine Office. We prayed the Divine Office some—once or twice a day together in a group—but I wanted to pray all seven hours of this Divine Office. In order to have the solemn vows, you're supposed to be bound to pray the Divine Office in community; that's a mark of the contemplative cloistered life. I could not stand not to have my life revolving around the Divine Office. And you can see that's mostly a lot of what made me want to get through that grate. Of course, I could get to Mass every day, that wasn't a problem. But if you're doing work, there are other schedules you have to accommodate; I was fitting in the Divine Office in all these odd ways and places. If I was in the back of a truck, I would pray the Divine Office. If I was walking from Point A to Point B, I would be praying the Divine Office. Maybe I wouldn't finish and maybe I would have to pick it up later. And if it was a work period, I couldn't pray it. It would have to wait until later.

So my spiritual director made arrangements for me to come back here for more religious training. The community also had to meet to decide whether or not they would allow this because it was very special if they would allow me to come in. And, of course, I had to have the permission of the bishop to come in for this training, being I wasn't asking to be a member of this community. They decided to let me try for a year. I really liked that and I asked for more time. And they said, "We'll only give you a year. You need to get your vocation going." I was here not the whole year, and I was getting this feeling inside I needed to go away and find my true home. So I left. And I was so completely miserable that in not much over three months, I was back here as a postulant. All I could think about was getting back here. I could pray the Divine Office, but praying it by myself wasn't enough.

In a cloister, a nun is dedicated to our Lord in a special way. An active sister has a postulate outside, but here 100 percent of our time is supposed to be with our spouse and we are allowed, because of the life we live in here, to spend more time in prayer. It's like a different tool. If you want to do very fine needlework, you're going to need a very fine, little needle. If you have a needle that's too heavy, maybe a very good seamstress could do this wonderful work, but it's easier with the fine needle. This is kind of the purpose of this life—that we are supposed to be dedicated 100 percent to Christ and to being His spouse. Here, we have an opportunity for silence. An active sister has to do a lot of talking with a lot of other people. Here, if you would like to get to know our Lord, it's going to be in silence and it's going to be with Him in quiet. There are a lot of different kinds of noise inside and outside of you. But the silence—there is where you're uncluttered and there is where you're free for God.

For a while, I regretted exploring the Divine Mercy Movement; I thought it was a waste. But maybe it did form me and form my spirituality. And it did form me as a person, too. And I learned more and more about my faith. God has a purpose. I find even here there is so much room for growth in me still. If I hadn't had all of that time being formed, I might not be even as good as I am now. And I really have a lot of room for improvement! God knows what He's doing. And maybe I was deaf and maybe He was trying to tell me a long time ago. But you know, He put that book in front of me, and it wasn't that long after I had that book, that here I was.

The words in the diary of Saint Faustina, it doesn't appear she knew anything about the Franciscans, but our Lord had said to her, "Your life is to be modeled on mine from the crib to the cross." Well, that's very, very Franciscan, very, very Franciscan. And the authorities have many theories about whether Faustina was being asked to start a community; there are a lot of theories on that. And I don't know. It doesn't appear that I'm called to be in that. But I'm called to live what she wrote and I can do that here: "Your purpose and that of your companions is to come into as close of union with me as possible." And that's what we're supposed to do here. It's interesting because the rule that Saint Faustina wrote is very similar to ours: "Through love, you will unite earth with heaven and soften the just anger of God." And, really, that's the job of everyone in the Church: Through love, we will reconcile earth with heaven the more we love and show mercy. My life and really the lives of everyone here and especially contemplative cloistered nuns, we are supposed to be intercessors. We are supposed to mediate.

    . . .

My family always knew my dedication to wanting to be a sister. They all, in their hearts, kind of thought of me as a sister even before I got here. They knew how badly I wanted this. And they wanted it so badly for me, too. It was so interesting when I received the black veil; my aunt and uncle and my mom said the black veil looked better because they all said, "Now you look like a real Poor Clare." You know they all thought of me as this, and so I guess they're happy to see me becoming what I wanted to be, and what they saw me as. They knew what my desires were. They've read the lives of the saints. They know the needs in the world.

My father died about a year before I came and one of the last things he said was, "Go for it." And I know he thought prayer was the only answer. Yes, it's a sacrifice, but they know why I'm here. And they know that I'm happy here. They want to support that happiness, and they understand this need. The world has a need for this. It was so touching, and I know it's happened more than once since I've gotten here. My aunt Marilyn asked me specially, she was crying and she said, "After I die, pray for me." So few people are prayed for after they die. She knows the need we have for that prayer, and she is counting on me that I will be praying for her.

My family only comes once a year. It's a long way, and my mom is older. It's a sacrifice for them, for assuredly it is. But I am blessed in that my family knows what I'm doing and why I'm doing it, and that's a great blessing; that's a great, great blessing. They, too, saw all the struggles and sufferings I went through with the Divine Mercy thing. They are so happy to see that I'm settled. I'm settled. I'm safe.

They know that I really am the Lord's spouse. And if I have made the promise to give up all I have—I have made these vows to God—can God give me less than He did before, or is He going to give me more? He's got to give me more because I gave more. And so I have opened myself to this relationship and said, "Okay, I am giving up my obedience, my will, my chastity, meaning I am your spouse. I am reserved completely for you. I don't have the freedom, nor do I choose it, to make any other choices. Poverty—I am going to live poor." If I am going to give Him all this and say, "I want to be your spouse," what's He going to do? He's going to have to reciprocate. And of course, He's the one that originated the desire in my heart in the first place. I couldn't have done it without Him. They understand the spousal relationship.

When I was first looking to do this, I was concerned about the family, but I did ask for the family, that the family could receive blessings, too. And there have been blessings to our family. They really believe in that power of prayer. I do, too. If I'm doing what I'm supposed to be doing, then God will bless those in the world and those I'm praying for more than if I was doing something else that might be more direct, hands-on, because I have to be where God wants me to be. We all do. If I'm not where God wants me to be, or doing what He wants me to do, then how can His grace be there?

If I have a person that I love especially, and if I deny myself and deny them our interaction and my presence, is God in justice going to bless that person more or less for that sacrifice that person had to give? He couldn't do anything but bless that person more. I know that they'll get more blessings from God if I'm doing what He wants me to do, even though it might seem less effective, and less gratifying even.

The biggest thing you give up? Your will. Obedience. That's the hardest of all—not to be able to choose what you want to do when you want to be able to do it. It's every day. It's all the time. We have a schedule. And sometimes maybe you're working on a project, and you're supposed to be doing it, but suddenly before you're finished with it they say, "No, stop doing that. We need something else done." That can be hard. You would like to get that thing finished and get it off your shelf. But, no, they said this. In so many little things, the hardest thing is that sacrifice of your will, and this is where your union with God comes in. If you want union with God, you need union with His will.

I need to be doing what I'm supposed to be doing, but not only that, I need to be like Jesus and Mary. Our Lord accepted the will of the Father, not as you like it, not as I like it, and He came to a complete peace with that, no matter what the suffering it entailed—and not to fight the will of God. And the Blessed Mother, you think about how she could be united with the will of God, watching her son die on the cross and not be fighting it inside herself. How united with God's will would she have to have been? And if I can take what I'm supposed to be doing in life and do it, and accept all that comes to me from God's hand with love—because He is all-powerful; everything that happens, he's allowing it to happen—therefore, I have to say,

"Okay, God, take it as Jesus." I should take it as Jesus would. Take it as love from your hand, and give it back as love and use it for what you want to use it for. If I'm united with the will of God, I need to always do what pleases Him and I will have union with God. So what else is there to worry about or to think about? But there it is. It's that will. So I know if I keep working on this will, and if I were ever to get to where I really was united in my will with God, I would have union with God. The closer I am united to the will of God, the more effective I am for me and everybody. The truth is, the more you are united with the will of God, the more you are going to have joy.

They say that the vows crucify you. Yes, they do. It's a crucifixion. Obedience is. If it doesn't cost anything, you know, it doesn't make a very good story, anyway! You want to watch the stories in the movies where someone had to struggle and work hard. If he just went and did everything without any effort, it would be kind of boring. He'd be an unreal Superman! Even Jesus, being God, He didn't show us that way. And it's a good thing He didn't because then we'd never be able to do it. He took our weaknesses and He worked with that human weakness and showed us how to do it. And God will help us to do it. Perfect joy is in receiving bad undeserved treatment with an interior disposition of love and abandonment to God's will, which permits it to happen. And the more I keep trusting in that and His mercy, the more I should be able to receive that mercy, as long as I am able to admit where I'm failing. That's the big thing—admit where I'm failing—because I can't get mercy that I don't think I need. I have to admit that I need mercy. "I'm not obedient, Lord. I'm not obedient." I need to work here. And the less I'm blind and the more I see myself, the more mercy. And I must trust God. See, that's the Divine Mercy message.

I'm doing what I want to do. I think the material things are so much easier to give up than that self-will. You know, the self-will is terribly hard to give up.

Maybe it would have surprised me years ago, before I thought about doing it, because it was hard, because obviously when I was younger it was the complete opposite. I started really realizing where the values were and where the worth was. The horses are wonderful creatures, and they're beautiful. They really are gorgeous creatures, but you know, what's really important and what's really going to help people? Really, let's help people get to heaven. And if you look at that, nothing else is really that important. What is it, whether you train horses, or have horses? It gets to be kind of empty;

if God wanted me to work with horses, that would be the way that I could help bring souls, but even then, Saint Paul talks about using the world as if you're not using it. And then at that point, I would have to have that same detachment of "I'm not here for the horses, I'm here for God, and I'm here for the people, and I'm here to help bring souls to Him and I'll try to be faithful and be a good horse trainer." But there's a detachment. I'm not here for the horses.

People thought that I was alive when I was with the horses. In a sense, it had become more fulfilling because I became better at it and I was better with the people and I was helping bring people to God that way. But the interest wasn't there in that my heart wasn't there. People didn't know that at all, but you know God had other things. Now there's more time for more serious responsibility and for things that can really make a difference and not just be for me. A lot of the time I spent with the horses, it was only for me—for my happiness and gratification. In the end, it wasn't for me anymore, which was a beautiful thing. But I can't live for me.

In the monastery we have a couple dogs, Melody and Harmony, to keep the watch. I take care of them—feed them, groom and trim them, and bathe them when they need it.

You get assigned those kinds of tasks. I really think it's a better policy most of the time to just let the community find out what you can do. If you have an ability, God will let them know if they need to know. It all started with trimming the dogs' nails because they didn't have anyone that could trim the dogs' nails and I could do that. They asked me if I could do it and that's how they found out I worked at a vet's for a while and I did dog training for a while, so they thought it was appropriate.

Before I came into the monastery, I had no real conception of what a religious, or a cloistered religious, or monastic life was like. Only here could I become what God wants me to be, and what I wanted to be, and what I'm called to be. I didn't even know what I wanted to be *was*, so here I found out what it was. The transformation is to become a religious, in this case, for me, to become a monastic, a religious contemplative spouse. I had some ideas of what it was—self-giving and those kinds of things—but to experience the monastic life and to live it, there is no way you could ever describe it without just living it.

It's rich. It's so deep and rich. And it's beautiful. Some people maybe think a lot when they're going to do something, "How's it going to be, how's it going to be?" Well, I didn't do that, and then when I came, I thought, "Wow!" It's like a beautiful old cathedral or an old building. It's almost like a work of art. The *life* is a work of art, this eight-hundred-year-old order. We have old prayers we've been saying from the start, and we have old traditions. We have a refectory! Everybody else has a kitchen but we have a refectory! The refectory is where we eat, and, primarily, the focus is on spiritual reading, not on eating. We happen to eat, but we're reading, doing the spiritual reading at the same time. Collation—the evening meal—that means small portion, so that means a smaller reading, a shorter reading.

It's a culture of its own. The monastic culture is a culture of its own. And we're following eight hundred years of tradition. We have to cook and clean and pick up after ourselves just like everybody else does, only hopefully we can do it for the spiritual reasons and for the love of God. That's what really makes the life because we all have the same needs in the end. But it's the dedication of *why am I here? What are we called to?* The spiritual idea is: I'm here for Jesus Christ and for His people.

We are separated from the world in order to be united with God and we need to have this barrier so that we can have our space to be with our Lord. We need to keep the distractions away, and yet at the same time, the Mother Abbess keeps us very up on what's going on and the needs and the prayers. Before our evening meal, the prayer requests are announced. We are told about all the earthquakes, and all the disasters, and the London bombings in the subway, and all the people who were stampeded and died, and in Iraq a little while ago, all those people were killed, and of course, the hurricanes. We hear about it all. I mean, I hear about this stuff more than when I was out there. We have very good connections.

We've set ourselves apart for God and for others, and from this place we can intercede so that, in the heart, the distance is not there. But there is a physical separation. We have to be wherever we are called to be. A mother, her place is with her children. If she wants to reconcile earth and heaven, she has got to do it where she is with her children. If she tried to go off and neglect her duties, if she spends a lot of time in prayer apart, that's not going to reconcile earth and heaven. It's where God wants you to be; if you're where He wants you to be, and you follow the duties with as much love and fidelity as possible, for love of Him and love of our neighbor, we all can do that reconciling of earth with heaven. But yet we have a special purpose: It's the special tool that our Lord has chosen. Contemplative nuns are supposed to be the heart of the Church. We are supposed to be there praying for and loving everybody.

This is a place dedicated to God. I really believe that's what the people who come here feel. I think that's the sense that the people have when they come here; they can tell this is a place of God. And that's a special and wonderful thing, to have a place that's dedicated to God. If I'm meant to be dedicated to God as His spouse, I need to be in a place like this. And it's got to be in the right place. Okay, we are Poor Clare Colettines, and there are Poor Clare Colettines in Cleveland. But He doesn't call you to be a Poor Clare Colettine even; He calls you to a certain monastery. This is the certain monastery that He decided, in His wisdom, that I belong here, and that this is the place that is the best for me.

I had to find my true home. And I found it, once I came here, because I was so miserable. And I've thought about that recently—I was miserable every other place I'd been. I can't imagine there being anything better than being the spouse of Jesus. I think it's a wonderful thing. And I know it's not for everybody, but I'm really glad that God picked me!

I wanted sisters when I was young. I had three older brothers. I prayed and I asked my mom and begged her and begged her and begged her for sisters. My mom had been told by the doctor, after me, "No more children." I think she almost died with each one of us. She was a person they thought never could have children. It was very hard on her. So the doctor said, "No more children," and my parents abided by that. I must have torn my mother's heart apart. I feel really bad about it now, although I didn't know and they didn't explain it to me. I was begging for a little sister because I wanted a sister to play with, not brothers. I think that was even a call back then, that I have sisters. So now I do!

I would probably be so completely miserable if I was anywhere else. Ever since I met here I've never liked any other place that I've ever been. I'm just not happy or satisfied anywhere else.

I will admit, I count for other people. I do. I think it's a wonderful thing and I think it's exciting. I'll count for other people and I look forward to the time of solemn vows, but I guess I am a real religious now. When you become a nun, when you take the vows of religion, you become a religious, and then every act you do becomes an act of religion, and everything we do in the cloister, or a sister out there who took the vows does, every little tiny act you do is an act of religion and it makes it even more possibly beneficial or detrimental if you don't act well. But I wanted this, to be able to represent God's people and to help God to bless His people, and to be our Lord's spouse—all of this is part of the same thing. I wanted that very badly.

The solemn vows will be a wonderful thing because it's permanent and there is a greater responsibility as far as the Divine Office; that's where you really become bound that you must pray this Divine Office. And then there is the Consecration of Virgins at that time, too. And you receive a ring and that ring says you are our Lord's spouse forever. I look forward to that very much, but my dream was to be a religious, and not just to be a religious, but to be a good religious. I think I have a long way to go to be a good religious, but I am a religious and that's what I wanted so, so, so badly.

I have to say I'm really plain Jane. I think that God speaks to me in the pots and pans. I think God is training me through the everyday life. I just need to be faithful where I am. There was a movie about Saint Faustina. They said she was a true mystic in that she gave up everything to be united with Christ. So there it is. A true mystic is someone who gives up everything to be united with Christ, and so in that way we all can be mystics. I don't think you're going to find a lot of experiences, and I don't think you're going to find many people that would want to talk about them if they did have them.

But the big experiences—let's live the life, and let's love God and neighbor. And I think God talks to me through all the people and through all the experiences, and that's how He teaches me and talks to me. It's not like you hear words. Sometimes you wish you did so that you would know more clearly, but I guess I hear my words through my superior, and in that way I know clearly God's will.

We're all mystics. We give up everything to be united with Christ. Let's just live the spiritual life. We're just simple Franciscans. Let's just live our Franciscan life. It's all about love and it's all about self-giving. And to be serious about living and being what we're supposed to be and about our duties and responsibilities that are very serious. But to me, God speaks to me in the daily life, just what I'm doing and what the people are doing and what I can learn and what I can convert and change in my life.

Now, my focus is on trying to acquire real virtue. And I guess that's maybe why I'm not counting days for myself—because I'm really trying to be authentically what I professed. That's a lot of work, and I need to do a lot of changing so that I am really a good representation as Christ's spouse. "Through love you will reconcile earth with heaven." The more I love, the more that earth and heaven will be brought together. God is love. I need to become like Him. I have a long way to go, so I'm really trying to work on that.

Part I

The Call

1

Community Life

Each person has her own responsibility for how she chooses her attitude toward others. Happiness is a choice, and we can't blame one another if the sister isn't the way I would like her to be. Even if you feel annoyance toward someone, you don't have to let that annoyance wreck your day. We choose how we're going to spend our day, and we can choose to think kindly of another person when we're annoyed. God gave us a free will. I think after living here for thirty-two years, you grow to understand those things better. It's a hard life in many ways. You can choose to live the life joyfully; but you can become bitter, too, because you don't have the things you had before, and it's possible that you make your vows and later you start to regret it, but that's all within yourself. You have to come to the realization that it's my fault if I'm not happy, and I can choose to be happy with this life.

Sister Mary Gemma of Our Lady of the Angels

After an early nomadic life, Sister Joan Marie has aged into adulthood and seniority within the same fourteen-acre enclosure. Decade after decade elapses, and Sister Joan Marie rarely leaves the Corpus Christi Monastery campus. She knows that she will die here, unless, she teases, they kick her out. "They overlook a lot, I hope," she says. "You know you're not under that tension. You know they're not going to send you away. They'd like to..." she trails off.

Sister Joan Marie ranks eldest in the community by longevity, having entered the Corpus Christi Monastery in 1950, before any other current member. She moved here at age seventeen; now eighty-one years old, she recounts her first impressions when she walked into the monastery, when life as a Poor Clare began: In the reverential moment when she first approached the tabernacle housing the exposed eucharist in the public chapel, she heard the novices and nuns who had already made temporary vows and final vows singing from their hidden choir chapel, which faces the public chapel but is separated and hidden from it by the sanctuary (past a swinging gold gate at the Communion rail that separates the nave, where the churchgoers sit, from the altar of sacrifice and altar of repose, where the priest offers Mass and the Blessed Sacrament is exposed). Sister Joan Marie and the other aspiring postulants walked single file, past the stained-glass windows that depict scenes from the lives of Christ, Saint Francis, and Saint Clare on both sides of the public chapel and under the frescoes with gold detail. The young women knelt before the Blessed Sacrament. "We were just overawed, and so all you could think about was, 'God and me,'" Sister Joan Marie says. "That's all you saw. I just thought I was in heaven. I just thought, 'There's God and here's me. Nobody else. Nothing else. I left everything.' And in a way it's true, but not quite so romantic. But I was in seventh heaven.

"I thought this is it. Live happily ever after. Oh dear. It was so different than anything you had imagined. When you get here, you realize more and more every day, I've still got a lot to learn."

Virginia (a pseudonym Sister Joan Marie selected for herself to represent life before she was assigned a religious name), was led to her new quarters, a cell that measured eleven feet, eight inches by six feet, nine inches. Seeing little more than a bed with a straw-stuffed mattress, she says, "That woke me up a little bit." She changed into the outfit for first-year postulants and then wound her way back through the corridors from the novitiate wing of the monastery to the parlor, where she met her parents and siblings to say goodbye. For the first time, the metal grille separated Virginia from her family and from the rest of the world. Debuting her uniform further startled the dream. "Here I thought I was all grown up, leaving my home and family," she says. "And when I came in with these cuffs and a big bonnet, I wonder, 'Am I a baby again?'" she laughs. Her mother told her she looked like the Dutch girl from a popular advertising campaign.

Before she entered the monastery, Virginia pictured life as a cloistered nun. She thought of Saint Colette, a hermit. "Of course, I was young and idealistic," she says. "I thought it would just be me and God. Nobody else. I didn't know about community. I had a lot to learn. You're that age, you're pretty idealistic, and even my parents—I don't think they knew exactly what I was getting into. We trusted the Church. We were so enthused by the Church, being converts."

Raised in an environment of upheaval that started with her father's job loss, followed by episodes of migrant family life and then periodic separations from her parents, Virginia believed her mother and father hoped she would choose her own religious preference. She took cues from her spiritual surrogate and stand-in mother figure—her maternal grandmother; Virginia claimed the Protestant faith but, after a successful campaign by her older sister, was baptized into the Catholic Church. Two years later, she joined the Poor Clare Colettine Order. Monastic life—her new life—seemed like a riddle. And she lacked the code to decipher it. "I just never knew what was going to happen next," she says.

Sister Joan Marie did not grasp the meaning of every custom or comprehend the significance of all the events she witnessed or participated in. She shares an anecdote about the predicament of observing monastic silence while adapting to her new culture: Every day, the nuns lined up in the refectory to confess their faults and weaknesses of that day before their community. Sister Joan Marie remembers standing with the other nuns, waiting her turn to step into the center of the room; the Mother Abbess and Vicaress sat at the head table at one end of the room, and the other nuns lined the two tables that ran the lengths of the room, their backs to the walls. Each nun stood before the Mother Abbess and recounted to her community her imperfections—confessing, for instance, if she accidentally broke a dish.

After the public admission, each nun prostrated herself on the floor facing the head table. Because they lived in such close quarters, Sister Joan Marie says, no disclosure was truly a revelation. "They knew anyway," she says. "It wasn't anything new." If a nun confessed that she forgot to perform a duty, she was given a broken clothespin to wear—presumably a symbol of the omission and a visual cue to remember the next time. If a nun was concerned she might have forgotten to mention a sin of omission or commission, she wore a "forget hat." Sister Joan Marie remembers one nun in her eighties always took the forget hat. Habitually, the elder nun recited her list of faults, adding, "Something else I forgot." A few minutes later, when she bent forward to eat her soup, the hat inevitably fell into the soup. "She forgot she had the hat on!" Sister Joan Marie says. "It was so funny!"

Following the communal ritual, one of the nuns walked to a chart and flipped the numbers. Sister Joan Marie assumed the nun was tallying for the scorecard the collective faults and weaknesses confessed that day. "Later on," Sister Joan Marie says, "this other postulant came to me and said, 'What does that number mean?' I said, 'I really don't know.' I said, 'There's some things you just don't ask about.' Well, she was smart enough she asked the superior, which I was afraid to do because everything was so mysterious to me." The postulant relayed to Virginia what she had learned; the number denoted the temperature outdoors so the nuns knew how to layer up for their manual labor in the gardens. "I was amazed it was so simple a thing!" Sister Joan Marie says. "I thought for sure it had to do with those faults or something mysterious!"

Virginia's new home, with its foreign routines and formal construct, baffled her. "It was so different than anything you had imagined," Sister Joan Marie says. "I guess that was good. In a way, if you see all that's coming, you can't adjust very well. I would have liked to have some relaxation. There was none. Like when you go home, you can relax. But there was no going home. There was no time when you could just be yourself. You were kind of on edge every minute. There's advantages to being young. I couldn't have done it later. I would have been too set in my ways by that time." Virginia arrived at the monastery directly from high school. She was accustomed to a structure bracketed by bells, and so she had no trouble responding when the monastery's bells prompted her to move on to the next activity—prayers, or work, or recreation. "You know the schedule is pretty tight," she says. "But in the evening, I would have liked to relax. You know, when you came home from school, you could be yourself, you know. You didn't have to be on edge. Well, there was no relaxing because you had work you were supposed to do. You had something you were always supposed to do—except when you went to bed; you were so tired, you dropped. What got me was there was no free time where you could just be yourself because I felt they were all looking at me, watching every move."

As the youngest member of the novitiate, Virginia led the group's processions into and out of the chapel. Another postulant directed Virginia to pick up all the "dust fuzzies" she saw on the ground, for love of God and mortification. This spiritual act, she was told, would prompt other young women to join the monastery. Whenever the postulant pointed out a dust ball for Virginia to stop and pick up, the line was forced to halt behind her in a pileup of postulants. "I just wasn't ready for all those little things, details," Sister Joan Marie says. "She was trying to help, but it just discouraged me because I couldn't understand why you had to pick them up." Virginia learned the postulants saved the "dust fuzzies" for Feast Days, when they counted them up, and she prayed that each ball of dust represented one woman with a religious vocation who would be called forth and hear her calling to enter a religious community. "I know it seems crazy," Sister Joan Marie says. "It seemed crazy to me, too." Still assimilating her conversion from Protestant to Catholic, Sister Joan Marie was moved by the teachings of Saint Therese of Lisieux, a contemplative nun nicknamed "the Little Flower of Jesus." The canonized Carmelite summarized the vocation of the monastic life not as a series of heroic acts of virtue, but as a process of honoring God in little acts that demonstrated great and steady devotion. "She always did something for souls," Sister Joan Marie said. "That's all we've got to offer—little tiny things. We don't have big martyrdoms."

Still, the senior postulant's unsolicited guidance frustrated Virginia, who eventually took the matter to her Novice Mistress. The Novice Mistress agreed the other novitiate was too "zealous," and she permitted Virginia to overlook the dust fuzzies when she was leading a procession. Virginia could, however, continue the practice of collecting wayward dust for prayers at other times, the Novice Mistress said, when she found her itinerary freer. "I could talk to her," Sister Joan Marie says of her Novice Mistress. "I was close to her because she was like my mother. Especially at that age, I needed somebody."

Sister Joan Marie says she was "ready to be formed" when she arrived, but she was also worn down by notations of her missteps. "They saw all your faults and all your defects," she says. "That's what they wanted to point out. They say the novitiate is the 'seed time' in life. They want to point it out so that you get a little better before you get with the professed nuns. Of course, the professed weren't all saints, either, but it seemed to us they were because we didn't recreate with them much."

Incongruous as this life seemed to Virginia, an outsider to the Catholic faith and a rookie at the monastery, she feared that she would be found lacking and would be asked to leave the premises. "I was just so afraid. They didn't realize how scared I was," Sister Joan Marie says. She witnessed, in Clothing Ceremonies, postulants become novices, receiving the habit and a religious name, only to be asked to leave months or years later. One novice refused to talk during the community's one-hour social recreation each day. The girl was moody, Sister Joan Marie says. "Well, that wouldn't work in a community. She got sent home. When she got sent home, I thought, 'Oh, I'm next!' As a novice, you're supposed to get a little better—at some things, anyway. I didn't either, but they kept me somehow. I guess they knew; they knew I didn't want to go back to what I came from."

Sister Maria Deo Gratias says,

Our love for God spills out, and it spills out on our sisters in community. When you have love, you can't keep it to yourself. We take
care of each other's needs, but when we're taking care of each other's
needs, we're taking care of the needs of Christ in that person. There's
that perception of that other sister as the body of Christ and that whole
mystical body idea. In community, we show our love for God by how
we love our sisters. We form a happy family, in the sense that the family is a group of adult women responding to God together. And people
are different. They have different personalities. But that's kind of like
a given. You know you're not going to find a perfect human on earth.

Even in a cloistered monastery, where like-minded women convene, for
life, after internalizing their common beliefs, and aiming together toward
holiness and perfection, there are conflicts. "You know, each person is so different, unique, and then sometimes we clash on each other; and sometimes
we agree," Sister Joan Marie says. "Most of the time we agree."

"I think men religious have different struggles than what women religious
would have," says Sister Mary Gemma. "A woman by nature likes to arrange
things and have her kitchen the way she wants, but in community you have
to learn to let go of that. I think that's one of the hardest things—you aren't
the woman of the home. There are twenty other women. That's something
you struggle with. It's more of a struggle when you first come. You have to
let go of the way you want things to be, otherwise you're just not going to
get along." Although Sister Mary Gemma has never heard "a bad word"
uttered in the monastery, she adds, "I would say probably what I found most
surprising was that once in a while there would be a couple of sisters that
would get into it with each other. Then later, I found that there's so much
forgiveness here. Later, that's what struck me more than anything."

The inherent tensions that can fester within an enclosed community have
been mythologized in oral tradition. The stories are like fables, or parables,
with morals. Sister Mary Gemma shares a story passed along from the early
days of the Corpus Christi Monastery's founding through the generations
of novices and nuns: Two young nuns were assigned to work in the garden
together, but they could never agree on anything, namely how they should
conduct their work. One day, one of the nuns introduced a novel attempt at

diplomacy, to quash the inevitable quarreling. She walked out to the garden and greeted the other nun. She had either filled her pockets with marbles in the monastery, or she picked up stones off the ground. She proceeded to place one marble or stone after another into her mouth, as Sister Mary Gemma says, "so that she would keep her mouth shut, because she had a hard time controlling her temper. In charity, she thought she had better put something in her mouth to remind her to be quiet when she didn't agree with something. She recognized that it was wrong of her to get so upset about things, and since she couldn't control herself that way, she did it another way."

This "real old story that goes way back," Sister Mary Gemma says, has been told and retold. Its themes strike at the core of the nuns' values: Discipline. Obedience. Silence. Love. Selflessness. Peacemaking. It illustrates the virtue of caring for someone else over the desire to express one's own opinions, or get one's own way. "Those are the kind of thing we share at recreation," Sister Mary Gemma says. "The sisters that have been here longer like to tell the stories that bring out the foibles of one another. It's a joyful acknowledgment. We're acknowledging that we're all struggling. You can look back and laugh, even though something was so hard at the time; and yet you can look back and laugh."

Sister Mary Gemma sees humor and truth in this now remote but still poignant teaching moment. "The thing is," she says, "we didn't choose each other. God chose. God chose who we were going to live with the rest of our lives and that's where we say, especially if women can get along together, can struggle together and get along, that shows the grace of God is there. It's God's grace that makes a marriage work. It's God's grace that helps us in community to be faithful and get along. Like marriage, you have to work at it."

"But our response to other people's personality is because of the love of God," says the Vicaress, Sister Maria Deo Gratias. "It's a little different than the divided life of a married another person. For us, we're all looking at God together. That would be a way of picturing it. All of us stand together looking in the same direction, focusing our life in the same direction and it's like a circle. We're all standing in a circle and the center is Christ and the more we come closer to Christ, the closer we are to each other.

"We are different people and we do think differently. But there is that unity—that core unity—that holds us together and it's a beautiful experience to live in community. The give and take that we learned as a kid, we apply that here." Having lived in another religious order before entering the Corpus Christi Monastery, Sister Maria Deo Gratias says this community exhibits a "beautiful grace," embracing the "essentials that we all treasure so much"—the same values and a "centeredness on living the life." "You understand that you're bound to have people make different choices, but our community is very united in our basic values—very, very much so, more than other communities, and I've experienced many of them. And that's a plus for us."

Sister Maria Benedicta first joined an active religious order, living with that community for five years before entering the Corpus Christi Monastery. "God has a special place for everybody," she says. "It's not just—religious life, go join wherever you want. He has a special place and a special purpose. And every community has what is called a charism—it's like their spirit—and you're created to be in that community. You have that spirit. God has given that to you. It's your home. It's where you will fit, where you will become holy. It's where my spirituality matches that of the community so we can strive together to holiness. Not that we're all the same because we're not. But we have the common spirituality and charism to strive together toward God."

Sister Maria Deo Gratias explains:

The higher you come into the spiritual life, the more you're able to accept differences because the spiritual life expands you. Whereas if you have a very narrow way of thinking, it all has to fit in that narrow little package, and if it doesn't, then you break out in some way—impatience, or you submerge yourself, or whatever. But the deeper you come into union with God, you come to accept people the way they are. There doesn't have to be any breakage. You can have union in diversity.

And we know—we certainly know—that our sister is striving to do the best she can. She falls short just like I fall short so therefore we don't take that amiss or against her; it's just we have a greater compassion to say, "I know what you mean, Sister. You fell today. I fell yesterday." And it's just that type of it's no big deal about it, but we do strive together and that's why at times, we hold ourselves accountable to say—every evening before collation, we say—"I'm sorry." We say that as a group because we know that we are human. We annoy. And we may not even know the annoyances we give another person. And it may be that on a particular day I didn't annoy someone, but I say sorry for anytime that I have. And you always are crystal clear with God.

For Sister Joan Marie, monastic life jarred her sense of self. Beyond the enclosure and the grille, in the chaotic world she inhabited until the age of seventeen, she was regarded as upright, a model student, daughter, and sister. "I think the novitiate was awful hard—being young, partly, being in a new culture entirely," Sister Joan Marie says. "Everybody's praising me out there. Before Vatican II, it was like coming to a completely different milieu. Well, when I got here, it seemed like everybody was on me for doing the wrong thing at the wrong time. So it was hard to adjust. In fact I don't know if I ever did. I got sick, mostly. Instead of adjusting, I got sick, the one way to adjust. I didn't do it on purpose, but God works it out."

She had endured much in her youth, upended by her family's many moves, jostled by her father's mental instability and the needs of her mother and siblings; she worked to protect her family from self-destructing. Before her parents married, her maternal grandparents predicted doom for the couple. She learned from her parents that they met when her father eyed her mother, a sorority girl in college, at a social. "I'll take that Kansas girl," he said. They married in a civil union; Sister Joan Marie's maternal grandparents were mortified by their quick pairing. Another daughter had married her high school sweetheart, and they "didn't think this could turn out."

Virginia's early years were sweet enough. She remembers visiting her father's office building in Detroit and looking down on the city below. "He would show me these little cars, and I thought they were toy cars. I soon learned it was because we were high up. I was just a baby," she says. She smiles at the memory and her juvenile mind's attempts to consolidate her perceptions and interpret her world. As a youngster, she and her older brother played the Lone Ranger and Tonto. Virginia always wanted to be the Lone Ranger and say, "Hi-yo, Silver!" Her brother relegated her to the role of Tonto. She aspired to become a "cowboy." The family vacationed at their beach house in Canada, and her father took her into the water to teach her how to "ride the waves." To Virginia, the phrase was married to the world of horseback riding; she tried to mount a wave, as if it were a horse. Her father laughed. Her family was "well off," Sister Joan Marie says, and each year she was proud to add one new doll to her collection, a gift from her parents.

If her grandparents' undisguised displeasure at her parents' union was not an omen, an ill-conceived object lesson at Christmas foreshadowed impending turmoil. A toddler at the time, Virginia watched her mother set the holiday cookies on the kitchen table, out of the child's reach. Virginia realized, though, that if she yanked on the tablecloth, she could get at the cookies. At first, her parents laughed at her cleverness, but they tried to stop it soon enough. "Well, Mother didn't like that because all the dishes came down," she says. "But I kept doing that because I got the cookie." Weeks shy of Christmas, her parents informed Virginia that she would not receive any presents if she kept pulling the cookies and dishes off the table; she would get switches, for spankings, instead. Her mischievous efforts continued to be rewarded, with cookies obtained. So Virginia persisted. And she wreaked havoc on her mother's dishware. On Christmas morning, Virginia watched her father hand presents to her older sister and her older brother. Then he reached behind the tree for a package, swaddled in newspaper, for Virginia. Inside the wrapping were switches. "Mother said she would never do that again to any kid because I was crying all day," Sister Joan Marie says. "Mostly, I was crying because Santa knew my sins. Santa knew how bad I was. I didn't mind the family knowing what was going on because they know me. But a stranger—Santa of all people—knew." Her mother tried to console her daughter with a gift of clothesline and clothespins so that the little girl could be like her mother. "It didn't help at all," she says. "I just cried."

When her father lost his job, Virginia experienced her family's downward spiral as an economic crisis. Her father began to unravel. When he filed for bankruptcy, signs emerged of his fragile grip on reality, his declining mental and emotional state. One day, the family packed their car and abandoned their home and most of their belongings. Her mother sold a few items to neighbors before the move, thinking she would replace what she sold after they resettled; she could not know then that they would never establish a stable family life again. "In those days that was a great disgrace," she says of her father's bankruptcy. Since Sister Joan Marie's older sister helped their father pack the car, Sister Joan Marie remembers they found room for all of her sister's collections. The car packed full, Sister Joan Marie was told to select from her possessions only what she could hold on her lap. She took one doll from her collection.

In time, Sister Joan Marie gleaned the backstory of her father's sad life: He was one of twelve children, and his mother died in childbirth when he was eight years old. His older sisters took care of the infant. Meanwhile, he and the other middle children were neglected. "Nobody loves you but your mother at that age," Sister Joan Marie says. Her paternal grandfather was portrayed in these stories as holding his children to impossible standards; he had overcome the dark years of the Depression in spite of the extra mouths and because of the many hands, his offspring toiling on his potato farm. "He worked them to death," Sister Joan Marie says of her paternal grandfather. Her father bonded with one of his brothers, who got a job on the railroad feeding coal to motor the train. In another tragic blow, her father's favorite brother was killed in a train accident. Still an adolescent, he ran away during World War II, lying about his age so that he could enlist in the military. A country boy with an aversion to rules, he clashed with authority. He made whiskey out of potato peelings and was about to face the expected repercussions from the military for his misbehavior when another brother who was "good to him" testified that he had lied about his age to get into the army. He was discharged.

Like his siblings, Sister Joan Marie's father did not want to work as a farmer, a result of their hard labor in their father's fields. "My father especially wanted to be a big businessman, and that was his ideal," Sister Joan Marie says. "He had worked himself up to this." After the financial collapse, Virginia bounced between the family's temporary shelters, including a campground one summer in Indiana, and her maternal grandmother's home in Kansas. At times, it seemed she was a character in a fairytale, inhabiting a campground complete with a backyard forest to explore, and a Hansel and Gretel–like cottage whose tenant kept pet raccoons and raised a blue jay named "Perculator." The owner trained the bird with milk and bread to land on her finger. "To us it was like a miracle," Sister Joan Marie says. Other times, Virginia was reunited with a patriarch who was succeeding either at business or at drink.

Her mother taught her children the Golden Rule. "As long as we were with her, it was okay," Sister Joan Marie says. Her father often left to search for work; his reappearance disrupted the calm and was "emotionally upsetting," Sister Joan Marie says. "And Mother always said, 'Forgive him. Forgive him.'" Once, her parents left their three children for a few days with a caretaker, maybe a neighbor, Sister Joan Marie says. Her parents did not explain in terms that registered to their youngest child where they were going, or why. "I think they said they'd give us each a quarter if we were good," she says. She doesn't remember receiving a quarter. "I don't think we were good."

Her father, never satisfied as an employee, "wanted to be on his own," Sister Joan Marie says. "He didn't want to be under anybody. He was kind of a tyrant." Virginia was terrified of her father. Her mother, it seemed, could talk to him, even during his rants. She warned her husband she was going to record his outbursts and play them back when he was sober and spent. "She should have," Sister Joan Marie says. "He liked to talk. When he got upset, he liked to talk. Just crazy. Wasn't reasonable. Unreasonable. But she could control him, pretty much. I think she was able to. But I was affected more than she. Because he would take it all out on her, it kind of got me."

Sister Joan Marie believes her father was a complicated figure. "Sometimes he would be so good," she says. "He would always stop on the highway if he saw anyone in trouble; he would stop to help. I guess he must have been real hungry when he was little because he always thought he should feed everybody. He wouldn't give you an ice cream cone unless he gave the whole group a cone. One time it was raining and we were soaked and we had to stay in the tent—we had a big tent that we went around with—and he got us all suckers. I think he came with suckers and it broke the day a little bit. He was real good with children. He always liked children. He had a lot of good points. But the sickness got him. When you're discouraged and it goes into depression, then you seem to take it out on the ones you love the most. It's terrible. But that's what happens. Suffering from Dad, I think we naturally turned more toward God because there was nothing else to turn to. Mother always said, 'Don't tell anybody, don't tell anybody,' because at that time you didn't have these groups—support groups. There was nobody we could talk to."

Sister Joan Marie remembers that her mother loved reading the melancholy Old Testament books of Job (the story of the holiest man alive, who experienced an epic plight, with his loved ones killed and his fortune erased, in a series of temptations to curse God) and Ruth (a widow who refused to follow her mother-in-law to her homeland, found love with a rich relative of her in-laws, and famously said, "Entreat me not to leave you, or to turn back from following you; for wherever you go, I will go; and wherever you lodge, I will lodge; your people shall be my people, and your God, my God").

With no one to talk to, no one to help carry her burdens, Sister Joan Marie turned to her dog, Suzy. She told her pet her worries.

It was in her maternal grandmother's care and in the United Brethren denomination, and their small, poor church with its conspicuous crack in the wall, where Sister Joan Marie felt safe and her faith took root. Sister Joan

Marie says her parents did not want to be "prejudiced," and so they left the matter of religion to their children's efforts. "I think they were hoping that we would choose some religion. My mother said she just thought it would take. She had been brought up in it. In college, I guess she just got that idea, that you should choose your own religion, you should bring your children up to choose. She was religious but she didn't know that she had to train; she didn't realize that you have to get some training."

Virginia was often anxious for her mother. Once, her mom disappeared in the middle of the night. Virginia screamed at her father, demanding to know what he had done to her. He laughed. The following day, Virginia was relieved that her mother had given birth, which explained why her mother had sent Virginia and her brother outdoors and out from underfoot in the previous months. Virginia's fear for her family grew, and this was justified: Her father, without any means and one more mouth to feed, experienced a psychological break. He told his family he was going to kill himself. He raged at them. One day, he held his newborn out a second-story window and threatened to drop the boy. He ended up carrying the child outside and walking the boy around the block barefoot. Virginia's mother sent her to follow them. "He went into different cars to try to take them away, but he couldn't get them to start," she says. "He didn't have the key, I guess. But then he came back. Thank God he came back."

Sister Joan Marie thinks now that her father was motivated to upset her mother. One day he held a knife to his wife's throat. He told his children he was going to kill their mother. The police were phoned, and Virginia's father was taken to a mental hospital. Asked if she would allow the institution to perform a surgery—perhaps a lobotomy—"so that he became like a vegetable," as Sister Joan Marie remembers it, "Mother would not allow that. She would not allow that. We all thought she should. She said, 'It changes their personality, and they're no longer human because they've got no passions. They've got no passions.'"

Virginia's mother tried to console her children, saying their father probably would not have acted on his threat to kill her. "Mother said he probably wouldn't have done it, just like he wouldn't have killed himself because he just would threaten. I couldn't understand why she would say that when she was pinned against the wall.

"Her love was too great, I guess. Some said she should have thought of the children. Well, she did think of us. I used to say, 'Divorce him. Divorce him.' She said he would just come after us because that's all he had. He didn't have a mother. His only love was for his family, really. But somehow it went haywire."

Her maternal grandmother's faith was a haven, cushioning Virginia through childhood. When her older sister enrolled in flight school, she converted to Catholicism after long talks with a priest-pilot. Virginia's sister began evangelizing her, which Virginia construed as an assault on her carefully guarded sphere. Virginia cried when her older sister professed she also believed in Darwinism, not the creationism that Virginia's grandparents instilled in her. In retrospect, Sister Joan Marie describes the thirteen-year-old version of herself as having "Protestant prejudice"; she was wary of genuflecting, which looked like the worship of Mary. Invited to attend her sister's Catholic church for Mass with her mother and two brothers, they laughed at the family convert who they said appeared to be swatting at flies as she made the Sign of the Cross. Embarrassed by their inappropriate responses, Virginia's sister said they were not welcome to worship with her anymore.

Aside from the theological disparities, Virginia liked her grandmother's church, a cornerstone of her upbringing. Her sister argued that she should not choose a religion based on feelings, but rather with logic. In the end, she gave up on Virginia and stopped arguing. She advised her little sister to find a priest who had the patience to explain theological matters to her. Virginia did seek out a priest at a local church, who explained genuflecting by association: "Now, you love your own mother," Sister Joan Marie recalls him telling her. The priest said that genuflecting was a sign of respect, that every other religion was founded by men, but Catholicism was founded by Christ. He suggested that Virginia pray, on her knees, for the gift of faith. Virginia walked out of the church, stopped on the sidewalk, a few feet from traffic, and she knelt on the pavement and prayed. She immediately wanted to be baptized into the Catholic faith. Her own religious fervor as a convert—the early risings for Mass and recitations of the rosary—attracted followers in her mother, her brothers, and even her father.

At the age of fifteen, Virginia was baptized. Moved by the poverty and simplicity of Saint Francis and his followers, the high schooler studied Latin at a junior college, took a job her sister lined up working for a two-person chemical company (helping test water on farms to be sure it was safe to drink), and read aloud at nights to her mother about Brother Juniper in *The Little Flowers of St. Francis*. They delighted in the stories of Brother Juniper, who was "always doing odd things," Sister Joan Marie says. As Saint Francis described him: "Would to God, my brothers, I had a whole forest of such Junipers." Once, Friar Juniper was asked to prepare a meal for the rest of his community. But because he considered food preparation an undesirable interruption that took friars away from their prayers, he produced a soup on a massive scale and in a less than conventional manner—"the fowls in their feathers, the eggs in their shells"—in the hopes the food would last two weeks. His time and efforts proved a waste of time; when "he set down his hotch-potch" in front of the other friars, "there was never a hog in the Campagna of Rome so hungry that he could have eaten it," according to *The Little Flowers of St. Francis*. Chastised initially for his abuse of resources, Brother Juniper was later commended for his simplicity and charity. "All those little stories were cute. It struck me, the simplicity of it. I wanted to be like Saint Francis," Sister Joan Marie says. She toted bread to work and then tossed it to the birds in the hopes of communing with nature. Drawn to the contemplative life of Saint Francis that was mirrored by Saint Clare, founder of the Poor Clare Order, Sister Joan Marie says, "I knew I wanted to be a Poor Clare right away."

Virginia's father was, at that point, baptized as a Catholic and focused on his next business venture. He worked two shifts at two newspapers as a linotype operator to raise capital for a system that would render obsolete shoveling coal to power trains—the job his brother had been working when he died. Her father carved the designs for his inventions in potatoes.

Although he was a new convert, Sister Joan Marie remembers that her father tried to dissuade her from a religious vocation. He told his daughter that underground tunnels connected nuns and priests. He drove her to a monastery surrounded by a high wall, and Sister Joan Marie remembers him saying, "You're going to be behind that wall. You won't be able to come out." It did look awful to Virginia. And yet she applied to join four Poor Clare communities. A friend of hers—Sister Rose—had entered the Corpus Christi Monastery in Rockford, Illinois, one year prior, and because Sister Rose was considered by members of the community to be very devout, Sister Joan Marie says she was invited to join without the requisite visit. The Mother Abbess only gave her one mandate: She had to wait two years from her baptism as a Catholic to enter. "They took me, thinking I would be that good," Sister Joan Marie says of the nuns' esteem for Sister Rose. "I wasn't quite that good. She was real vivacious. One sister told me, 'You're just the opposite and you'll never last.' Big help! The ones that didn't want you to go really helped you more." Sister Joan Marie says the harsh words gave her more resolve to endure the trials.

In their cumulative centuries of life within the Corpus Christi Monastery, as adherents to a lifestyle that Sister Mary Monica describes as a "work of art," the nuns have developed philosophies about community living, as well as opinons about who is capable to endure it. Sister Sarah Marie says that the strict rules and intense emotional demands of mandated silence and interrupted sleep would self-select members who must be completely normal, immune from psychological abnormality. "I think when you enter an enclosure, if you're abnormal, it's going to come out if there's something wrong," she says, laughing. "In the active world, you can keep it under for a little bit, if you've got a little psychological disorder. Not here! Not here.

"That's why, I mean, when people think they must be a little bit dingy to be back there, it's just the opposite," she says. "We're more psychologically healthy here than most people out there because you have to be, because you get a little ding-dong here. See, there has to be that calling, there has to be that calling from our Lord for this particular life, this vow of enclosure.

"Sometimes we get ones that come here and think they have a calling. And that's what you should do if you feel that you're being called—well, come!" Sister Sarah Marie says. "Find out if this is where our Lord's calling you. That's the only way you're going to know. And after a couple of days, if they say, 'Gee, I miss going to Wal-Mart,' well, it's kind of an indication, because we're not going to keep someone here if they're dying to go to Wal-Mart, you know! Well, then, maybe this isn't where God is calling you to."

In a separate, later conversation, Mother Miryam says that a young woman called to religious life could really miss Wal-Mart but still belong in a cloistered monastery. Mother Miryam remembers, as a novice, glancing toward the wall encompassing the cloister's acreage, hearing the traffic, and wishing she could hop in a car and drive somewhere. Anywhere. She, too, believes, though, that psychological disorders and emotional issues make for a difficult pairing with religious life. Years might lapse before a disorder emerges or a repressed issue becomes visible, she says, but it will become apparent in the enclosure. Mother Miryam gives an example: Humans, in general, need self-esteem; in the close quarters of a cloister, if a woman has poor self-esteem, she might think another nun is ignoring her, or trying to hurt her, or doing something to get under her skin, when, in fact, the woman has not even registered on the other nun's mental radar. Mother Miryam says that God often works not on the spiritual level, but on the human level.

It's like in relationships on the human level. You really can roman-ticize, "I love God, I love God, I love God." But He says if you don't love your neighbor, you don't love me. So on that level, you can't kid yourself. You can't kid yourself, "I'm just going to go pray and I love God so much," if you can't get along. And of course there are going to be times when it's going to be hard to get along. That's just normal, because we're all different. But you have to grow in that. You've got to grow in tolerance. You've got to grow in sensitivity. You've got to grow in gentleness—all these things will make it easier for others. You've got to grow in self-sacrifice. Are these on the human level? Yes, they are. They are on the human level. But you're lifting yourself to another level. That's the only way we can really grow is on this human level. A wounded person—maybe they can't do a lot of that. But maybe God will use them. He'll work with them and sanctify them in their own way. You never know.

It may take years for someone to arrive at a moment of self-honesty and clarity, Mother Miryam says, following a pattern of problems relating to oth-ers in community that actually points to a problem that needs to be resolved within oneself. Mother Miryam believes the full picture of these hiccups in relationships can emerge only with an admission of one's own emotional hangups and shortcomings; this acceptance of one's defects can allow one to move past them, no longer under the illusion of perfection, or the pow-erlessness due to denial.

Those who are mistrustful by nature remain mistrustful in the cloister, and the same holds true with social butterflies, confrontational personali-ties, and critical spirits. It is easy to conceive of ways that these qualities and imperfections can affect others in the cloister. I became privy to the magnification of such traits creating tensions—with conflict and drama inserted in community life—when one nun pulled me aside in the kitchen during one of my visits to tell me she did not know what Mother Miryam wanted to tell me, but she thought I should learn the story of the statue overlooking the gardens. Mother Miryam happened to walk in as I was trying to clarify what she wanted me to ask the Mother Abbess, and the

nun in question was startled and flustered, as if she were being discovered mid-transgression. She put her finger to her lips, indicating silence,
and her face turned red. I forgot, in subsequent visits, to ask about the
statue. A few months later, the same nun talked with me one-on-one in
the parlor and told me that other nuns had a question for me, and so
she would take notes and relay my words to them; I suggested, instead,
that she retrieve the Mother Abbess, the authority of the community, the
elected channel of practically all external communications, so that she
could take part in the conversation. The nun informed me she did not
want to bother the Mother Abbess. Later, I explained the interaction with
Mother Miryam, and I learned that even in an atmosphere of monastic
silence the telephone game emerges as a means of moving information,
stirring conflict. Mother Miryam told me there is a saying, "the angel afar,
and the devil within." I am sure that I appeared shocked by her use of the
phrase. Mother Miryam quickly added that each individual possesses her
own set of issues that she must contend with; all are fallen. She quoted
the Catholic Church's historical perspective, that "holiness is wholeness,"
a notion that was finally—and rightly, Mother Miryam says—dismissed
in light of the examples of "wounded saints" who overcame many weaknesses and flaws in their struggle for, and attainment of, holiness.

Vicaress Maria Deo Gratias suggests another prerequisite for adapting to
cloistered communal living: A woman must be able to detach from her own
vantage point, her own personal desires. Joining a religious order might
imply that a woman is willing to disavow her own interests and cede her will
to the vows and the direction of her superiors. But Sister Maria Deo Gratias
believes, from her interactions with young women visiting the monastery,
that today's youth are deprived of skills such as negotiating relationships,
which are essential for community living. "Let's say a person comes in and
they find in the novitiate a novitiate sister she clashes with personality-wise.
And it isn't that either one of them is causing it, that's just the natural way
it is; then because they're not used to living with people, it's like they don't
know how to handle it, where it can be handled very well if you have the
natural ability and then the grace can build on that."

Negative emotions naturally well up and might spill out, unchecked, she
says, but growth in the spiritual life derives from reflection. "What is it, when
we fail, that we need to change?" Sister Maria Deo Gratias asks. "Two wrongs
don't make a right."

In what might appear to be an inversion of the natural order, Sister Maria Deo Gratias says that if life were to play out smoothly, without trouble, she might make the mistake of believing she possessed more virtue—more patience, for example—than she could actually claim, and she might not concede there was room for improvement. "Then you develop that virtue and you thank God for that opportunity, that I was able to acquire a greater practice of the virtue of patience because there was the opportunity," she says, "and you don't hold it against the person because of whatever it was that tried you. It's just one person will try one person one way. And we all try each other. We all have flaws."

Sister Maria Deo Gratias has transferred to communal living a pattern of relating to others, built upon a childhood dictum she learned from her parents: "You stood for the person you were and you make the person you are. You are who you are because of your own choices." As a high school student in the aspirature, Sister Maria Deo Gratias says she learned that everyone arrives at any given moment from different personal histories and frameworks. If she could not understand the actions of one of her religious sisters, she always asked, "Could you tell me why you did that?" She says she has gleaned, through their disclosures, "My mind didn't go that way at all. But if my mind went that way, I can obviously see her behavior now. It was so clear. Then you say, 'If I had a mind like that, I would come to that conclusion, too.'"

"You know, so many things don't matter," Sister Maria Deo Gratias says. "It just matters that we love God. It's just a beautiful way to live. We all strive to live that way." She refers to her visual image of nuns standing in a circle, directing their attention to Christ at the center, and conceding their own rights. "When you have somebody coming in that's not used to that, that's used to everything revolving around them, as center, you have to say, 'You have to step on the side with the rest of us and let Jesus in the center.' But they're not used to living that way because everything has to be around them. That's the way the culture is now. When they come into our community, we're all on this side together and Christ is in the middle. The closer we come to Christ, the closer we come to each other."

In a process of mutual discernment, an aspirant and her community might discover they do not make a suitable match. "I think more women today have a different idea of what it's really about," Sister Maria Benedicta says of religious life and the cloistered monastery. "They are unconsciously seeking something else—acceptance or something else."

When Sister Mary Nicolette, the Novice Mistress, first arrived as a Poor Clare postulant, she was one of thirteen women training together; of those, seven stayed and professed final, solemn vows. She says this is a high ratio; typically, fewer than 50 percent of women who enter as postulants join the order permanently. When a woman comes to the monastery "for the wrong reasons, or the wrong motives," Sister Mary Nicolette says, "then obviously they're not bound to stay, and they can't stay because it wouldn't be right. You know, our intention and our motive is a big thing. We could be doing the correct things, living poverty. But if we're doing it for the wrong reason— 'oh, this sister is going to think that I'm really poor and great'—well, that's the complete opposite of what poverty is for. You can be living this life for completely the wrong reasons. Or someone might say, 'I'm going to live perfect poverty,' but not make it interior, and then it's completely pointless."

"Obviously, if you're staying and this is not your expression, it's going to agitate you," Sister Maria Deo Gratias says. "And even if you wouldn't say anything, the atmosphere is there, and so you don't want to contaminate the atmosphere with agitation. If the shoe doesn't fit, you take the shoe off. It's as simple a thing as that."

Asked if she reflects on her experience in the monastery as an entirely different milieu, as Sister Joan Marie experienced it, Mother Miryam says, "I wouldn't see it that way myself at all. I suppose it was. Maybe. Maybe she's right. I just experienced it as a gradual change. I would have to think about it, but I wouldn't make a statement like that myself. I really don't see it that way. I can see it that way and she's a simple soul. She really is a sweet and simple soul. I could see why she... but I couldn't."

Even though Virginia's father detested the notion that his daughter wanted to become a nun, her mother helped usher her to this place, conspiring to keep secret her daughter's plans to enter the Corpus Christi Monastery. The mother and daughter tucked behind the couch a few belongings Virginia planned to bring with her to the monastery. When her father discovered the small stockpile and he registered his daughter's intentions were real, he stopped objecting. "My father—he always said a lot of things, but in the end he brought me up," Sister Joan Marie says. "He was proud of me, really, but he wouldn't let on to it. They had brought us up to choose our own religion, so they couldn't complain when we did."

When she left home, Sister Joan Marie says she did not think at first to pray for the family she left behind. "I'm afraid I was all wrapped up in myself," she says. "It was such a new experience and I thought I was doing something so great. And they all thought I was a saint because I was a teenager and most teenagers were looking for a good time and I wasn't. I wasn't. But I soon got that out of me. It didn't take too long to go out."

Before she embraced monastic living, and the constant alternation between manual labor and prayer, Sister Joan Marie does not remember ever being asked to pitch in with family chores. "To work was a shock," she says of the monastery. Having overcome bronchial pneumonia and the measles shortly before she entered, Sister Joan Marie says, "Mother kind of babied me, I guess, and I just laid around and read books before I came."

Still, she found stability, if not comfort, in the cloister. "I always loved everything about it," Sister Joan Marie says, "because, I guess from having trouble at home, I was so grateful to be away from that—that emotional upset all the time. I think it made it seem like heaven, in comparison, except I was young; that was the trouble. I mistook things. I was afraid. I was scared to death to ask anything. I thought they would send you home. I was scared I would get sent home; mostly, I was scared of that than anything else."

As she struggled to figure out what was expected of her and scrambled to keep up with the physical demands, Sister Joan Marie was stricken with a series of illnesses. "You think the harder you work, maybe they'll keep you," she says. "No."

She enjoyed preparing meals, but she was domestically deficient. Her mother never taught her to cook. Believing she needed a break from their troubled family life, Virginia and her brother were encouraged to play outdoors. When she was assigned to work alongside the monastery's cook of fifty years, she failed to measure up. "I did more or less whatever she told me," Sister Joan Marie says. "I tried. But then I got the pan in the wrong place and there was always something I was doing wrong. I tried to write down everything she was doing to learn to cook. She said 'Sister...' She didn't like it. She wanted me to work, not write things down. She said, 'Sister, you'll never be a cook because there's always somebody that comes that will know how to cook.' And she was right."

In time, Sister Joan Marie learned that for years after she left home, her mother continued to set her place at the dinner table every night in front of a long-vacated chair. Virginia's absence was observed daily. Decades the wiser, Sister Joan Marie interprets the experience of loss from a parent's perspective: "I think what was hard was when they got home and you weren't there. We went to a new life, thinking, 'Each day is new,' you know, and each day you learn something new. And here they are left with an empty nest. It's almost like a death. They're left empty until you write your first letter. I think once they have visits and they come, then they get adjusted, then they realize that you're happy, and then they're happy. But it does take time, I'm sure."

After sixty years in the monastery, Sister Joan Marie cannot say for certain if she has adjusted to monastic living.

When you get older, it gets a little easier. Seems like. I mean, now I'm not too sure yet. I've been sick so long.

I think the beautiful thing is praising God. And you're called to that seven times a day and at night. But that's the hardest. That was the hardest for me because I had to break my sleep. And I couldn't. I had a hard time adjusting to that. In fact, I thought they were going to send me home because of that. I just slept. In fact, I still do at Mass because I couldn't break the sleep. It wasn't my cycle. Anyway, I had a hard time with that. I guess you have a hard time with everything when you first enter. Well, I think you just think more of God, what He got out of you. It wasn't much. And pleasing Him and praising Him—and you're happy that you were able, that He let you do that. Nobody else can take the time. And it's not so much the work; the work is more of a penance. Any poor person has to work, and so that's part of the life. But that's part of the life in the world, too. I would have had the same trouble. Had the same, maybe more....

A lot of it was to find out that you are your biggest enemy. Yourself. To realize that took a long time. I was pretty critical of others, and you think, "Well, they shouldn't be doing that. They shouldn't be doing *that*.' " You have to look, "Well, am I always on time? Am I always...? No." When you really try to see yourself, you realize they're doing pretty good. And, you know, in sickness and everything else, they can keep going. And can you? No.

From within the same fourteen acres, Sister Joan Marie's perspective on the world, herself, and God have changed. "You get a different view of things," she says. "The whole thing is terrific, sort of like what God must feel sometimes. You take in the whole world. I think you kind of get God's view of things, because you see all these terrible things to pray for. There's plenty to pray for. It's a wonder He doesn't destroy us, but He loves us. Loved us all. Love makes it seem easy. And it was easy, when you think of it, compared to what He did for us—the crucifixion. We didn't have to go through that. Nobody could. Nobody could. Really, He spoils us more or less. We're spoiled little children, especially us, because we're in the cloister, because we're His, because we belong to Him entirely. We gave everything up for Him. I guess He spoils us in many ways."

Sister Joan Marie lists what she calls her "consolations": The monastery's pet dogs that "keep us going," along with a cat that turned up in the dumpster. These are some of the ways that God has provided. Sister Joan Marie adds that the nuns do find joy in their lives. "When we celebrate we really celebrate," she says. "There's no limit. I mean, according to our life, there's no limits."

Still, she does not think she can ever expect, in this lifetime, to acclimate to the rigid structure and the severe Rule of Saint Clare. "It's just a supernatural life and it's not natural," Sister Joan Marie says. "You would rather live a natural life. The body would rather sleep when it wants to sleep and forget the bells. It's just so different. You really have to have a supernatural outlook; otherwise, you can't persevere. And you have to keep it. You know, you have to somehow realize that there is an afterlife and you're going to get rewarded. And it's going to be nice. It's going to be wonderful. All your dreams are going to come true, but not until you die. You have to die first."

Sister Maria Deo Gratias of the Most Blessed Sacrament

My mom was a re-weaver. She mended clothes at home. She went to school when she was sixteen in Milwaukee to learn this trade. It wasn't real common. Most of the people that called themselves re-weavers didn't really re-weave the cloth. She was a re-weaver in the true sense of the word, in that she re-wove cloth that she'd take apart from the hem. Under the lining, there would be cloth that she would cut out and she would fray the edges, and then she would re-weave each thread into that so you didn't see the hole. She did a superb job. She had an art that not many people had.

Different customers would go to different re-weavers and they would do a patch. And then it'd come off. She never advertised. She always had enough work because people would see her work, and they'd say, "We'd like ours done." She did it in her own home. She did that purposely because she wanted to be there when the kids came home from school.

She wanted us to take it up and I tried, but I don't have good eyes and you had to have good eyes for that. I was born with a very high nearsightedness. In fact, when I was born, I would scream every time that I was fed, and Mom and Dad were just frantic, trying to figure out what was going on, trying to find out what was wrong. And no doctors could find anything. All of a sudden Dr. French says, "Did you ever check her eyes?" And Mom found out I couldn't see the bottle until it was an inch away from my face, and then I screamed because it was there. That's how they found out that I needed glasses. Of course, I was put in glasses when I was two years old. It was really a real trip for my mom to try to keep glasses on a little kid because I was quite active. I'll never forget, when I was older—I must have been in third or fourth grade—we were helping Mom clean up the attic and we found those glasses and my sister said, "Mom, look at these glasses. Aren't they cute? They're little!" My sister Mickey said, "They're a doll's glasses." She said, "Whose are those?" And Mom said, "Those are *my* dolly's," and then she pointed at me. Those were my glasses that I wore when I was two and three years old. That was kind of clever: "Those are my dolly's."

We came from a very good family. It wasn't overly Catholic. We went to Mass every Sunday. Other than that, we were a very good, very close family, but we weren't overly religious.

My vocation is quite unique because I have the exact day that it started: It was a Friday afternoon at a quarter to three. We were at spelling class in sixth grade. We had just taken our test and we were checking the answers. The teacher had a little extra time, so she was writing on the board the different spellings. At a quarter to three, all of a sudden, I got this inner desire: "Go to church." I didn't pay too much attention. But it was very strong. I looked at the clock and my heart was pounding. It was, "Do I go? Do I don't?" Back and forth.

The inner voice was getting stronger and stronger. "Go to church. After school, go to church." Three o'clock, the school bell was going to ring; we were going to get out. I thought, What am I going to do? So I thought, I'll go.

My sister and I usually walked home together. I thought, "How can I tell her I'm going to church?" I told my sister that I was going to stay after school for a little bit. She said, "Why? Did you get in trouble?" I said, "No, I want to stay after for a little bit." She kept on me, "Well, what's the matter?" I said, "I'm going to go to church." "To church?" I said, "I don't know myself. I don't know anything about this. I'm just going to go to church. So then you just tell Mom that I'm going to be late. I'm just going to go to church for a while."

Well, then I went to church and I knelt down before the Blessed Sacrament. It's very hard to put something like that into words, but two hours went past in just a flash and I experienced God as I had never experienced Him before. It was just awesome to experience God that way. I knew I would be His the moment I knelt down. It's very hard to put into words. It wasn't that I didn't see anything; it was more of an experience of God in one's heart and that you knew He was speaking to you—that inner sense of His presence, there in the Blessed Sacrament. It was very, very, very real. It wasn't so much an emotional trip or an experience. I had experienced God in such a way that I wanted to give my life totally to Him and there was that firm desire to be

His alone. And that was it. It was just that experience with our Lord that I came to know Him as a person and wanted to give my life totally to Him.

When I looked at the clock, it was five o'clock. I had a half-hour walk home. I got home and Mom said, "Where were you?" I said, "I went to church!" Well, she didn't believe me, of course. I'm not going to spend two hours in church!

From that day on, I went to church after school and I developed a deep relationship with our Lord and I felt Him calling me to Himself. We went to a Catholic school and I knew the sisters were always called "the brides of Christ," and so I wanted to let Him know I would give my life totally to Him. I didn't know what that was called; I was only twelve years old. We didn't talk too much about the terms, just that they were the brides of Christ. I promised our Lord I would be a sister. I promised Him that I would be a virgin and never drink or smoke. I just would give Him my whole self, totally.

After this experience, I told Mom I wanted to go to the convent. I went home and told Mom, "Mom, I'd like to be a sister." She said, "Well, you can think about that." She thought I would change my mind. Mom would always say, "You'll change your mind. You'll change your mind." The funny thing, too, she said, "You'll always have to wear a dress." I said, "That doesn't matter. That's a habit, that's not a dress." I wasn't one to wear dresses. I was very active, did all kinds of things. I wasn't one to sit around. The other thing she would say was, "You're going to have to get up at five every morning." Now that was a real stickler because I like to sleep in. But I said, "That doesn't matter," because I just thought it doesn't matter what I have to give up. I didn't think so much about giving up; I just knew that I was going to be His and that was more on my mind. And it's good she did put this other stuff on me. It made me think, "It will all take care of itself."

There must have been something prior to that because when I think back, in fourth grade the principal gave me a nun doll. She called me to the office, and I was scared to death because I didn't know what she was calling me to the principal's office for. The thing was—she wanted to give me this nun doll. She must have seen something in me, but I never formulated it. I always admired the sisters but I never formulated my view that I can consciously remember.

After a few years, in eighth grade, I said, "Mom, I would really like to enter the convent." So she said, "Well, you can do what you want." I wanted to enter right after eighth grade, and I did. I was very interested in the cloistered life but my mother was totally against that. She said, "You can write to different orders." I got a book that had the different orders and I wrote to all kinds and got all kinds of mail back. On one of them, she noticed a Carmelite order on the return address. "Not there," she said. She didn't have any use for cloistered life, and so I had to put all of those aside. I didn't know anything about Poor Clares at that stage. I didn't know they existed.

Mom wanted to make sure I knew what I wanted. There was no doubt in my mind, but she didn't know that. And looking at it from her perspective, that's a little different than looking at it from my perspective, but Mom never believed in the cloistered life. "God never wanted anybody to live a life like that," she thought. And down the road in my story there is that point when I told her I was entering the cloistered life and she just couldn't see that God would call anyone to that life. Teaching, yes; you're serving people. That's fine. But to live in the cloister, no; she couldn't see that at all.

I had an older brother, but I left home first so that was an adjustment for Mom, more than I think I could ever realize at that time because I was just a child.

My dad, he had no problem understanding. Not the cloister—he didn't particularly care for that either—but he never voiced his opinion because he felt that your life is yours; you do what you want with it. The active life, he liked that. He was quite proud of it.

My mom didn't stand in the way because she always felt that, too—our life was our own, and you have to make of your life what you think God is calling you to. So she never stood in the way, except, being young, she wouldn't allow me to enter the cloister. But for active religious life, she wouldn't stand in the way. And so I entered. And I remembered when she said goodbye, I knew it was harder for her than it was for me and I can understand that. I have the vocation. She doesn't. My brothers and sisters would always say, "She kept on setting a place for you to come home." It was very hard for her to adjust because I was the first that left home and I think when the first one leaves home that's always the hardest on parents. And I think part of it, too, is we won't be getting married and having grandchildren for them; I kind of think that might have been behind my mom's mind. She never mentioned anything like that, but I think that might have been something that she probably would have considered. I think Mom said later she didn't want to build it up in me so much that if I decided this wasn't my life, that

I would feel uncomfortable saying that; I think that was her whole idea, you know, "You're always welcome to come home." And that was a good thing for Mom, on her part. I said, "I'm not coming home," but I always appreciated her saying that. And I would tell her, "It's always nice to know that, but don't count on it because I'm really solid in this vocation. I have no qualms. No way am I going to leave."

Of course, I was not the typical type to go into a convent. I only found this out years later: The relatives had a bet on me, whether I would make it or not! They didn't tell me that until my solemn vows, my perpetual vows. They said, "You know, we lost our bet." Whatever they bet, they gave to Mom and Dad.

When I was a kid, I was very active, the daredevil type, and into a lot of things. Most of my friends were boys, growing up, because they did things like build forts and ride stock cars—all kinds of things that I liked to do. I wasn't one to sit around and play with dolls. That's probably why the relatives didn't think I would make it. But Mom had us go over to the relatives' house and stay there for a week so we were used to back and forth; we weren't always home. That was another wisdom that she had, that we could be independent. Later, it was something that I desired; I was just very eager to learn the customs and the way of life in the convent.

We didn't just sit around when we were at my aunt's farm. I would go out with the boys and take turn with the boys riding the pigs to see who could stay on this big pig the longest. We would put the food in a pail and when the pig would put its head down—these were huge pigs, huge sows—then we'd put a rope over the neck and we'd jump on. The other one timed how long you stayed on because this pig would try to buck you off. And then, of course, when you're bucked off you have to get out right away because you'd get mauled to death. My grandpa had a bull. When we were kids we'd watch Toro on *The Lone Ranger*. So I thought I'd try that sometime. I got out there with a bull and I was just fascinated because it worked just like it said on television. He would make his feet like that and the smoke would come up from the dirt in the yard. It would be just like TV. He'd charge at me, and I'd step aside. Then he'd get on the other side and charge. I had a great time. My sister Mickey came and I said, "You try it." Mick got out there and got scared, and the bull almost got her. Of course, she told Grandpa and that ended my fun.

My dad was a prankster, too. He sometimes would tell us the things he would do. He worked until nine o'clock because when you first start a business you have the long hours of work. When Dad came home we always wanted to spend time with him, so we pretended, "Mom, I'm hungry." So then she'd say, "Come out and get something to eat." We just wanted to be with Dad a little bit, and he'd get into telling stories of what he did as a kid. And Mom said, "Frank, don't tell them that; they're going to do it." But none of the pranks were mean; they would just be innocent. One time, when he was at my aunt's restaurant, he said, "Oh, Fran, let me wait on the next customer." She said, "You can't wait on people. You don't know how to do that." He said, "Let me just try." He put on the apron. A couple sat down. She said, "I'll tell you what to do. You give them a menu, and then you..." She didn't want to lose her business. He went to the table, and of course he was a card. He gave them a menu, and then the lady asked, "Do you have frog legs?" And Dad said, "No, ma'am, that's just the way I walk." He's just a joker like that. It ran in the family. Us kids—three girls and three boys—enjoyed life. Cindy was born later, after I entered the convent. But the five of us were kind of close, within a year apart, all the way down. There's the song that was real popular with the line "creeping like a nun." Whenever that was on the radio, my brother blared that real loud, and he said, "That's you, that's you!" I just teased him back. We could tease about it. I don't know that they really took me too seriously until I entered. They just said, "What's the matter with you?"

Just after eighth grade, I entered the convent, the aspirancy. I went to Mass every day from that experience on, and I said the rosary every day. And I looked at religious orders, whenever I saw a sister with a different type of habit. At that time they were all wearing a habit that was distinct to their order so you could distinguish and tell when a sister from a different order came to Mass at your church. I noticed that there was a sister of Saint Agnes and I had never seen that type of sister, and so I went up to her and I asked her if she would be kind to send me some information on their order. And she did. Different ones that I met in church would send things, too. I think that's where I found most of the brochures. I was very taken with the Sisters of Saint Agnes. They were beautiful—their brochures and everything—and I had the sense that's the one that God wanted me to join. They had exposition of the Blessed Sacrament a lot, and that's what I liked. So I think that was the drawing card. In brochures, it said they were a very prayerful community. That's what drew me. I applied and I entered right after eighth grade. It was August of 1968 when I entered their community.

When I entered the aspirancy, I just loved it. We lived at the convent, and we would take a bus to the parochial high school, a Catholic high school in Fond du Lac. We lived a religious life for those four years. After those four years, you went to the next stage, the postulancy. I just told Mom and Dad to take my money out of my banking account and put it in theirs. Other nuns say, "I found this so hard to give up." I didn't. I didn't. In fact, I didn't even think about those things, like my bike; anybody that wanted my belongings could help themselves.

My family was always very eager to have me home and show me stuff. My brother got his license and he bought a car. I didn't even get in the house and he said, "I want to show you this car," and of course he wanted to drive me around. I said, "You think we should say hello to Mom first?" The joy of having me home was always there.

When I was on home visit from the aspirature for the summers, my mom said, "You have to date." I said, "I don't care. I can date. I don't mind." Whenever I went on a date I would say, "I am going to be a sister so it's just a friendship." I would think that was only fair to that other person. It would be kind of hard because sometimes I would come for home visit and my sisters' boyfriends would come to the house and they would want me to come out with them. We joked, so it was like, "Have her come along." Sometimes I would, and sometimes I would say, "You two go."

I always felt comfortable with boys. In high school, when I was home we would go bowling. I wasn't much for just sitting around. Sometimes they would just want to sit around and drink. I remember thinking, "This is just so boring." Then they gave me a drink. I don't like the smell of the stuff, let alone the taste, so I would say, "Oh, look at those stars. Isn't that something?" Then I would pour it in their drink. They didn't know they had a little bit more. I didn't get into drinking or anything. Being serious and expressing love to a date? No, because I loved our Lord and my love was for Him. We were just going out to have fun and we were good friends that way, but there was nothing serious because I had my mind made up.

Mom was really interested in one boy having an interest in me, so she'd invite him up to the cottage. Fine. He was a very nice person. He did ask me to go out. I said, "I have to pray my holy hour first," so he would meet me over at church. One night, he wanted to give me his ring. I said, "Oh, yeah, I'll take your ring." He was quite surprised. Then I took it and I put it by the altar. I said, "Everything I get, I give to Jesus." He went up and he snatched it, and he didn't ask again. He knew where I was at. I said, "I told you at the beginning that I'm not interested in dating in a serious way, like steady, because I'm not for marriage. That isn't where my calling is. We go out, that's fine. But if you give me your ring, I give it to Jesus."

The last year of aspirancy, our aspirancy closed so I was home that last year and went to a public school. Mom said, "You can go to the Catholic school," but I said, "That's a lot of money." I wanted my money to go back into the convent, so I just went to a regular high school for my senior year. I could adjust. I didn't have any trouble with that. When the aspirancy closed, I always considered myself still in the convent. We would go once a month; it was a nonresidency aspirancy for the few of us that were in this program, but it was no problem for me because I had my prayer life. I went to Mass every day, I had a holy hour every day, and I kept the schedule that whole high school year.

We were a close family, a very, very close family and we did a lot together as a family, played together a lot when we were little and even when we were older. We were always very close.

Both Mom and Dad were very easy to talk to. If there were little difficulties, Mom would sit down and talk it out with us. I think that was a very good thing, growing up, that you handled your own problems. She'd sit down and say, "What was the problem here?" And then we had to figure out: What was it? And then you could work it through. You didn't blame the others; you just worked it out yourself. And there was that give and take. We didn't really fight that much, but if there was a disagreement, well, "You work it out. Don't come running to Mom. You work it out." We'd work it out together, and then we'd be friends again. We never held grudges that long. Half the time you forgot about it and you kept going on with life.

Mom was a good psychologist, even though she didn't use that term. She was just very basic in dealing with life. You made the best of it. And she was a good example of that. Both parents were good examples of that. They had good psychology without even knowing what it was. It was just common sense. I think that's what I would say with both parents: They both had good common sense, how to live. If you got upset at what somebody did and you said, "They made me do it because they did this," my parents said, "No. You chose to get upset by what they did. You could have chosen not to. It might take a little virtue." But of course they never used those religious terms. They weren't that type, but they were just very upright and honest, and so they made you responsible for who you were.

They would never say right out, "Do not drink and do not smoke." But they realized we were getting older so one of them once said, "We've got to deal with you. If you don't smoke until you're eighteen, you get a hundred dollars. And if you don't drink until you're eighteen, you get another hundred dollars." That was a motivation for us. And it was a motivation for them. They didn't want us to get into those habits while we were children, so instead of saying, "Be sure you don't take drugs, be sure you don't do that," they did it this way. You were kind of looking forward to the hundred dollars as a kid. Now, when I was eighteen, I was in the convent four years already. So what did that mean to me? My brothers and sisters—that was something for them. But for myself, I made the choice after my experience at the altar; I didn't have the desire to do any of those things, so it wasn't fair. I told Mom it wasn't fair for me because there was no temptation to do it. So, therefore, I said, "You keep your $200. I don't want to take your money."

One time, I was on home visit. There was a school close to us and the kids were walking past our house to go to school. And I thought, boy, those kids are small. And Mom said, "Well, they're in sixth grade." And then it dawned on me that I had made my life decision when I was their age. Other than that, you were just growing up so you didn't think of yourself as so young. You just thought of yourself as yourself! But that's one experience I had where I realized, my gosh those kids are babies and I made my life decision when I was their age!

I've always had the desire to be a cloistered contemplative but because I was only fourteen years old when I entered, twelve when I made the decision, I had to obey my parents and they wouldn't hear of it. And I figured God wouldn't call it if it wasn't granted by my parents. I knew I had to respond because He was calling me to respond now, so I thought maybe He's calling me to a prayerful active community; I entered that and I loved it. I can't say I left that because of anything I didn't love while I was in that community. I was very happy there serving the people in different ways, first as a gym teacher and later as pastoral associate in the hospital. But then God in His way said, "No, I want you to go further." Also, the superiors at that convent would say, "Have you thought of the cloistered life?" They could see it in me that I was probably called to the cloister. They could discern that I have the gifts to be a cloistered contemplative nun. And they said, "It won't be long; you're going to be a cloister." One superior told me that and I said, "If that be, that would be very fine, but I myself I don't know at this point whether He wants me to be a contemplative in action, or truly a contemplative." Did He want it, or did I want it?

My mom wanted to steer me away from a cloistered community. The other community, I think that that was all right with her. You could be a teaching sister; that was all right. She was a re-weaver, and so she had customers come to the door to fix garments, whatever they had holes in. One day, a priest came and he wanted his suit coat fixed. And so Mom said, I'll ask him. In fact she came out and said, "God would never want anyone to enter one of the cloistered kinds of orders," and then the priest said, "Oh, yes, He would." And that helped my mom because she could talk to him and he talked to her about the value of the cloistered life. I just think how humble my mom was to share that with me. Because I wasn't home, I didn't know that that experience had happened. She shared it with me. I think that had helped her. I was here already when she shared that with me.

I think I can do more for people in the cloister than I could ever do out there, even though I did a lot out there, so to speak. Touching people's souls, you do that through your prayers. We don't see the results of that in the hidden life, but we have the faith to know that is what is happening. Here, it's kind of like the powerhouse of prayer going out into the community and touching people's lives in a way that we're not aware of, but that we know it happens. And so to be a part of that, to give yourself totally to God, I think is a real privilege. To be together and have a life provided by the Church—that frees us to do this. There is a real freedom because of our customs; we don't have to follow the protocol that you would have if in the world. We have our own monastic culture here. And we live side-by-side, respecting each sister's union with our Lord. In that living together day in and day out, knowing that we do keep silence and in that silence, she's communing with God, I'm communing with God and somehow developing our own relationships with God. But more than that, that's our apostolate—to pray for others, and God gives graces to others that they would not have had otherwise. That doesn't put it on us. It's not us, it's Him.

That's the purity of the life of being one with Him. It's a union, the contemplative prayer and whatever you're doing outside of chapel; it's not two separate things. It just flows into each other and it's just the life of union.

Now, our life is a perpetual Lent really, and I love it. I love Lent. It's more simple. So in a sense, it's probably my feast day because I love it. The simpler, the better. I just happen to be that type of person that I like that.

I'm only an instrument, as each of us sisters are. But we have the responsibility to be good instruments in our apostolate of prayer. We don't work it through with people like I did when I was a pastoral associate, but I work it through in a different way. I say, "I pray for you, and I asked God to give you the special graces and the nudges you need to think things out." That's what I think my role is now. I think it's a very important role that I can't take for granted.

Even those who don't call us and don't contact us in any way—that don't believe in us—we can touch their hearts.

2

The Claustrophobic Nun

In the monastery, everything is directed for the search for the face of God. Everything is reduced to the essential because the only thing that matters is what leads to Him. Monastic recollection is attention to the presence of God. So when you think of how the media, mass media in the different forms, can distract and be like a noise that can interfere with communion with God, we try to reduce that; most, we reduce to zero. We don't listen to the radio or watch television, but it's not because we're against progress, or we're against information, it's just because of the effect that that can have on an environment that is silent, and what it can do to a recollected mind. It would come in and would just totally disrupt.

Sister Mary Nicolette of the Father of Mercies

To Sister Mary Nicolette, it is a familiar refrain, a now-old family joke: It is for the best that the Corpus Christi Monastery sits on South Main Street and that no mountain can be seen on the flat midwestern landscape; otherwise, the travel-hungry Sister Mary Nicolette might be tempted to run for the hills.

Sister Mary Nicolette laughs when she retells this jest of her relatives, which is funny because it is true. She was a child from Texas who grew up in Europe. The Alps were her backyard. When her family lived in Italy, and she was still known as Monica, she met Pope John Paul II twice. Once, he patted her on the cheek. When her father took a job in Lichtenstein, she learned German. In Austria, she hiked the mountain trails. There, she says, nature spoke to her of God. Her family moved and she thrived in each new culture. Because Sister Mary Nicolette managed to pick up languages like other teenagers pick up boyfriends, she considered studying etymology in college. And then she discovered the perfect outlet for her love of traveling and her talent for languages—a career as a flight attendant. "I had thought of being an airline stewardess because I love travel and wanted to see the world," she says, "and I thought that would be a great way to do it. I knew that wouldn't be a permanent thing, but that was a dream. And I thought, well, maybe I could even be a pilot." At twenty, when she became a postulant of the Poor Clare Colettine Order, Monica was fluent in English, Italian, German, and French.

Although she is allotted up to four family visits each year, her siblings are scattered across the globe; she usually sees only some of her family members once a year. She has a large family: three sisters and two brothers. In their transitory upbringing together as expatriates, the siblings bonded through humor. Once, when her younger brother arrived at the monastery for a family visit with his wife and children, Sister Mary Nicolette reminded her young niece that she is the big sister to the girl's dad. The child did not buy it; her father is six feet tall. Sister Mary Nicolette looks petite, by comparison, especially when seated, talking to her family from the enclosure side of the parlor—a metal grille between Sister Mary Nicolette and her relatives. Sister Mary Nicolette climbed on her chair; her ankle-length habit hid her advantage from her niece's side of the grille. Her niece was fooled and awed.

Sister Mary Nicolette's brother travels for work. He has told his sister that he thinks of her during these trips; when he stood on a mountaintop in Peru, he was startled by the amazing view and the fact that his sister would never have the chance to hike up that mountain or take in that scene. Sister Mary Nicolette remembers him saying that he feels sorry for her because she is missing out. All joking between the siblings stopped then. Sister Mary Nicolette says she told her brother, "That's really sweet to be thinking of me. But you know, I don't think, 'I'm here and I'm never going to be able to go out again.' You don't think of it as something restricting. It's something that's freeing. I'm freed of the worries and of all the exterior things."

Sister Mary Nicolette realizes that the cloistered monastic way of life is difficult to understand, to translate to her own family. She received the calling to this life, she says, and so has been granted a supernatural grace to value and accept the vocation.

Sister Mary Nicolette's journey to this place began, she says, with a lie. Her parents raised their six children Catholic. Sister Mary Nicolette believed she could become whatever she wanted; any path she chose in life, her parents told her, she should do with her whole heart. Her parents encouraged their children to consider any vocation, including the priesthood or sisterhood.

In childhood, Monica encountered religious figures regularly; nuns taught her at Catholic school, and when the family lived in Rome, the birthplace of the Catholic Church, sisters dressed in the full habit were a common sight in public.

From an early age, Monica wanted a family of her own. She planned to get married and have eight children. "It was a beautiful ideal for me to be a mother and a wife and have a lot of children," she says. Above all, she wanted to give her life for others. She says, "I wanted to do something that would really make a difference and help. I always wanted to help." This aspiration fit with her conception of marriage and motherhood.

Monica became what she jokingly refers to as the "black sheep" of the family when, instead of following the path of her two older sisters who had followed in their parents' footsteps and attended the University of Dallas, she enrolled at Franciscan University of Steubenville in Ohio. Her parents' and sisters' alma mater is also a Catholic institution, but Monica heard of its reputation as a party school and she thought the Franciscan university would be the better place to meet someone who shared her beliefs, someone with whom she could spend the rest of her life. "Something in my heart told me this decision was going to be important for the rest of my life—if I was going to meet the man I was going to marry, or if I would discover the vocation God had for me," she says.

During her first year of college, Monica was put off by the religious fanaticism she encountered in the other students. Her father, a Fulbright fellow, had moved his family overseas to teach at universities; during Monica's teenage years at a restored monastery they referred to as the Sistine Chapel of Central Europe, her peers were older philosophy students. At the Franciscan university, Monica befriended but debated a student who believed that every Christian should evangelize the world aggressively, preaching the gospel with the intent to convert people. Monica agreed, to an extent. "His approach was, everyone has got to do this and if you don't do it, you're going to be lost. My approach was, I can save souls and help further the kingdom of God by prayer," Sister Mary Nicolette says.

Back home in Austria the summer after her freshman year, Monica told her mom she was thinking of transferring to another college. Monica was turned off by a polarizing, judgmental message: "You're not good enough and we want to convert you." She says, "They were out to convert everybody," Monica included. She decided to try one more semester at the Franciscan university before making a final decision about transferring. Her sophomore year, Monica had a much different, much better experience. Now, in retrospect, she ascribes the pushiness and zealousness as acts of "misdirected charity."

During her sophomore year, she and two friends worked together in the college's conference office, helping organize a massive event, Pentecost in Pittsburgh. When their work was complete, the three sat in their dormitory, exhausted. They needed a break. One of them said she knew just the place where they could rest—a cloistered monastery in Ohio. She picked up the phone right then and called to arrange a visit. The Mother Abbess said she could not offer a place for young women to stay if they simply wanted a vacation, but the monastery welcomed visits by those interested in the cloistered monastic life. In that case they could stay across the street from the monastery with an active order of nuns, and they were permitted to attend the cloistered nuns' chapel service and Divine Office.

"We were all three sitting on the bed," Sister Mary Nicolette says, "and I remember my friend covered the phone and she said, 'Mother wants to know if we're interested.' We all said, 'Oh, yes, we're interested! We're interested!'" Sister Mary Nicolette laughs. "So this is how I got my vocation— through a lie. I was interested in knowing how Buddhist monks lived, too!"

Sister Mary Nicolette says her two friends "played their part a lot better than I played my part" because they asked for private interviews with Mother Superior. Monica did not. "Uh-uh!" she says.

Sister Mary Nicolette does not question her friends' sincerity in asking for those private talks. "They were very, very, very spiritual so I'm sure they spoke to Mother about spiritual things, their spiritual lives and what-not," she says, adding that the two were not interested in becoming cloistered monastic nuns.

In the monastery's chapel, the Blessed Sacrament was exposed perpetually. Sister Mary Nicolette spent hours praying before the Blessed Sacrament, the host that, once consecrated, Catholics believe becomes the very presence of Jesus. She says, "I remember I was praying there and I felt a strong sense in my heart, not an audible voice, but a voice speaking to my heart, kind of, saying, 'This is where I want you. You don't know where, you don't know how, and you don't know when, but this is where I want you.' And I was shocked. This is not what I was expecting. At all! Not right now. I was expecting to relax from my busy, stressed work and instead God hit me over the head and told me this was really what He wanted for me."

Monica talked with an extern nun, who maintains a unique role in an enclosure, as the one responsible for communicating with the public and with the world on behalf of the cloistered nuns. The nun explained the mission of the Poor Clare Order: Cloistered contemplatives dedicate their entire lives "for the salvation of souls to the complete love of God without any distraction, or without a divided heart." The extern sister told Monica that, in the enclosure, there are no distractions, and so their hearts are not divided because they are separate from the world, devoted to God alone. For Monica, this description—this life—seemed like an answer she did not know she was seeking. "It's all about this deep relationship with God, for your own salvation but also for others," she says. "And I just thought, that's always what I felt deep in my heart. I wanted to live for others. Everything she is saying is what I feel God created me for. I imagine it's what someone would feel when they meet someone they love and want to marry: God created me for this person and this person for me. We were made for each other. It was the same thing for this; everything she was saying, I thought this is the whole reason God created me."

Introspective and reflective Monica took stock of all that the cloister denied—traveling, marriage, motherhood, talking to and visiting her parents and siblings. Hugging her loved ones at will. "It just seemed so radical to me and so drastic," she says, "and I didn't know if I could do that. In my mind at the time, I'm just working through it and I'm just saying, 'I'm really attached to my family.' I'm giving all these reasons to God why this isn't a good idea. I'm like, 'Lord, you know, you *know* me. You know I can't do this!' "

Monica's proficiency with languages offered little solace; rather, it was a lens into yet another obstacle. The words "cloister" and "claustrophobia" both derive from the same Latin root, meaning "to close" or "to lock." "That's where the word 'cloister' comes from—being shut in," Sister Mary Nicolette says. "That was very ironic. I get claustrophobic in an elevator. So I'm like, 'Lord, the cloister? I'm going to get claustrophobic!' That's the word that comes to my mind. You know being shut in and not being able to travel. I just thought, 'How am I going to be able to do this, Lord? You're asking me to do something that's just completely contrary to my nature.' "

Monica never learned if her two friends asked for applications to join the Ohio monastery, or if the Mother Abbess offered the applications during their private meetings. "All I know is that when we walked out of there, they had application papers and I didn't," Sister Mary Nicolette says. "I didn't dare ask for the application papers."

Over the next couple of weeks, Monica wrestled with an unsettling prospect: She might have stumbled, unwittingly, upon her vocation—to be a cloistered monastic nun. "To my human, limited view, this was something that just seemed so contrary to what I was expecting of life," she says. "And it was beautiful; I wasn't against that, but it just seemed so much bigger than what I could do." She told God, "You know, I thought you knew me. Why are you asking this of me? You know me better than I know myself."

Gradually, Monica engaged her own desires and her will in a mental exercise, a question of faith. She became convinced that if God truly called her to this vocation, He would also grant her the ability to embody it. Sister Mary Nicolette says she took a "stab in the dark." She asked one of the two friends for her application papers to the monastery, since neither of the other young women planned to apply, and Monica submitted her own application to join the Poor Clare monastery in Ohio.

She was rejected, though, for health reasons. In childhood, Monica was diagnosed with a rare autoimmune disease after antibodies, which had been called forth to fight a virus as they should have, turned and fought her own body, devastating the healthy muscle cells. The monastic community's physician thought that someone with her disease could not live the physically demanding Poor Clare life of fasting and manual labor and interrupting sleep at midnight for the Divine Office. "I was on medication, but I was stable. I was crushed," Sister Mary Nicolette says.

"I thought, 'This is what God created me for. This is my life,' and I had come to a peaceful acceptance of saying, 'If God wants me to do this, He's going to help me.' And then it was, 'No,' and it was just like everything, my whole world, came down. I just thought, 'Oh my goodness.' "

She says she cried for two days after hearing news of her rejection. Monica worked to interpret the twist; maybe she was mistaken in thinking she was called to the cloistered contemplative life, or maybe the monastery in Ohio was not the right community.

Again, Monica enrolled in college courses at her Franciscan university. She remained open to the possibility that she might be called to become a nun. Sampling religious orders and communities became her weekend pursuit. "There was a group of us at school—seven at first, and twelve by the end of the year—who were interested in a religious life," she says. "We'd go convent-hopping, or make 'nun runs' on weekends and we'd visit these convents."

Monica was impressed when she visited a convent in Kentucky. She was taking everything into consideration. "I loved their habit," she says. "I just thought their habit was so beautiful. It's all black and they had a head covering that doesn't go across the forehead; I think it goes a little bit higher and it covers the ears. But it's all black and they have an insignia of the Sacred Heart of Jesus. The austerity of it attracted me for some reason."

She thought the Poor Clare habit was beautiful, too. "It kind of captured my whole idea of a sister who is consecrated and set apart," she says. "It's a sign, a very tangible sign to me of that. And I loved it."

Monica kept thinking, "The Poor Clares is the place. Poor Clares—it just kept coming back to me." On her birthday, a Sunday, a piece of mail was delivered to Monica's dorm room. She thinks it could have been dropped in the wrong mailbox the day before, then left at her door when the error was detected. The return address on the envelope listed a Poor Clare Colettine Order in Rockford, Illinois. "The fact that it was my birthday and it contained the address of this monastery I don't think is a coincidence," she says. "I think God works through little things like that, just little touches in our life here and there you can see all along the journey. It was just the special touch I needed that day from the Lord. So it was a beautiful birthday present that year." The form letter served a simple function—calling Monica's attention to another Poor Clare monastery—yet Monica felt, because of the unique timing and situation of the letter's arrival, she might be fated to go there.

Monica wrote a letter to the Mother Abbess. She wrote about her visit to the Poor Clare monastery in Ohio, that she had asked to join that community but was turned down because her health was not deemed adequate. Monica thought it prudent to be honest from the outset about any potential obstacle. She informed the Mother Abbess she wanted to live as a Poor Clare. She assumed that this candor about her medical condition and the other monastery's rejection would sabotage her acceptance into the Rockford community.

On Christmas break while home in Austria, Monica received a response. The Mother Abbess explained in her letter that the process of joining a religious community should start with a visit; she invited Monica to spend a few days at the Corpus Christi Monastery. Monica replied that she would love to visit when it could be arranged. She did not mention at the time that on a student's budget she could not afford the $110 round-trip flight from Franciscan University of Steubenville in Ohio to Chicago, or the $98 bus fare. After the holidays, Monica returned to college. About ten days before spring break, while she was working in the conference office, a friend walked in and announced to everyone within earshot, "Does anyone want to go to Chicago?" Monica shouted, "I'll go!" She figured a group was taking a road trip and she could split the cost of gas and tolls. Monica learned the student had found an airline deal called "Friends Fly Free"—two tickets for the price of one. The two split the cost of one ticket, each paying $60 for the round-trip fare. "You wouldn't find that normally so I said, 'this is a godsend,' because I could pay for that," Monica says.

She flew to Chicago. A relative picked her up at the airport and dropped her off at the monastery so she could stay for three days during Holy Week, leading up to Easter. "I spoke to Mother Abbess and a few of the sisters and I was so afraid," she says. "I was just scared to death. I was terrified. I think I just sat in the chair and listened most of the time to what they had to say to me. I didn't say much myself. I was just so terrified. You would never know it, but I'm a shy person!"

Before Monica left the monastery, the Mother Abbess told her she could return to join the community if she wanted. The ease of this acceptance stunned and frightened Monica. "I didn't expect that," she says. "I was like, 'Whoa.'" She told the Mother Abbess she still had a year of college left before she graduated. "I guess I was scared of being hurt again, of it not working out and putting all your hopes in something, and then it's just crushed," Sister Mary Nicolette says. "And I think it was just a defense mechanism; I didn't want to commit myself."

Back at college, Sister Mary Nicolette solicited advice from a priest whom she had sought out earlier to help her discern her vocation. She conveyed her confusion. "This is the life I want," Sister Mary Nicolette remembers telling him, "but when I was there, I felt nothing. It was just, like, blank." She told the priest that maybe God was treating her differently in this situation than during her visit to the monastery in Ohio. "Maybe this time," she told the priest, "he's not going to whisper in my ear, 'This is where I want you.' Maybe he's going to say, 'This time, you make the choice.'"

The priest pointed to a park bench and instructed Monica to sit there until she heard a directive from God. Sister Mary Nicolette says, "It was a lovely day to sit on a park bench!" She explains, "The priest wanted me to come to a conclusion for myself, you know, because he knew he couldn't tell me what to do. He couldn't tell me, 'You go and try.' He thought, 'You have to figure this out on your own.' He was very wise. And I remember just feeling in my heart, 'Now, the first place the door was closed to me. Here, the door is opening to me. So the choice is up to me. What am I going to do? Am I going to give it a try and if it doesn't work out, well, at least I tried? Or am I going to spend the rest of my life wondering if that's where God wanted me?' "

Monica was up from the park bench, decision made, within an hour. She tracked down the priest—with his long white beard, he looked to Monica like a jovial Santa Claus—and she told him she planned to join the monastery. He gave Monica a "bear hug" and congratulated her.

That summer, when her junior year came to a close, Monica flew home to Austria for two final months with her family before joining the Poor Clare Colettine Order. "A lot of people probably think we spend the last month thinking, 'This is the last time I'm going to eat ice cream, walk in the mountains, hug my parents,' " Sister Mary Nicolette says. "And most of that is true. Most of that is true. It is the last time you do a lot of things.

"I had a few minutes where I thought, 'What am I doing? I'm crazy.' I had moments that I wavered. You get cold feet. But when you get past moments like that, there was just a real eagerness; I know this is it, I'm not going to let anything stop me—fear or the uncertainty."

Sister Mary Nicolette repeats and laughs at another nun's joke, that a few of them who did not finish college become members of the Dropouts for Jesus Club at the monastery. Her new life, her hidden life, began when she gave up her shoes and was given a new name. Sister Mary Nicolette is not, in fact, this cloistered contemplative nun's real religious name. Humility is integral to the Franciscan spirit, and anonymity is treasured as a virtue of the enclosure. Sister Mary Nicolette is the name she chose as an alias, a condition for disclosing this story of her life.

Sister Mary Nicolette discovered when she entered the monastery that God indeed equipped her to live as a cloistered monastic nun when He called her. "It's a mystery," she says. "There's really no way to be able to explain that, but when you get the vocation, you get the strength to do it. So it was a sacrifice to leave my family, and it was a sacrifice to leave everything, but at the same time there's something so much deeper that fills you. It's like it makes up for everything else. It makes up for that sacrifice. And you know that it's worth it. There's a reason for it and it makes it all worth it."

Since entering the monastery, Sister Mary Nicolette has heard from the friend she argued with in college about evangelism. He wrote to her that he understands the point she was trying to make: Someone can have an impact on the world quietly, behind the scenes, praying for souls and for the conversion of souls, praying that a missionary will speak the right words at the right time. Sister Mary Nicolette says, "You need both. You need the prayerful support of the religious—of cloistered contemplatives—to support those who go out and evangelize, to prepare the way for them so that people to whom they are speaking will be receptive. And a lot of times that's only going to come from someone praying for them. We don't know who they are, of course, but we can pray that souls will be receptive to God's message."

Ironically, this worldly woman does not know the layout of the city beyond the cloistered grounds. She does not know the neighborhood just past the monastery's stone wall. One winter night, when traffic was light, Sister Mary Nicolette went outside the wall with a novice to shovel the driveway and the parking lot next to the Shrine of Mary. A car stopped. The driver asked the two for directions. Sister Mary Nicolette smiled and told the driver, "We don't get out much!" She imagines the driver might have been searching for a street around the corner from the monastery, but she had no context for her physical environment.

Having embodied her gifts and hopes in a life she did not realize she longed for, Sister Mary Nicolette says that her question to God as she debated, internally, the veracity of her calling—if He really knew her personality, if He might be placing impractical demands on her God-given temperament—has also been resolved. "That's the thing," Sister Mary Nicolette says. "He knows us better than we know ourselves."

Although claustrophobic, Sister Mary Nicolette has never felt restricted in her private seventy-eight-square-foot cell, or in the 25,000-square-foot cloistered monastery, or within the fourteen-acre enclosed complex.

Sister Mary Nicolette, who once hoped to have a family as large as the one she was born into, believes her desire for motherhood was not abandoned, but satisfied in the cloister, which she describes as a "powerhouse of prayer." "I love the whole idea of spiritual motherhood, that we're the spouses of Christ—another name for sisters—and our fruitfulness in the Church is to bear spiritual children," she says.

"That's one of the things that struck me very much, that struck a chord in my heart, is that you're not only responsible for a few souls, like you would be in your own family if you had your own children; you would be responsible for *these* souls. But you're responsible for a multitude. It's something that's very deep in every woman's heart, probably, to give herself for others. I think that's a part of our nature—to give yourself for others, and even that is fulfilled in our vocation. You know, we're not physically mothers, but we are mothers to souls. And that's something that's very fulfilling in our hearts." It's a paradox, Sister Mary Nicolette says: Cloistered nuns leave the world in order to be for the world, albeit absently and anonymously. She has removed herself from the world in order to give herself wholly to others.

During an especially harsh midwestern winter, Sister Mary Nicolette and Sister Maria Benedicta, shoveled for hours to remove piles of snow from the monastery's premises. During communal hour with the other nuns, Sister Mary Nicolette shared a lesson inspired by their manual labor. She showed them a cartoon she had drawn with the caption, "You don't have to go to the North Pole to reach all four corners of the world." It is Sister Maria Benedicta who recalls and tells about the cartoon. "Here," she says, "your heart can expand to the whole world."

In her spare time, Sister Mary Nicolette deploys her language skills to translate religious texts. She is translating into English a compilation of writings by Poor Clare nuns over the centuries. The journeys of this thoughtful, seasoned traveler are now entirely internal.

Sister Mary Michael of the Hearts of Jesus and Mary

Both my father and mother were German. We lived right in town, just a little town—five hundred people, and only eighteen in my high school senior class. My dad owned a garage and filling station. They had a little restaurant with one counter, one booth. My mother worked there. I just got in the way.

My dad could fix almost anything. He was a workaholic. The garage was right next to the house, a few steps down, and he was there at all hours. It was hard to get him to come in and eat; he worked very hard.

We were the first ones in town to get a television set. The neighbors would come over and watch on our "snow TV." You had to put the antennae up high, and all the neighbors would come over when we'd say, "It's good; it's clear tonight. Come on over."

They were good parents. They got along well and it was a good thing my father died first because he couldn't have gotten along without my mother. I couldn't see how he could live alone.

They were just always there. My mother was always home. We came home from school and she was always there. Our home was *everything*. You always wanted to be there. Our Christmases were great; we had our tree and the gifts were way out to the middle of the floor. I'd go to our friends' houses and they didn't have many gifts, but we always had lots of gifts. We weren't wealthy, but I never felt I was lacking anything.

I was a tomboy. I should have learned about fixing cars, but I didn't. And I didn't learn anything about cooking. My older sister's a great cook. I don't know what happened to me. I really don't. My sister would go shopping and see things in the store and bring things home. Not me; whatever was on the list, that's what I came home with.

I think there were thirteen years between my older brother and me. And then my younger brother, he was five years younger. It was like two families.

We were always trying to get away from him, when we were doing things we didn't want him to know, like smoking under the railroad cars. We had a lot of fun. We went swimming down in a crick, a river. We had to track through all this grass and woods to get to this hole—a swimming hole. Then we'd build grass huts down there. Can you imagine? And then we'd crawl in there. I just can't imagine. There must have been snakes. I'm just petrified of snakes. That would be a good place where we would do our smoking, too.

My family was real easygoing. Even friends I played with, we just didn't have all their rules. We were fussy kids with eating, but my mother just tried to fix something we liked. I didn't eat much; I was just in a hurry to go out and play outside. As I was running out the door, I would grab candy. We didn't have to do the dishes or anything like that. They were good parents but they weren't real strict. I'd be running down to get my friends to play and they had to finish dishes. Well, we didn't.

We didn't have a Catholic school because it was just a small town, but we were good practicing Catholics and went to church every Sunday. Some of the nuns came to teach us in the summertime, and I enjoyed going to classes but I didn't have thoughts about becoming a nun. Some of the girls from our town would go there to a boarding school for high school, maybe forty miles away. They stayed the week and then came home. My sister-in-law did that. The thought was too much for me. To be away from home, I couldn't think of doing that at that time. I couldn't see how the other girls could leave home and go there for school; it wasn't something I would ever think of doing. It frightened me. I just couldn't imagine doing that.

During high school, I was a cheerleader. That was fun. We went to all the basketball games and I liked that. In fact, I was a cheerleader all four years.

In high school, I wanted to be a doctor, so I went to the University of Wisconsin–Stevens Point for the first four years. I studied a lot and worked hard to get good grades. I wasn't involved in a lot of things; I was concerned with studies and getting good grades. Then I applied to medical school. At that time, I think there were only seven in the class—just a few—and I was accepted. I guess I had these ideas of helping people and being a missionary doctor. When I went to college, I still went to Mass. Sometimes, I would go during the week. I didn't have any devotion to the Blessed Mother. I didn't even pray the rosary after a while. But that all changed later.

My younger brother lived with me in a small apartment when I was going to medical school. He was completely carefree, and I was working so hard and spending all my time studying and trying to get good grades. Maybe I envied him because he was so carefree. He worked in a florist shop and he had these crazy friends. One drove a hearse!

This was during the Vietnam War, a kind of wild time with a lot of demonstrations. I remember getting involved, and the tear gas, which burns. I went a couple of times when they were hooping and hollering, or they'd be stopping traffic, but I was never that involved. I observed more than I took part. I was against the war at that time. My father was against it because he didn't want my brother to have to go.

In medical school, you're assigned a cadaver. It's in a large container. And to work on it you just crank and it comes up. You start and you work from the outside, every part of the whole body. That wasn't any problem. That didn't bother me. You get kind of cold. You don't think about it too much. It's something you have to learn to work on. It's not like you're thinking this was somebody's father or somebody's brother.

I had a real close friend—Bill—in medical school. We worked on the same cadaver. I can remember when we'd finish at night—the fat tissue it gets under your nails–and I can remember a lot of times we'd go to a restaurant nearby.

It was getting into the clinical work, working with people, that I found hard. I don't think I had the personality for it. I wanted to leave my first year. I was having a hard time and didn't want to go anymore but my older brother came over and talked me into staying. We weren't close. We got along okay but we weren't real close; not like with my younger brother where you can say almost anything and you think along the same lines. My older brother was real nice. He was just trying to help me out.

It was a disappointment for my parents, for my family, because they were going to have a doctor in the family. I don't blame them, I suppose. It was a disappointment. It was hard to say, "I don't want to do this." There was one class I had a hard time with, but I stuck it out. I kept going.

In my third year, I left. It was traumatic. It was hard—the whole thing, telling them you're leaving and quitting medical school. It was a hard time. I mean, I'm glad I left. I mean, I didn't want it, I just didn't want it. In the third year, I guess I was kind of panicky about doing an externship at a hospital. I got panicky over the whole thing and I couldn't take it anymore. It was too much for me, so I said I want to leave. You had to talk with the head of the different departments. They question you up and down. It was awful.

They try to figure out what's going on in your head. And why you really want to leave. And they have other ideas. I can remember one saying something about where I was going to go. He was accusing me of something about my parents. I can't remember—insinuating something about being close to them. I just remember it was upsetting. I guess he thought that maybe I was letting other people control my life; I wasn't in charge, something to that effect. Maybe he thought I was too close to them, that I couldn't do things on my own. I just remember it was an unpleasant conversation.

After med school I went to a technical school for a little while to learn the computer. I went to Milwaukee, and I was going to work on a graduate program, but I didn't carry that through. I stayed in a crummy apartment. Actually, now when I think of it, it was really scary; the apartment I stayed in, they said that somebody was murdered in it. I think it was on a bad side of the city. It was the east side of Milwaukee. Then I went to Chicago and I found work at a large insurance company in the Loop, right on Lake Michigan. You looked out one side and you could see the lake. It was a real good job. I worked there almost eighteen years. That's where I was working when I got this call.

I liked my job. I didn't have any reason to want to leave. I really loved that work. I couldn't wait to get there in the morning. We had "flex time," so we could come in during a range of time in the morning as long as you put in a certain number of hours. You didn't have to be there at seven; you could come between seven and nine. And your lunch break wasn't just boom-boom. Some days it was longer, and some days it was shorter. It was a beautiful job. I just loved it. I was a programmer analyst. We wrote the programs, designed the programs to pay insurance bills.

I've been lucky because the twenty years I worked, I enjoyed it. Not everybody likes their work. If I had it to do over, I wish I had gotten into that right away rather than go to medical school. I had some training in computers already, and the insurance company gave me some training. At the time, women weren't being paid equally with men, so to catch up to make us on the same level, all of a sudden, every little while, I got a pay raise. It was really funny; I would come home and I had another pay raise! They were big chunks!

In the meantime, right across from where I worked there was a Catholic church, and almost every day I went to Mass down there. I had this thought that I should start praying the rosary again. After high school, the rosary was in the back of a drawer in my bedroom and there it sat. I don't think I prayed the rosary at all during college. I don't know where this inspiration came from, but I thought I should start praying the rosary. I started trying to do it when I went to bed. That was a mistake; you start praying these prayers when you get into bed and you just fall asleep. So that didn't work.

One Christmas, I think I was down at my mother's house. She lived a block away. She was in her late seventies. Her brother used to live with her and he had left some books in a cabinet, including *The Song of Bernadette*, a book of fiction about Saint Bernadette of Lourdes.

That's where it all started. I read that book and something just clicked. I got interested in her life, which started a desire to read other spiritual books. I started going to Mass all the time. During the week it was in Chicago, where I worked, but then on the weekend where I lived in Indiana I would go wherever they had Mass early in the morning. I had this real desire to pray. I wanted to pray a lot.

I was so excited about this new thing that was happening to me. At lunchtime, I couldn't wait to get out and go to a Catholic bookstore; I'd spend almost my entire lunch hour browsing the books and buying some new ones. I was just so excited about all this.

I remember that I loved baseball. I loved the Chicago Cubs. My mother did, too. She noticed that I lost interest in that. The Cubs game would be on at her house and I'd be outside reading. Things like that were changing. My family noticed that, and my mother would get upset because I always wanted to be at church. I'd take off to go up and just pray by myself. It was just such a strong desire to do that, to be alone.

One morning as I was coming out of Mass, an older woman came up to me. She noticed I was always at Mass. There is a statue of how the Blessed Mother looked at Fatima. Some people would take that statue into their homes and they'd invite people in to say the rosary and prayers; the statue would stay for a week and then go on to another house. She invited me out to her home because she had it in her home, and so I went out there and then I got to be real friendly with her. She read a lot of spiritual books and biographies of saints and we got to talking a lot. I was having all these desires to read about saints and spiritual things, and so I had someone to talk to and share my experience with. I couldn't share with my family; they were concerned. I couldn't relate this to them because they were upset that I was being so taken away by wanting to go to church all the time and wanting to pray. I had this lady I could talk to. She mentioned one time when I was out there one evening, "Maybe you have a vocation to a religious life." I thought, that's impossible because of my age. I said, "What kind of religious group would I go to?" Sisters that serve the sick with nursing, or that teach—I didn't have any of those qualities. I didn't understand it, but I still had this desire to pray and dedicate myself to God. It went on like that for a while. She knew a priest, and it was a real coincidence because he had just been up to *this* monastery teaching the sisters Gregorian Chant.

I got up enough courage to call him and I went to see him and while we were talking, he just came out after a while and said, "Maybe you're being called to the contemplative life." That wasn't a shock because I had that feeling. One time I was reading a book about monks and the contemplative life. I had this feeling, that's what God was asking me to do. I can't explain how it was; it was interior. Deep down I knew that's what I was supposed to do. It was a real coincidence, the priest had been up to this monastery teaching the sisters here Gregorian Chant. He mentioned this monastery to me. I said, "I'm probably too old, though." He said, 'Well, we'll call." Then I got information.

What impressed me when I got the pamphlet was they all wore long habits and there were pictures of them at night, kneeling before the Blessed Sacrament. I saw all that and said, "That looks great!" It made such an impression on me. I got up enough courage to call here and that was real hard, to pick up that phone to call and make an appointment, because this was all so strange. I had no idea really what the monastic life was all about. It was all new to me. I just knew that God was calling me. I knew for sure. There weren't any doubts. In some ways, I had it easy because a lot of the women that come here are looking; they're searching; they don't know quite what they want. They go to different monasteries, look into the active life. I didn't have that. I knew I was supposed to come to this—to the contemplative life, for sure.

My mother, when I approached her about the contemplative life and showed her the pamphlet, it just really hurt her. She didn't want anything to do with it. That was hard because she was so much against it. She was older. And she was sick. Since I wasn't married, I took care of her a lot. I was close to my mother, and she was getting older. She had a bad heart, but I think she died of some kind of cancer. She was always getting blood transfusions. But I knew God came first. It was really hard, but that was just the way it was. I'm sure now she understands.

The second time I visited the monastery, I just wanted to ask some questions about what I had to do to get here. I was so anxious to come and so afraid they wouldn't take me and it was like, "Let me in!" I kept wanting to know, "What should I do next?"

I had a strong conviction that I knew I belonged at the monastery. I was supposed to come here. It was what I was supposed to do. It was just I had to hurry up and get here. I couldn't wait; I was just real anxious to get here. I really was confident, even though I didn't know much about the life from reading the pamphlets. It's not the same as coming here and living. I can't understand why, but I was very sure that this was it. I knew for sure I was coming. The Mother Abbess gave me a list of things you have to bring and I started on that. It's kind of funny things when you think about it. It was real funny because I needed a white blouse with sleeves and I had the hardest time finding one. I had to go way up the north side of Chicago; a religious store sold them for kids. I made such an effort, such a big thing out of this. They have some of the things at the monastery, and if I didn't get them, it wouldn't have been the end of the world. I needed a blue blouse for working outside in the garden as a postulant. I was wanting to get all this stuff—a sewing kit—exactly what was on the list. It wouldn't have been the end of the world if I hadn't gotten it; they would have gotten it for me.

It's all so interior it's hard to put into words. When you have doubts, you know that. But this was just so clear. You have that inner peace, so you know you're doing the right thing when you don't have turmoil, when you're at peace.

This made my life meaningful. It gave meaning to my life. Such a crooked path. I don't know why it was me. It's hard to understand. God wanted me, so I guess He loves me the way I am, so that's all that counts. It's all past. You can't change it. Not everybody's life is perfect. Things fall into place. Anyway, I'm here and that's something. That's special. Not everyone is called to this life.

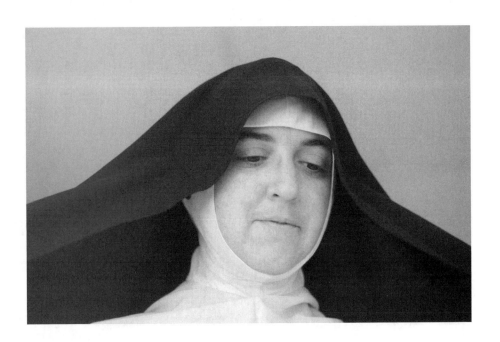

A novice harvests cabbages grown in the monastery's gardens. She smiles, caught using hosiery—a novel gardening method—to protect the vegetables from worms.

In general, the nuns observe monastic silence, a custom in which they speak only what is necessary and in a low tone in order to complete a task. One hour a day, during recreation, they can talk freely.

The Mother Abbess was not particularly pleased to discover the holy graffiti that turned up on the greenhouse. Set on the nuns' cloistered premises, it could only have been their handiwork.

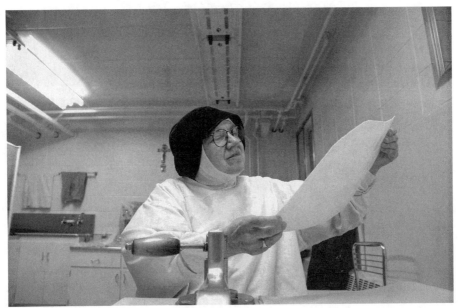

Rockford Poor Clares make and ship the host. Here, a nun stamps out the host after it has been baked.

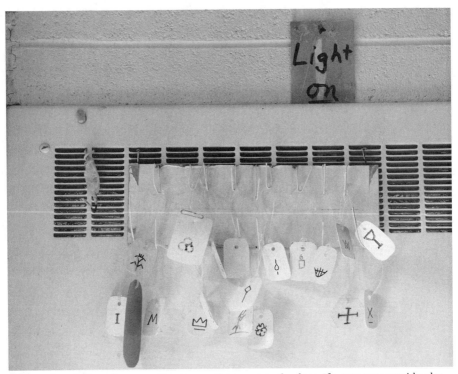

The nuns' marks hang by paperclips on a radiator next to the door. If a nun goes outside, she indicates this to the rest of her community by removing her marker. When a postulant enters the Rockford Poor Clares, the Mother Abbess assigns her a mark.

Part II

The Life

3

Monastic Living in a Throwaway Culture

It is a mystical life. The more that God gives to us, the more we give back to Him. And we are freed, because the structure of our life is such that we don't take on work that is over-encompassing in the mind; the reason for that is so the mind and heart can be with God.

Sister Maria Deo Gratias of the Most Blessed Sacrament

The corridors of the monastery are dark, as usual, the lights off. Mother Miryam walks out of the nuns' private choir chapel after the Divine Office. She opens a closet and finds her mantle—a heavy cloak. The woolen artifact is a vital layer at the Corpus Christi Monastery in the winter; it keeps the nuns warm in the drafty building, which is heated by a boiler that dates to the building's construction in the 1960s. The nuns clean and repair the boiler themselves, as much as possible. Mother Miryam has used this same mantle since she entered the monastery in 1955; green-thread stitching denotes her mark—the letter R. (Mother Miryam was assigned this letter when she first joined the community; the Mother Abbess at that time was partial to giving each postulant a letter for her mark—a letter from the name Jesus, Mary, Joseph, Francis, Clare, or Colette.) The cloth in Mother Miryam's mantle is worn and thin. She jokes about these "old rags" that she loves. The garment has been mended many times, the fabric unraveled and reused; it is precious because she helped make the mantle more than fifty years ago. "I hate to give it up," she says. "Then I wonder why it's worn. That's what amuses me. You wonder, 'Why is it wearing out?' It's been a long time! We expect things to last a long time around here."

According to the Rule of Saint Clare, the Poor Clare Order was granted the "privilege of poverty" so that the individual members as well as the community as a whole would not own property. Sister Mary Gemma quotes the novel credo, "without anything do I own." Literally, this means a nun cannot borrow anything from one of her religious sisters because, she says, "it would acknowledge ownership by the other sister of something." Mother Miryam does not own the mantle; it is for her use. Poor Clare nuns look to God, their superior, and church patrons for sustenance.

This absolute poverty, a pioneering concept at the order's inception, hails from Saint Francis, the forebear of the Franciscan order of Poor Clare nuns. Saint Francis wrote of his community of friars, "Let the brothers not make anything their own, neither house, nor place, nor anything at all. As pilgrims and strangers in this world, serving the Lord in poverty and humility, let them go seeking alms with confidence, and they should not be ashamed because, for our sakes, our Lord made Himself poor in this world. This is that sublime height of most exalted poverty, which has made you, my most beloved brothers, heirs and kings of the Kingdom of Heaven, poor in temporal things, but exalted in virtue."[1]

The future Pope Gregory IX tried to relieve Sister Clare and her followers, the Poor Ladies, of the harsh tenets, but she held fast, earning approval in decree for "Privilegium Paupertatis," issued September 17, 1228:

As is clear, by your desire to be dedicated to the Lord alone you have given up your appetite for temporal matters. For this reason, having sold everything and distributed it to the poor, you propose to have no possessions whatsoever, in every instance clinging to the footsteps of Him, who was made poor for our sakes and is the Way, the Truth, and the Life. The lack of goods from this *propositum* does not frighten you, for the left hand of your heavenly spouse is under your head to uphold the weaknesses of your body that you have submitted to the law of the soul through your well ordered love. Accordingly, He who feeds the birds of the sky and clothes the lilies of the field will not fail you in matters of food and of clothing until, passing among you, He serves Himself to you in eternity when indeed his right arm will more blissfully embrace you in the greatness of His vision. Therefore, just as you have asked, we confirm your *propositum* of most high poverty with

apostolic favor, granting to you by the authority of the present document that you cannot be compelled by anyone to receive possessions.[2]

As elected Novice Mistress at the Corpus Christi Monastery, Sister Mary
Nicolette is responsible for overseeing the training and formation of postulants and novices; she buffers young women from a cultural clash. Sister
Mary Nicolette helps women make the transition from the outside world;
she was nominated and then voted into the position because the other nuns
recognize she is uniquely situated, as one of the younger members, to understand the current challenges of adapting to monastic life, and to relate to the
young women. "The monastic culture is a culture of itself, of its own. Of its
own," Sister Mary Nicolette says. "So while we have many different sisters
coming from different cultures, we all learn the monastic culture when we
come." To this end, Sister Mary Nicolette says an aspiring nun must shed
presuppositions and routines, in order to arrive at the monastery with an
open disposition to relearn even the simplest of tasks. "When they come
we explain to them that you're relearning everything and you just have to
be very humble, you know, and willing to listen," Sister Mary Nicolette says.
"And teachable. Be very teachable."

Each member of the cultural time capsule that is the cloistered monastery is a product of her upbringing, her familial context, and her geographic
framework. Within the enclosure, novices and postulants are integrated
gradually into the rest of the community, as required by canon law; they
reside in a separate wing from the cells of the professed nuns who have
made temporary and permanent vows (typically three and six years, respectively, after entering). Today, the contrast between mainstream culture and
the cloistered monastery is so stark, and departure from the world outside
to the ancient rules so radical, that novices are given more time than they
were given in past decades—one extra year before making final vows—so
that they can adapt to monastic life. This steady and gradual immersion
is intended to allow them adequate time to discern if they truly are called
and to learn if they can adapt to the deliberate environment of unceasing
prayer.

"You're just so used to functioning in a normal way," Sister Mary Nicolette
says. "Eighteen is the youngest a woman would come. But already, at eighteen, nineteen, twenty, you're used to functioning a certain way. Usually, the

younger women find it easier to adapt because they're not as set in their ways as an older woman would be, perhaps, who's had a career and a home. But still, at that age, it's like, 'Hold on!' You know?"

They say only what is necessary, in a low tone, in order to complete a task, and ask another nun to step out into the hall for the conversation so as not to disturb anyone else in the room. Anything a nun says must serve a purpose; otherwise she must refrain from talking (except during the daily evening recreation, when they are allowed to socialize). "Obviously, sometimes we slip," Sister Mary Nicolette says, "but it's a discipline that we try to cultivate and foster, and it's a learning process because when you first come, you're not used to that. So the novitiate is good for that."

As a novice, Sister Maria Benedicta describes the process of integrating into the monastic community as "a time of orientation and learning." "It's really kind of unraveling for everybody," she says. One evening as a postulant, Sister Maria Benedicta took her assigned seat next to her Novice Mistress for collation. When the dish of potatoes was passed, two portions remained—a full potato and half of a potato. Sister Mary Nicolette told her, "You may take a full potato." She was not hungry enough to eat a full potato, though, and thought, "I may, but I may not." She served herself the half-potato. "And then I realized, I think 'may' actually meant, 'Take the full potato,'" she says. "It was like, 'whoops!' You realize what this really means is, I need to give my full consent, but I need to take a full potato. Even though you have the fundamental attitude that I'm coming to do God's will, it's really in the small things. Talk about countercultural from independence and doing things your way, to say, 'Okay, I'll eat a full potato.'"

Sister Maria Benedicta explains,

It's a life commitment and it's very different from anything in the world, so it's in the wisdom of the Church to say, "Live this life. See if it's for you." In Saint Clare's day, a woman would come for a year and then make final vows. But gradually, the Church has said, "Let's just take our time and say the person can decide over time, the community can decide, Is this person called here? Do they fit? Do they have the right dispositions to strive for holiness, those sorts of things it takes?" So you can take the commitment and have it be informed. It's not just, "I love it! It's great!" I have time to experience the difficulties I'm going to encounter and ask, "Can I live this? Can I make these sacrifices over time?" And it's the wisdom of the community, too. You're gradually incorporated into the community life. We get up at midnight, but when you first come, you don't get up at midnight every night. You would just crash. So it's gradual; everything happens kind of gradually. You lead certain prayers at certain times, with a gradual incorporation into the fullness of the life.

Forty-seven years old when she began to learn the ways of the monastery as a postulant, Sister Mary Michael pondered the unbending peculiarities. Working in the kitchen, she wondered, "Why do the vegetables need to be cut this way? And prepared this way?" But she accepted the structure imposed on her, and she deferred to tradition. She has seen others resist the tutelage. "They might be used to a better way, or may even know more about it than I do," Sister Mary Michael says. "You notice sometimes they find it hard not to say something and to just do it. The work is done a certain way. I think that's what some find hard; they know how to do something but we do it a certain way, and so you should follow the way we're doing it. Maybe they question that, why it's done that way."

Sister Mary Michael attempts to convey the challenge of subjugating one's own volition to the monastic customs: "It's so restrictive, especially starting out. You have to.... You can't.... There's some place you're supposed to be all the time. Somebody's telling you what to do and where to go."

"It's just a different—very different—culture that, at first, you're just like, 'Wow,'" Sister Maria Benedicta says. "You know how to do normal things, but here we do it differently. With monastic life, you do things a certain way so that it doesn't take a lot of conversation to discuss. It's just, there's a way that we do it, but it makes it more peaceful and run more smoothly and we don't have to talk about a lot of things so that our hearts and minds can be on God."

Any domestic idiosyncrasies Sister Maria Benedicta possessed when she entered the enclosure have been undone during her tenure. She has relearned how to make her bed the monastic way, folding the blankets lengthwise in thirds—a symbol of the Trinity and also a practical measure that keeps the blankets from dragging off the low beds, sweeping against the floor, and getting dusty. She has relearned, too, how to hang the laundry outdoors with her Novice Mistress silently, crisscrossing the courtyard in sync; how to clean her plate with her bread, then wash her dishes in a tub on the rolling cart in the center of the refectory, and then replace her dishes in the drawer at her assigned place at the table. "It's like, I thought I knew how to do dishes," she says, remembering her first impressions of the monastery. "But it's like you don't even know how to do dishes anymore! You don't know where anything goes, you don't know how anything is done. We have a very systematic way and it goes very smoothly, you know. But it's like every aspect of your life you're relearning and it's like, 'Wow, you know.' And at first, it's really like, 'How do we do dishes again?' Everything in your day is like this: 'How do we do this? How do we eat? What's the ritual for eating?' You take out your plate at a certain time. You know, it's very, very different."

Failing to register each new instruction, Sister Maria Benedicta told her Novice Mistress, "I know you told me how to do the dishes yesterday, but you also told me how to do five hundred other things. It's really overload at first. My goodness! And you forget. It's like, 'Oh, I heard that, but I forgot.'" Sister Maria Benedicta, the most recent member of the community, is supposed to lead each procession. She recalls her confusion when the Divine Office would end and nuns began leaving the choir chapel. "All of a sudden everybody's up and it's like, 'I'm supposed to be first!' It's like, 'Ahhh!' It's like, 'Bye, God, we're going! I don't know where we're going!' All the time, we're going somewhere and, okay, gotta go, and they're tripping over you. They're coming, they're expecting you to know, but I don't know where we're going!" Confounding the normal routine were the alterations to the schedule for feast days and during certain seasons in the liturgical calendar.

Through the daily upheaval to her own habits, Sister Maria Benedicta slowly became familiar with the monastic customs. She drew consolation by reframing her foibles within the grander schema. "We know it's between us and God," she says. "In Scripture, it says, 'Man looks at appearances, but God looks at the heart.' That's very comforting. I can be messing everything up, I can be doing everything wrong, but trying to do what God wants, and He's pleased with us. And that's very freeing. He doesn't ask us to be these perfect beings all the time. Yes, we try, but He looks in the heart and He knows that we're trying. That's all we have to do. It's so simple to live for Him."

In this built and controlled environment, twenty women with varied experiences and personalities attempt to undertake radical lives. "If you really have the call, you won't feel hedged in," Sister Maria Deo Gratias says. "If you don't have the call, then the rules are burdensome. But, really, the rules are just a loving response to the Lord who called us to the life, and so there have to be some guidelines. That's what the rules are. And there have to be some challenges of, okay, you said 'yes' to God, you said you would give yourself to God, so there has to be something to give." Until making solemn vows, a nun can petition the community to leave the monastery.

Sister Maria Deo Gratias says that the monastery's dwindling population has not altered the community's recruitment strategy or diluted the customs; one exception is the raised age limit for women wanting to join. "The community won't hold onto anybody and say, 'Well, we'd like to have numbers,' because sometimes numbers—if you're not living the life the way you're supposed to live the life—can be a detriment to community," Sister Maria Deo Gratias says. "So adding to our numbers isn't the answer. It's the quality of life. That's the most important thing."

"What draws you here? What makes you stay?" Sister Maria Benedicta asks of the hiccups and frustrations she has encountered. She answers her own question: "Love. At first, it is unsettling, but once you learn it, you can really settle down and really, like, enjoy the benefits of the life, rather than being puzzled by it. Your mind and heart can be on God. It is like a fundamental motive; as much as we can, we think about Him. But the love grows—love for Him, rather than love for ourselves, so that we're not still wanting to say five years later, 'But if we did it my way, it would still be a lot faster!' No. You give that up. Or you may still be thinking about it five years later, but you say, 'Okay, Lord, you can have this again. I'm doing this for you—just for you—not for myself,' even if you don't agree with it. It's all for love."

As Sister Mary Nicolette explains, "We've set our hearts on God—love of God. So even the work that we do, some of it is very common and mundane, you know, cleaning and keeping house. But it's done for the love of God. And when everything is done for the love of God, that sets kind of a higher standard because you won't do it sloppily if you know you're doing it for the Lord and for the love of God. That's what keeps us here and would keep us doing the same things—that desire to love and serve God. And also—this would be secondarily, but it always comes in—is it's for the good of community. We serve community. In Scripture, the two greatest commands are to love the Lord with all your heart and to love your neighbor as yourself. God is first, and then neighbor. But they really go together because our way of expressing our love of God often is in the very common day-to-day life with one another."

Prospective nuns are initiated to the daily rhythm of work and prayer, meals and sleep with the sounding of two bells. One bell is called Peter, for Saint Peter, whom Jesus described as the rock on which the Church would be built; the other bell is named Paul, for Saint Paul, a Jew who persecuted Christians before he was blinded on the road to Damascus and then became a follower of Jesus. "Peter does the most work," Sister Mary Clara says. That bell signals the start of Mass and summons the nuns working outdoors to the chapel for the Divine Office.

In an early lesson in cultural adjustment, postulants and novices are taught that obedience is a free choice. Sister Mary Nicolette explains that a superior—a Novice Mistress in the novitiate, or the Mother Abbess for the entire community—always first "invites" a woman to undertake a task; rarely would a superior need to word the request more strongly or directly by making a command. A superior might ask, for example, "Would you like to go outside today and prune the fruit trees?" "It's an invitation so the person can make the free choice to obey," Sister Mary Nicolette says.

Today, the nuns are amused by anecdotes when previous newcomers simply accepted the strangeness of monastic culture, miscalculated their environment, and exhibited unquestioning obedience to a humorous conclusion.

Sister Joan Marie says that when she first arrived in 1950, the culture was stricter: In the spirit of anonymity, the nuns were not allowed to share personal information about themselves, and they were supposed to begin any verbal exchange with "Dear Sister." "We still try to," Sister Joan Marie says, "but we had to say, 'I humbly beg, sister, would you do this or would you do this?' Or, 'I humbly beg, sister, can I have your pencil, can I borrow your pencil?' We were supposed to say all that. One sister—another postulant—thought that we were saying 'Honey Babe.' She thought the Mother Abbess was saying, 'Honey Babe, would you do this, would you do that?' That was really funny! I knew that right away; I knew she would never say 'Honey Babe!' Well, I knew we were supposed to say, 'humbly beg,' 'humbly beg.' She was older, see, so I think it's harder to come when you're older. I don't know. That's just my theory."

Sister Mary Gemma's all-time favorite story—"the funniest story I've heard since being here," she says—dates to before her arrival, to the 1950s. At the time, the novitiate was on the second story of the building, furnished with a large round table for studying. The Mother Abbess told the postulants and novices that she would like the round table brought to her on the first floor. "So all the novitiate sisters were struggling to get this round table down the stairs," Sister Mary Gemma says. "They were narrow stairways. When they finally got it to the Mother Abbess's office and she saw, she started to laugh so hard tears were coming down her face! She said, 'I meant the book!' There's a book called *The Round Table* that was up in the novitiate. The sisters just love to tell that story. The Mother Abbess laughed and laughed and the tears were just going down her face!"

A chasm has always existed between secular culture and religious communities. In the lapse from the order's founding eight hundred years ago to postmodernity, a continental drift has widened the distance between mainstream popular culture and the cultural oasis that is the Corpus Christi Monastery, described by Mother Miryam as "a whole different secluded world." A fundamental unity of purpose and values prevents any significant culture war within the monastery between women hailing from different eras of the past century and different experiences around the globe. When Sister Mary Nicolette was a novice alongside women her mother's age, she felt an unexpected kinship she does not think would be possible beyond the enclosure. "We shared the same ideals, and we were striving for the same thing—living the same life—and so what was dearest and closest to our heart was what we shared, and so that kind of transcended any kind of generation gap as far as what we were striving for," Sister Mary Nicolette says. And yet it is no small feat to knit together several generations of women from a range of personal experiences, who departed their own versions of contemporary culture. The difficulties have intensified over the centuries for would-be-denizens willing themselves to release their fascination with what popular society suggests is significant.

An oft-stated adage at the monastery is that the nuns know, when they arrive, that they must adapt to monastic culture, and they should not expect the monastery to adapt to their individual desires and personalities. Sister Maria Benedicta embraces the dictum; even if her fresh eyes find room for improvement in the ancient order, she would not presume to suggest the community revamp any customs. "It would be totally contrary to what we're supposed to be," she says. "I'm not coming here to do things my way, you know what I mean? I need to fit into the life. We're fitting in; we're not trying to make the life fit us. And that is something you have to learn. Because you can say it. They can tell you before you come and you can say, 'Oh, yes, that makes perfect sense.' But then it's really in the little details. I have to even fold the laundry the right way, with all the nametags in the same place."

Sister Maria Deo Gratias believes that young women arrive at the Corpus Christi Monastery today from a world of immediacy, with a mind-set of "when I have a headache, I take medicine right away." "It's always instant. They want instant answers, instant gratification. It's like the level of suffering is very low. So, here, say you have a headache, naturally, if you need medicine you take it. But you don't jump to that as your first solution. Sometimes, by just being calm, then it's gone. On the emotional level, it's more a sense of keyed-upness, and I think it's probably because of the fast rate of society—everything at them all at once, everything is always action, action, action. Where, if you come here, it's a different culture, so they have to learn. Not that they can't; most of them that enter are very welcoming of this, but because they don't have the experience from the world, then they have to learn how to slow down, or they have to learn how to combat difficulties or struggles that they may have within themselves in trying to adjust to the silence and to the life."

Seventy-four-year-old Sister Mary Joseph is known as the mechanical nun who fixes what she can and calls in repairmen for the rest, often to teach her how to make the repair herself next time. Born in the aftermath of the Great Depression's financial reserve and material minimalism, Sister Mary Joseph's transition to the monastery felt simple. What she learned at home was reinforced at the monastery; with tools, she was taught to handle possessions "as they should be," she says—leaving them in good condition so that others could use them after her. She joined the Rockford community as an eighteen-year-old in 1957. Her understanding of modernity has developed from watching and listening to the tales of novices. She has seen young women who are the products of emerging technologies—objects she has never encountered in person or virtually—try to assimilate with her religious family. "They're coming from a different world, a different society than we came from," Sister Mary Joseph says. "It's sort of a throwaway society, where you use a thing and throw it out. We use a thing and take care of it, and keep on using it and use it so the next person is able to use it. It's a respect for things, and handling them carefully. And the younger ones weren't taught that. They use a thing and maybe that's the only one that can use it. It's not useable after that." Aghast by postulants' destructive tendencies, Sister Mary Joseph recites a lyric that captures the religious approach: "You can tell a monk by the way he sits and stands, the way he picks a thing up and holds it in his hand." She explains that the monastic way of caring for material possessions means knowing what pressures or demands the tools should take, how they have to be handled—"what they are, and using them for what they are and what they can do, and not pushing them too far. It's something you have to have or learn. And it seems they're coming from a world that just doesn't have that, for the greater part."

As religious communities have discovered that women need more time to adjust to life inside a cloister, Sister Mary Monica says the Rockford Poor Clares have revamped the black-and-white time frame of progressing from postulant to novice one year after entering the monastery; the three-year temporary vows two years later; and then final vows, which are permanent. At the Corpus Christi Monastery, temporary vows can be extended by one-year increments if a nun needs additional time before making solemn vows, which are permanent.

Although Sister Mary Joseph cannot relate to the newcomers' approach to the monastery's equipment, or condone their unrealistic demands on the tools, she does not judge the women. She knows they bring into the monastery only what they learned in the world. "They don't realize it because that's what they did; they just used things and then threw them out, and when they needed it again, got another," Sister Mary Joseph says. "Each generation will have to find their own ways to overcome what distractions are brought about by the people that are living in them at the time, because each person is different; each person comes from a different background."

Sister Mary Clara leafs through the pages of an album; at one time, a superior gave one of these small photo albums to each nun. She has turned hers into a book of memories, filling the transparent folders with cards and mementos, including a prayer card following the 1963 assassination of John F. Kennedy. She has also kept, since 1982, the piece of paper on which she wrote, in precise cursive, the final, solemn vows she made the day she became a Poor Clare. Ever since she made those vows, she has recited them again each day. In another transparent folder in her album is a card, and inside the card is a poem written in calligraphy—a gift from her best friend, Sister Michelle, the last time the two saw each other in 1978. The poem reads: "May you be kept in safety in the hollow of God's hand, no matter where you wander, over sea or over land; under His protection may your life's heights ascend, is the prayer that's offered daily, the benediction of a friend." Sister Michelle and Sister Mary Clara were teachers in an active religious order. Sister Mary Clara lived with that community for more than two decades before she decided to join the cloistered contemplatives at the Corpus Christi Monastery.

Clutching her memory book, she explains how her view on possessions has changed. "It's not that they become less important," she says. "You draw away from them. You know where your treasure is: It's up on the altar and the Tabernacle. If I was asked to give this up, if one of the sisters wanted the book, I would be able to give it to them." She pauses, then adds, "I would take some things out, of course."

When she was a teacher, most of Sister Mary Clara's wages went to her community's operating expenses; she received a ten-dollar monthly allowance, which she spent on the brand of toothpaste she liked. Sometimes, she saved up to buy a book. The more austere lifestyle of the Poor Clares still startles her at times; she believes that the gradual immersion into cloistered monastic life from an active order, in which she could make personal purchases and own a few items, afforded a more fluid transition than she might have experienced otherwise. "That's why the young people have such a difficult time," Sister Mary Clara says; "because they haven't experienced anything religious in their life, and so they have a harder time making the switch giving up things or not being able to hold onto things, not possessing things."

Sister Maria Benedicta's path from college softball pitcher to the youngest member of the Corpus Christi Monastery, when she joined in 2006, might appear unlikely. She knows this and smiles when she explains she was drawn by the poverty. Sister Maria Benedicta was a twentysomething active nun with the Marian Sisters, a Franciscan order, when her religious community made a pilgrimage from Nebraska to Assisi, Italy, where Saint Clare had followed Saint Francis; there they founded the Franciscan Friars and the Poor Clares, respectively. Sister Maria Benedicta toured San Damiano, the run-down church that Saint Francis and the Friars Minor turned over to Saint Clare for her budding order to use as a monastery.

"They were so poor!" Sister Maria Benedicta says. "But they were so happy because they had Jesus, and I thought, 'They never had to do anything but just love Christ.'" She shows a photographic postcard she kept of San Damiano, the Poor Clares' motherhouse where fifty sisters lived together, cramped in the stone quarters. Sister Maria Benedicta muses that she is not sure how they all fit. Some of the nuns must have slept on the floor. "Talk about only staying for the right reasons!" she says. "It's no comforts. But that's like how God puts it in your heart, because I think most people would see this and think, 'Uh, what? Yuck!'"

Sister Maria Benedicta aspired to the life of simplicity that Saint Francis and Saint Clare modeled—the giving of oneself entirely to Christ in utter poverty. In the Franciscan template for monastic living, poverty is not merely an external demonstration, with indifference to physical signs of wealth; poverty in religious life means divesting oneself of other status symbols—power and prestige and looking good to others. "That's the true poverty," Sister Maria Benedicta says. "Yes, it starts with the material things; I don't need all these things that lead me away from God, but it's also in giving up my own self, my selfish ways, my selfish desires in order to just live for Christ. The material poverty is a start; we don't want all these things that are going to lead us away from God because the more you have, the more you want.

"Jesus said, 'Blessed are the poor in spirit; theirs is the kingdom of God.' He didn't just mean, 'If you don't wear shoes, you'll go to heaven,'" Sister Maria Benedicta says. "Obviously, there's something behind it. There's so much more to poverty than not having the latest modern conveniences or the most comfortable whatever in your life. It's being stripped of everything that's not God. It's an interior stripping. The exterior stripping helps to make the interior possible. If I'm always seeking things that are going to help my comfort, it's not going to help me strip of all my selfishness. It's going to feed it. But the purpose is so that God can fill me rather than be filled with self. That's what poverty is: It's not an end in itself. Not wearing shoes is not going to get me to heaven, unless I see the purpose that, you know, it's very selfish that I always want to be comfortable, to seek self."

Her Novice Mistress, Sister Mary Nicolette, teases this concept further: In and of itself, she says, poverty has no value. "Poverty can even be an evil. It can even lead people to be bitter, or away from God. But when it can be used as a means, as an instrument to a deeper reality, then it becomes a good. But never in and of itself—poverty is just a means to something greater."

In what has become her third and, she hopes, final home with her second religious family, Sister Maria Benedicta feels affinity for the older nuns in her community. She senses few hindrances relating to the older nuns because of age differences or generation gaps. All share the same values, motivations, and desire for simplicity. "I think in the world, I wanted *this*, I wanted *this*, then *this*," Sister Maria Benedicta says. "Those things don't satisfy." She reflects on the postcard of the San Damiano Monastery that triggered her countercultural transformation. "Poverty," she says. "It's a good thing. It's not what the world thinks is a good thing."

Although she has not yet made permanent vows as a Poor Clare Colettine, Sister Maria Benedicta is already a zealous protector of her ancient order. Assuming that a new wave or trickle of postulants and novices follows, she will contend with any relics and mind-sets of contemporary culture that disrupt the carefully guarded terrain of the Corpus Christi Monastery.

Sister Mary Joseph
of Our Lady's Joys

Prayer was part of the family. I can't say when I first realized it because it was just part of our life, an integral part of our life. We said the family rosary every day.

I must have been around three when I started telling Mom, "Mom, I want a little sister." I had six older brothers. I wanted a sister, someone like me. She said, "You'll have to pray about it. You'll have to ask God." I prayed to God, and I did have a little sister!

In fact, I only had the little sister until I came here, and then she died ten days after I came. I had a sister while I was at home. Here, I have quite a number of sisters.

With my life, it should start with Mom and Dad.

I don't know as much about my father's family as I do about my mother's. Mom belonged to one of the better families in Milwaukee. And yet she was quite different. She was very advanced in school, and she liked to play with the boys in the sandlot. She'd play baseball with the boys in the sandlot, and she was doing that up until the time she got married. In fact, she said when she was going to Marquette University she still played ball with the boys. The boys asked her where she went to school and she said, "Marquette University." She said they were so hurt that she wouldn't tell them where she went to school because they had told her where they went to high school. They thought she was their age, but she wasn't. She looked much younger than she was. She was only eighteen, but she looked younger. I was always like Mom; I looked way younger than I am. She never looked old until she was really old.

Her father owned his own business—a baker supply business. He went to work every day of his life until he was ninety-one, when he died. Two weeks before he died, he got sick and stayed home. They were nursing him at home. I remember going to see him then. I was in sixth grade. Up until then, he had gone to work every day of his life.

Mom married Dad at eighteen, but she was a very bright, intelligent, young girl. She went to a private school, to Milwaukee University School. She skipped a couple of grades, and so she graduated early. She was not a Catholic at that time but she wanted to go to Marquette University. Her father was a Mason and the Masons are not in favor of the Catholic Church. Her uncle was a High Mason and he told Grandpa he could not send his daughter to Marquette. Mom said she was real happy then; she knew her father would let her go because Grandpa wouldn't let his brother tell him what he couldn't do!

Mom met Dad there at Marquette. Dad was studying; I think he had a fellowship. He was teaching while he was studying. She started going with Dad; my grandparents didn't like that. They offered, if she would quit school—because then she wouldn't go with Dad—to give her a fur coat. So she quit school. And then she got married. She got her fur coat and married Dad. I really don't know why they weren't in favor. It might have been religion. It was a real quiet wedding because they weren't in favor of it and also because she converted to the Catholic faith. She said it wasn't because of Dad—he didn't convert her—but Dad's parents had a good marriage. She didn't want to get married outside the Catholic Church. She saw there what she would want in marriage so she converted before she married Dad.

One of the hardest things for her was she knew when she got married she couldn't play out in the sandlot anymore! She had to stay home and take care of the house and hopefully raise a family. That was one of the hardest things—hearing the kids out in the sandlot playing and she wasn't able to go out.

Dad was studying to be a teacher. Mom read all the books on education, on educating children. She gave Dad the books she thought were worth his reading. Really, she read all of the books and she gave him the best. In a way, she got quite an education even though she never had a degree.

Mom started raising boys and she had boys and boys and boys. She wanted a girl all along. But she kept on getting boys. She wanted twins, too. After she had four boys, she was praying. She prayed to Saint Joseph for twins. The next ones were twins. Mom thought the doctor knew she was going to have twins because he told Ma when she went to visit him, "Sometimes these things happen." He told her what to do and that she wouldn't have to come back as much because he knew how hard it was with four kids out there in the waiting room. He was not expecting twins, but there were twins! They were born at the Deaconess Hospital. One was much smaller than the other; Joe was the smaller of the twins. I guess the nurses decided he wasn't going to live. At that time, the children didn't stay with the mother in the hospital. They were in the nursery after they were born, and so Ma went to the nursery to see the children. They had put Joe up by an open window, no blankets or anything. Mom was really upset. She put covers around him and she insisted he stay in the room with her. When it came time to go, Joe must have been a little underweight. They let Mom and Dad take him home because they were afraid of her reaction. And he survived fine. Mom decided then she would never have a baby in a non-Catholic hospital again so I was born in Concordia, the Catholic hospital.

We moved to Elm Grove, Wisconsin—near Milwaukee—when I was a year old. Before that they were living in Wauwatosa. I think because of the size of the family, they wanted to move out where there was more room for the family.

It was just a very good family life with brothers and my little sister. It was at the time of the Depression, back in the '40s when you didn't do much driving around because the gas was expensive. Mom and Dad saw an ad for a cottage on Lake Michigan that was for sale. They went by bus to see it and they bought it. It was very reasonable at the time because dad was teaching at a Catholic school, where the salary was way less than you'd get at the public school. During the summer, we would go to the lake, back and forth. We were just very frugal. We grew as much of our own food—produce— as we could. I know other children always had allowances. We never had allowances. If we needed money, we'd ask Dad and he'd give us whatever we needed for school, but we didn't ask him unless we really needed it. The boys would sometimes get a job and go bean picking with the migrant workers and the farm children around, or they worked for the cannery in Belgium. That would be their summer job if they didn't work in Elm Grove. Some of them, when they got older, worked at the brewery in the summer. The boys would also get babysitting jobs. I don't know whether other boys babysat, but I know my brothers did and the people liked them. They baby-sat for the family that owned the brewery. The people liked my brothers. They always felt safe with them and they were good boys, so they got a lot of good babysitting jobs. When I was old enough, I babysat, too, but I had my own clients.

I have a lot of memories with my brothers—being with them, playing with them, living with them. We had an acre and a half and we did quite a bit of gardening to raise food for the family as much as possible. We had apple trees, pear trees, plum trees, and cherry trees, and so we spent a lot of our time during the summer months picking fruit or taking care of the garden. My father was a teacher and so during the school year he was going to school when we were going to school, and during the summer he was home with us and working in the garden. His master's degree was in botany and so he was really into gardening. He loved the iris. That was his specialty in the garden—crossing the iris to develop other varieties. Now, when I see the iris today, I think, oh, he would have loved it! They've developed the iris so beautiful now that he would have really delighted in it.

Dad was also very interested in music, and so all of us played instruments. Some of us played piano, but if we played the piano we also played another instrument. A few times we all played together. I think my oldest brother played saxophone; he was twelve years older so I don't remember playing with him. I played flute. My sister played flute. One of my brothers played flute, another played clarinet, and the twins played trumpet. Dad was also the band director at the high school, where he taught chemistry until he had a heart attack.

My sister was four years younger than I was. We had our differences. When she was real little, with our family size, there were a couple of us in each bedroom. It was a big farmhouse and the boys were in two rooms. After Mary grew up enough, she came into the room with me. I must have been five or six by the time she came in. It was just a little room. We quarreled a lot. When the boys began leaving—my oldest brother got married when I was in the seventh grade and my second oldest brother got married when I was in high school—we could move to the bigger bedrooms. When the boys were gone, we had separate rooms and we got along better.

My brothers were everything to me. Since there were so many of us, I can't remember many times when they had friends over. They stuck together, though, so they didn't need a lot of other company. I looked up to them and they were wonderful. There was nothing better than being with my brothers. Being with them meant more to me than anything. Whatever they did, I wanted to do. In a way, my life was sheltered because they took care of me and made sure nothing ever happened to me. I was the youngest in the family for a few years, and that's why, when my sister was born, we didn't always get along; she was the youngest then, and she was the one getting spoiled. I didn't consider myself spoiled but they said I was.

I went to a Catholic school and I admired the sisters. We had the Notre Dame Sisters at the parish school. I got along really well with them and I admired them. Around seventh grade, during noontime, I was just daydreaming and looking out at the country woods near the school. I was praying and looking at the woods, praying about having a big family. I wanted to get married and have a family—a great big family—and one of the sisters came by and said, "Did you ever think about being a sister?" I said, "No," but then I began thinking about it and praying about it and I began to feel the call. My family went to daily Mass, six o'clock Mass every morning after I received Communion in the second grade. With our Lord, you have a daily relationship that you develop in prayer. The sister suggested it, but then in listening to Him, I did feel that He did want me.

The Notre Dame Sisters used to have an aspirature over on the Mississippi River in western Wisconsin. After eighth grade, I said to Mom, "What would you say if I wanted to become a sister and I wanted to go to the aspirature?" Mom didn't want that. She said, "You have a good family life. There's no reason to go over there. Wait until after high school." I would have had to go to a boarding school to go to their aspirature. I went to high school and there were different sisters, the Divine Savior Sisters, a different order than the Notre Dames. In a way, I liked the Divine Savior Sisters more and I admired them; I saw things in them that I liked better. I think the Notre Dame Rule was way stricter than the Divine Saviors', who seemed to have a more personal relationship, a human dimension rather than a focus on the rules. I thought, maybe I'll try the Divine Savior Sisters. I went to a guidance counselor and she encouraged me, but she didn't encourage me to join them.

In high school, I always read a lot. From the time we wanted to read, Mom had signed us up to a Catholic book club for children, so we always had good books to read. She got me books about Saint Therese of Lisieux and Andrew Jackson's daughter. My brother and his wife gave me *A Right to Be Merry*, which is about the Poor Clares. It was that book that sparked my interest in the Poor Clares, especially the chapter about the Rule of Saint Clare. The Rule of Saint Clare was to live the holy gospel. That was what drew me—the simplicity. There weren't any other pious practices, just the simplicity to live the holy gospel in poverty, chastity, and obedience.

And so I became interested in the contemplative life. The guidance counselor had books on the religious orders, and I read through all of the contemplative orders and I didn't like any. Right off, I didn't want to join any that had lay sisters doing the work, and the other sisters praying. I didn't want that; I didn't want someone else doing my work for me. I thought the prayer and work should go together. I didn't think there should be two standards, like the rich and the poor, or the publicans or the peasants and the nobility and more educated socially or elite—all those different standards in social life.

I think the guidance counselor gave me the names and addresses of orders that were already reformed. She thought I should join one that had already reformed. I came down to visit the Poor Clares. That was what I was interested in. The Colettines were reformed Poor Clares and that's what we are— Colettines. I looked at the addresses, and they had monasteries in Chicago and Rockford and Cleveland. Mom said she wouldn't want me to be in Chicago. Even as a contemplative, she didn't want me in Chicago; Chicago is a rough place, so I came to visit Rockford.

In a way, I didn't want it but I did believe it was what God wanted for me. It's where He wanted me to be, and so that's what I wanted.

Before that, I was planning to go to Marquette. I sent in my registration but when I had to finalize it, I said, "Do I need to send this in? I really want to enter the religious life." Dad said, "That's all right if you're sure." When he found out I wanted to come here—to a contemplative order—he wasn't so happy. He said it would be the end of my education. He said I should have more education. He was teaching at a Jesuit high school, and he said all the Jesuits he asked said the same thing: I should go for at least a year of college or university before I entered here. I don't know that anyone here has, but you can take courses by mail; theoretically we could, and I think some do. He didn't realize that. And then it was too late to finalize my registration for Marquette.

A number of my classmates, or in the class ahead, or the class behind entered the religious life. None entered the contemplative life. In a way, I could have been anything I wanted. I could have been a doctor, or I could have been a teacher or a nurse. In fact, they called me a dentist in high school. I knew I was going to enter the religious life but during vocational days for different professions, different people would come to see what you were interested in.

Although I was planning on entering here, I had never been here for an interview. I came down here for an interview at the end of the summer. That was my initial visit. I came down on the bus and I got lost in Rockford. They said to take the bus, and so I got on the bus. The trouble was, the bus I got on went the wrong direction. It went out to *North* Main Street. I was about to get off and I said, "It doesn't look like a monastery." I asked the bus driver, and he said, "Oh, you're in the wrong place," and so he gave me a transfer to come back down to South Main. I can't remember whether I was drawn to the building or repelled by it. I must not have been repelled by it or I wouldn't have come back. I was just happy I got to the right place. I rang the doorbell and it was dinnertime, noon. Wrong time. I was very young and I wasn't used to being out alone, but I wasn't scared either. I was just doing what had to be done before I came. You had to come for an interview, so I came for an interview.

I didn't realize they would make me wait until November before I could enter. They gave me a date in November—the sixteenth—where, if I wanted to come, I could come. It was the novitiate's Patron Saint Day for Saint Agnes of Assisi, Saint Clare's younger sister, who followed her to the religious life. Saint Clare followed Saint Francis, and then a few weeks later, her younger sister followed her.

They gave me a list of things I would need: towels, blankets, underwear, nightgowns, and shoes for the garden. I can remember Dad helped me with that. He took me to the shoe man, and that way I knew what size to get in the Sears catalog for the boys' shoes. The Poor Clares said garden shoes could be high shoes. Back then, girls didn't have high shoes, but I ordered them in the Sears catalog. I got a real nice lightweight pair of shoes for the garden. I don't have them anymore; I think they did give out.

They said you could bring along anything you needed or would want so I brought along a few books and a flute and sheet music. I had time to clean up my room before I left. I can remember everyone was going to school or their jobs. I was still at home. I felt bad because when the boys were cleaning up their things, I always considered it an honor to have their junk; but when I offered Mary some of my things, she wasn't interested. But, of course, she didn't need them. It was at that time that the boys discovered stuffed toys. Mary and I got all these stuffed toys that had character. I got a monkey and a couple of dogs. I had a number of those that they had given me, and so I had Mom give those to my nieces and nephews after I came.

I cleaned everything up and left it in the closet. Later on, Mom said, "If I had known all that you left in that closet, I never would have let you out of the house!" I left some artwork, some sketches, and I had some of Mary's artwork and letters and drawing pictures. She was a better artist than I was. She was very talented, very gifted, both in looks and otherwise. I left some of those in the closet. Mom appreciated those, I think. She didn't appreciate all of the other stuff I left—the *Better Homes and Gardens*. I was interested in architecture and building my dream home. I just didn't know what to do with all of my stuff. It was too good to throw away! And clothes I left because I thought Mary would have needed them sooner or later. But she didn't.

I remember my junior year, I went to a lay apostolate women's group over on the Mississippi River in western Wisconsin for a summer course. They had a lot of good courses for women. I got sick with a gall bladder infection and had to come home. I went to the hospital because our doctor was gone at the time and our substitute would only see me in the hospital. Usually, it was Mary that was in the hospital; she came to see me. She was too young to come in. They didn't allow children to visit in the bedroom, but they allowed her to come in. They were so used to seeing her.

My sister contracted leukemia when she was in sixth grade after she had her tonsils out. Mom thought that somehow her bone marrow had been poisoned by the ether when she had her tonsils out. That was Mom's guess. The type of leukemia she had was pernicious. She shouldn't have lived more than six months or a year at the most, but she did. She lived. Mom and Dad had her go to school, and they kept on her to go to school because they wanted her to have as much of a normal life as possible.

So she went to school and her teacher knew. They let the teacher know because she missed so much school. When she was sick, she was sick and she couldn't go to school. They never told Mary then what she had. We knew; the family knew. But they told Mary she had anemia so if anyone asked her, she said she had anemia. Otherwise, people would have always been asking how she was doing, like people do. But my parents wanted her to have as much of a normal life as possible.

When Mary was feeling well, she'd want to do anything she usually did and the doctor told her she could do whatever she wanted. Of course, he didn't realize she was like me—a tomboy—always wanting to do what my brothers did. She was like that, too, maybe not as much as I was. He didn't know what she was used to doing. She went out and played on the trapeze and when she came in, Mom looked at her—because the blood vessels began bursting—and she knew Mary couldn't do that again.

The thing was, sometimes in the end the disease didn't act like acute leukemia. Sometimes the red blood cells were produced correctly. Mom watched very carefully the medicines the doctors gave her; if she saw any bad reaction, she told Mary not to take it. Mom said the doctor said that, too. She said, "He gives the medicines to others and they take them like candy but they're dead." She'd go back and see that other patients wouldn't be there anymore because the medicines they were experimenting with were poisonous in the end. They had to be very careful. Mom watched very carefully, and so Mary lived. After a while, Mary knew the things she couldn't do because of the reactions. After a while, when we would go out to the cottage she couldn't even go wading because of the difference of the pressure of the water.

Mom and Dad didn't tell her the name of the disease but she understood she was very sick. The bone biopsies she had to have were painful. They weren't anything that you wanted to go through. She had long hair—long beautiful hair from the time she was little. When I was born I didn't have any hair. When I was one year old, they put a ribbon around my head so that people would know I was a girl, not a boy. But Mary had hair when she was born, and by the time she was one or two, she had long hair. She had braids when she was little—just two or three—long blonde braids. She was beautiful. She had pigtails when she started high school. I always had short hair. I never had curly hair. Mom didn't believe in trying to curl your hair if it wasn't curly so I just had a bob. They did give me a permanent once and when I came home, it was curly so my brother, Father Tom, who was in the seminary, told Mary, "You should cut your hair like Josephine." She had long hair and because of the medicine, she was losing it. But because of the braids, you didn't notice. I told her, "Don't pay any attention to him. You're fine." If she cut her hair, it would have been noticeable that she was losing it.

Mary knew she was very sick. And when she was real sick, she knew; she knew she was deathly sick. She knew how she was feeling. At times, when she was very sick she would wake up and say "mercy killing" because she was in so much pain. She was tempted, because of the pain, to want to be killed.

Mom, Dad, and Mary came with me when I entered here, and I remember seeing her in the parlor. I came in and I was dressed as a postulant and I was thinking, "This might be the last time I see her." And it was. I remember the sisters asking her if she wanted to enter the monastery. She, like myself, from the time she received First Holy Communion, went to daily Mass. In fact, I think she might have wanted to be a religious. I can't remember what she said to the nuns, but I knew she wouldn't live that long. I was sort of resentful that they kept asking her because I knew she wasn't going to live long enough to be a religious.

When they went home on Saturday, Mary felt awful sick. She went to school that Monday because she knew she was going to see the doctor that afternoon and she knew he was probably going to put her in the hospital for more transfusions. He put her in the hospital and she never went home after that. Mom was with her in the hospital; she always stayed with her. The day before she died—she died on November 26—Mom said the doctor came, and Mary told him she didn't want any more transfusions. And then she thanked the doctor and she thanked the nurses that had been caring for her because she knew she was going to die.

One of my friends was a nurse's aide in the hospital, and she said to Mom, "What's happening? Everyone's coming out of the room crying." It was because Mary was thanking them all for their help and what they had done. Mom said she didn't want any more transfusions, and so they all came out crying. Mary must have known that she was getting near death. And, no, she didn't resent that. In fact, in the end, she really was longing for it, to go and be with God. In the end, she wanted to die.

Usually, November is our time of Lent of Saint Martin and we don't have family visits or letters from November 2 until Christmas. I entered during that time and so I wasn't expecting any correspondence until after Christmas. But I was told that Mary had died. My family sent word and they told me. I knew she was ready, and I knew she wanted it because she had been so sick. But for Mom and Dad, it was terribly hard for them because I had come here, and then ten days later, Mary died.

I didn't know if I could go home for the funeral. I didn't ask. Usually, once you enter you don't go home for a funeral. I hadn't made a vow of enclosure then, but when you enter you observe it. I think they told me when the funeral would be, and I prayed during the time when she was at the funeral. My parents told me afterwards that Mary's entire class went to the funeral because she was in school until nine days before she died. She was a freshman.

I realized later that it was a good thing that I entered and didn't go home for the funeral because the public opinion would have been very hard. To come back here would have been very difficult; it would have gone against the public pressure. People would have said, "How can you leave when...? How can you leave now that your sister's...?" I think the Lord worked it that way. I asked Him for a sister, He gave me a sister. I came here, and she died right after. He gave me a sister for as long as ...

I prayed for a cure. Really, I did. I wasn't looking forward to entering. I thought it was what He wanted. And I tried to bargain with God: "Well, I'll answer if you make Mary well." But I knew I couldn't bargain.

That Christmas, when my parents came to visit, it was hard for them. It was even harder for them than it was for me. There were very few times I've seen Dad cry. Once was when they came back from the doctor and he knew what Mary had. I saw him reading *The Merck Manual*, and he was crying. And it was hard that Christmas when they came. Dad asked Mother Petra to pray for them because it was like the bottom had dropped out of the family. And it's true. It was like that. The two youngest were gone. But they got through it and so did I. Just remembering, though, it's hard.

But that's the way life is. And, you know, God's ways are not our ways. His thoughts are not our thoughts. And you see that, too, with the crucifix: God's ways are not our ways. That's what His son had to do for love of Him, for love of us, to show His love of us.

I think in every Christian's life, for everyone who's trying to follow Christ, they're going to experience it. It will be according to their vocation, according to whatever state of life they are in—they will all experience it in some way. It's a sacrifice He asks. It's the sharing in His suffering. And it's the share He gives to all of us, to all His followers. You can refuse, but then you're not being like His son, and He sent His son and His son gave us the power to become sons of God, to become God's children through baptism. He makes us like His son and if we're like His son, we'll be like Him in the different experiences of life.

You ask me, "Why the contemplative life?" I felt I could be anything I wanted to be. Really, if I wanted to be a doctor, I had the intelligence; I could have if I wanted—or anything else I wanted to be. Here, I thought, I could help more by praying, I could help people in every walk of life; it wouldn't just be one walk of life. Here, it's helping in all the professions. That's why I chose this.

4
Little House, Big Heart

It's a whole different world that we're living in.
Mother Miryam of Jesus

There is a scene that Sister Mary Gemma conjures easily. She has slipped back to this visual memory many times. When she was nineteen years old, she flew to California to visit her aunt, uncle, and cousins; it was her first—and second to last—trip by airplane. She hoped the vacation might save her from what she believed to be her calling to cloistered monastic life. She had pictured a "romantic encounter" during her trip to the West Coast. Raised in the country, she reveled in her relatives' sophisticated and uninhibited lifestyle; they partied with friends and drank alcohol. The trip ended early, with tears.

It is not this memory that Sister Mary Gemma recalls so vividly, though. Finding language for her experience in California takes time; in her recounting, she stops and starts, she pauses, and then she revises the timeline and events. She has not rehearsed the story with multiple retellings.

The series of images she knows so well, and the feelings resurrected by the visual memory, took place before she visited her relatives in California. The scene is not from her own childhood in northern Illinois, near her monastic home of almost four decades. The memory is her own. The experience is not.

Sister Mary Gemma describes what she sees: An open prairie and a family fighting to survive, uncertain if they will outlast the winter. It is the late nineteenth century. Sister Mary Gemma remembers that the family is waiting out a blizzard in the hope the rails will clear so a train can deliver necessities in time. They grind wheat in a coffee mill all day in order to make bread, which suffices until dinner the next night. The family labors for their daily bread; each day, they grind more wheat and then bake more bread to last one more day. At night, the mother sits with her baby on a rocking chair, unable to fall asleep because of the cries of "natives." Sister Mary Gemma sees the children sweeping the dirt floors of their cabin; because they cannot afford shoes, the children go barefoot from first thaw to first frost.

Sister Mary Gemma loves the dramas of the Ingalls family. She loves reading about Ma and Pa and Laura—the simplicity of their lives, the hard manual labor required to pioneer unsettled territory, the constant threats to their existence, the characters' faith in powers outside themselves, and their closeness and dependence on one another.

As a child, Sister Mary Gemma's family drove west through South Dakota, and so she can imagine the lake the Ingalls lived near, the birds that slept on the lake when it froze, the noises they made in morning. "I can picture it," she says. "I don't know why. It seems I must have seen it or heard it before, heard these birds. It's so real to me." When Sister Mary Gemma first read *Little House on the Prairie* as a child with an active imagination, the books gave shape to her fantasies. They carried her away from sometimes trying family dynamics. In grade school in the late 1960s, her father moved the family from Rockford to a rural village in the next county over. "He thought it would be a healthier bringing up for us if we lived out in the country and had animals to take care of," Sister Mary Gemma says. "He got us into a farming community where the kids were all farming kids and town kids. It was a completely different atmosphere." They had pet cats and dogs. They raised ducks and chickens. They hiked and camped. With this move, Sister Mary Gemma felt more connected to the Ingalls family.

Today, tears surface when she describes the challenges the pioneers faced. She knows that the *Little House* books were written for children. But, she says, "They're so simple and beautiful." Poor Clare Colettines at the Corpus Christi Monastery do not generally read novels. During the limited time that is unscheduled each day, in between meals and chores and prayers, and when they retire to their cells at night, they sew baptismal gowns or make prayer cards using dried flowers plucked from their gardens to be sold in the store. They read biblical and inspirational texts. Sister Mary Gemma assists in the monastery's infirmary; her primary charge is the only full-time resident of the infirmary: Sister Ann Frances, bedridden with advanced Alzheimer's disease. Sister Ann Frances speaks a language the other sisters cannot comprehend. At times, she grows distressed. She demands time and attention, often keeping Sister Mary Gemma from other duties or attending the Divine

Office. To soothe Sister Ann Frances, Sister Mary Gemma reads aloud. Sister Ann Frances smiles—the best smile in the monastery, Mother Miryam says.

At times, it has seemed like Sister Ann Frances might pass away soon, in a matter of months, but each time she has rallied and recovered under Sister Mary Gemma's watchful eye. Meanwhile, as Sister Ann Frances has become more needy, Mother Miryam says she does not know "quite how to entertain her." Mother Miryam says that she is happy to visit with Sister Ann Frances, who "talks back a mile a minute," and even though the nuns do not understand what Sister Ann Frances says, listening appears to comfort her.

"She's mystifying us," Sister Mary Gemma says. "She could last a long time yet. She takes a lot of my time, though. I do spend a lot of time with her because she gets confused and she gets restless and it's best to keep her entertained. I'm good at entertaining, I guess. And I'm pretty good at calming her down if she gets upset. Right now this is the necessity of the community."

Sister Mary Gemma's assistance in the infirmary is a blessing, Mother Miryam says; she does not know what the community would do without her. Maybe Sister Mary Gemma's voice or face suggests a memory. Maybe Sister Mary Gemma remains unfamiliar to Sister Ann Frances, yet she still manages to bring solace.

Like the rest of her community, Sister Ann Frances made lifelong vows to the enclosure. She committed to remaining until she died. And so she stays, even as she no longer knows where she is, no longer understands the symbolism of Communion, or why she must wear the small veil worn by the ill. She may no longer know herself or the vows she made.

Sister Ann Frances enlisted in the Marines during World War II. Ever since she transferred to the contemplative order from an active order, she has depended on others. While the public relies on the Poor Clares for prayers, the nuns pray for donations and gifts for their own sustenance. The cloister's inhabitants depend on benefactors from the outside world. Doctors, dentists, and chiropractors pay house calls to the monastery. Locals donate food. One delivers salmon he buys in Chicago. Other food requires effort to salvage, for instance cutting away the wilted parts of vegetables. All of this supplements fruits and vegetables the nuns grow in their gardens. Sister Joan Marie says the donations sometimes appear to be a miracle of redundancy. "As soon as we eat something, the same thing comes in. So it's miraculous, really!" Sister Joan Marie laughs. "I think, 'We ate that! It's at the door! We ate all that!'"

Just as the nuns hope for provisions, Sister Ann Frances looks to Sister Mary Gemma, who indulges her love of books, especially children's stories. "Sometimes it can seem like if you haven't read the stories for a while, you can tell her mind can't comprehend what you're saying to her," Sister Mary Gemma says. "And of course she can't express herself at all anymore. But when you start reading the stories to her, somehow there's some part of her mind that takes it in. She laughs at the right time. She smiles when I show her the pictures. She's so happy. I show her the picture on the cover: 'I'm going to read this to you today.' She remembers and she gets excited. She doesn't remember what we read exactly, but she remembers the picture when she sees it. It's so good for her. It's probably good for me, too, but I do have the joy to care for her and I do have the gift of gab and that's good for her."

The *Little House* series and Sister Mary Gemma's love for the plots and characters have unfurled a new drama, a present-day conflict for Sister Mary Gemma within her own psyche. "After reading those stories to sister, I get fascinated by the history of it," she says. "So much of the history I never knew before, and so I start looking up things in the encyclopedia, or I'll go look up on the map to see where this Indian Territory was, which was actually Oklahoma. I get so fascinated with it. I have to be very, very careful that I don't let it grip me so much that it takes me away from my relationship with our Lord. You admire this family's faith in Providence. Even though they had these worries, they had a great trust in Providence."

In caring for Sister Ann Frances and trying to keep her own appreciation for the Ingalls family in check, Sister Mary Gemma submits to the hierarchy of the Poor Clare Order: In living out her vows, Sister Mary Gemma waits until Christmas each year to ask the Mother Abbess for permission to ask her parents for one more book in the *Little House* series. "I have to keep asking myself, 'Am I getting these books for myself, or am I getting them for sister?'" Sister Mary Gemma says, "Because I really do love those books very much. That's a struggle for me. I often wonder if I should be asking for something like that. Sister is getting to the point she can't understand anymore anyway. She does all right, but you could keep reading the same book to her over and over again; she doesn't remember that she already heard it, but she enjoys it. That's something I struggle with right now. I love books, and stories like that are so interesting to me."

Even as Sister Mary Gemma recognizes her mixed motives and worries about indulging her imagination, she can hardly wait to read again what happens next, to learn again how the plots are tidied up, the characters evolved, the conflicts resolved. "We don't realize how hard it must have been for people who pioneered the United States and made the beginnings of America," Sister Mary Gemma says.

The Ingalls family left a culture known to them, foregoing comfort and convenience for a life of simplicity and faith. This mirrors her own narrative: Sister Mary Gemma has embraced with monastic life the traditions of a bygone era. Sister Mary Gemma is a pioneer, staking her claim in an unseen world to come. "Here in the monastery, we're living in a different world than what so many people are living in," Sister Mary Gemma says. "Because the Christian message is countercultural. What our Lord teaches us in the gospels is countercultural. There's just no two ways about it. And that's our vocation. Our vocation here is to live the gospel life to the full. We're not distracted here, and we have the vows of poverty, chastity, and obedience, which help us tremendously to live completely for God." Like the Ingalls family, the nuns are usually barefoot.

Sister Mary Gemma was drawn to enact the ideals and virtues in the Ingalls books—to embrace, generations later and voluntarily, a life of poverty. But although a cloistered monastery strips away many material distractions and creates the space to focus on God, Sister Mary Gemma names a vice: She daydreams too much. She always has, she says, and her grades were poor in school because her mind often wandered from the teacher's lesson. She believes she missed out on a lot because of these mental flights. When it was time for her to become a novice, Sister Mary Gemma gave one name to the Mother Abbess as her selection for a religious name, not realizing she was allowed to submit three choices. (She was given the English version of the Italian name she requested.) Sister Mary Gemma struggles to stay focused; when the nuns gather for the Divine Office, she says, "something we're praying will make me think of something else and then my mind will be all over the place before I know it."

Sister Mary Gemma is accustomed to admitting her weaknesses publicly. During the Chapter of Faults, the sisters confess aloud their imperfections and weaknesses that have defied the Poor Clare customs. Sister Mary Gemma often admits that she talks too much. She loves to talk. She has learned to appreciate silence, yet she is often tempted to speak in the company of others because she is, by nature, social. "It is a paradox, I suppose," she says of her calling to observe monastic silence. She adds, "God can call anybody, you know." It has been challenging for Sister Mary Gemma, now fifty-seven, to live decade after decade attempting to adhere to a strict code of speaking only what is necessary outside of the community's one hour of daily recreation, when they can socialize. "I did fail in silence many times, and I still do sometimes," she says.

Sister Mary Gemma entered the order when she was nineteen years old. Before she was Sister Mary Gemma, she was Teresa. As a child, she learned she was placed on earth to love and serve God and that her true home was in heaven. Her father, a strict disciplinarian, imposed many rules on his children. Sister Mary Gemma shares a few of the rules: Do not lie. Sit up straight. "That was one I had trouble with; I was always slouching," Sister Mary Gemma says. Clean the house before their father arrived home from work. Go to bed on time. Say the rosary every day, and if they stayed overnight at a friend's house, her mother told them to say the rosary while they fell asleep.

If Sister Mary Gemma's parents went out and left the children home alone, they were always admonished, "Don't fight!" "We usually did anyway," Sister Mary Gemma says. "So we weren't terribly obedient that way. We weren't supposed to hit each other, which we did all the time. We were good friends, but we picked on each other a lot."

When she was five or six years old, Teresa saw a nun for the first time. She was visiting her older brother at school. She learned then that nuns give themselves completely to God; she felt that she, too, wanted to belong completely to God. "I know that I was attracted to her in some way. I thought that's what God wants me to do," Sister Mary Gemma says. "I don't know why I felt that way. Somehow, I knew I had to give Him everything." Her father approved. "He would have been willing to give all his children to the religious life," Sister Mary Gemma says. "I think that's just the way my dad is."

Her childhood religious inclination waxed and waned through her turbulent teenage years, when desires incompatible with life as a nun stirred. These tensions became tangible when Teresa began sleeping with a photograph under her pillow of a boy she had a crush on, a boy she says did not know she existed.

"I was actually afraid of falling in love because I felt—I felt so sure God was calling me," she says.

As Sister Mary Gemma describes it, she was on the fence, sometimes wanting religious life, sometimes wishing desperately against that fate and crying herself to sleep, hoping it was not her destiny. On Christmas vacation during her sophomore year, Teresa read a spiritual book that served as the tipping point. Sensing that God was "calling me in a deeper way than I felt as a child," she reached under her pillow, tore up the photograph, and threw it in the wastebasket. She felt happy then. This relief stayed with her when Christmas vacation ended, school resumed, and a friend, in tears, told Teresa that her own boyfriend had broken up with her over the holidays. Teresa thought, "Well, Jesus, I know I never have to worry about you turning your back on me." Feeling pulled back and forth by her own unsteady whims until that point, Sister Mary Gemma says, "I knew I didn't know whether I could trust myself, but I knew I could trust Him."

The summer after high school graduation, Teresa went to work at a nursing home. When an aunt—her godmother—invited Teresa to stay at her home in California for the winter holidays, Teresa imagined what the trip might yield, particularly how her life might unfold if she met a young man while visiting her family on the West Coast.

Teresa's aunt was married to a doctor; Teresa admired the family's home, their parties, and their outgoing personalities. Her aunt asked if she was sure about her vocation to the religious life. "Don't you want to get married?" Sister Mary Gemma remembers her aunt asking. "I said, 'Well, I do feel that way,'" Sister Mary Gemma says. Her aunt replied, "That's a sign that you don't have a vocation." Another aunt interjected: "That's not a sign. That's a sign that she's a woman. She could still have a vocation." Asked if she wanted to be home for Christmas Day or stay longer in California, Teresa answered slowly, "I'd like to stay here." Before she finished her sentence with "but I think I should go home," her aunt said, "Well, then, you'll stay here." Teresa was shy, afraid to offend her host. She also felt persuaded to the other side of the fence—the possibility of marriage and a family. "I was hoping something would rescue me from going to the monastery," she says.

Her reverie was temporary. It ended when Teresa phoned her father and explained she planned to stay with the relatives for the holiday. She added she might wait to enter the monastery. Sister Mary Gemma remembers her father saying she should do what she felt she should do. "Somehow, even though I didn't say much, he knew I was struggling and he was afraid I would end up not following my vocation," Sister Mary Gemma says. "He understood me. My dad and I were real close spiritually. We had an understanding."

After talking with her father, Teresa regretted agreeing to stay in California. If she joined the monastery, as planned, this would be her last Christmas with her parents and siblings. Teresa told her aunt she was homesick. An airline strike almost prevented her return home, but the strike lifted on Christmas Eve. One of just a few passengers on the flight, Teresa cried en route to Illinois, knowing she would probably never see her California relatives again.

Her father installed new carpet in her bedroom. Her parents settled on the Christmas gift after considering she might continue living with them and find a job, or leave for the monastery. "I really think this is a temptation," Sister Mary Gemma remembers her father saying. "If you have felt God calling you so often, you should really enter the monastery and just put the temptation behind you. You have felt this call for so long." He may have understood her heart, Sister Mary Gemma says. But in struggling to define her father in precise and charitable terms, she says, "I should say he's Irish. That makes me Irish, too. But he—how shall I say about my dad? He's delightful. Really, we tease him so much. He's overly optimistic, I shall say.

"I told him, 'Dad, I'm a little worried about my laziness, entering the religious life.'" Sister Mary Gemma remembers him replying, "Oh, you can overcome that." "But my dad was a very disciplined person," Sister Mary Gemma says, "and I think he couldn't see why anyone else couldn't be the same way he is. I think in that sense he didn't have an understanding that people were made differently. I think he was a little that way; if he had a headache, we all had a headache and had to go to bed early, something like that. 'We have a headache, let's go to bed.'" Sister Mary Gemma says her hardworking father probably assumed she was, too—or could become that way.

Her mother, meanwhile, thought that Teresa was not equipped for cloistered monastic life. "She saw that I liked to talk," Sister Mary Gemma says. "She saw that I was kind of lazy. In a way, I had a stormy relationship with my mother. I was struggling with myself and I was taking it out on my mother, stomping, slamming doors, and so she had doubts about my vocation. She didn't think I would persevere, quite frankly. She was happy to give me to God, if that's what God wanted. She was just afraid I wasn't being realistic about whether I would be able to live the life."

Three months after returning from California, Teresa entered the Corpus Christi Monastery. Her three years as a postulant and a novice were painful. Sister Mary Gemma attributes the challenges to the age difference between her and the next youngest nun and to the culture gap between her and the rest of the community. When she joined the monastery in 1976, she was the first new postulant in fifteen years. At the time, the nuns still made their own straw beds with rye and wheat that they cut and dried themselves. It was the first time Teresa had slept on a straw mattress. "It was very hard for me in the beginning, I must say. I know I found it hard to wait until recreation when I came. It was just so wonderful when recreation came and I could just start talking." During recreation, Teresa told stories; she asked and answered questions, and the older nuns began to grasp just how different her experiences were from theirs. "The kinds of presents I got for Christmas, the sisters were horrified—'You got *that* many presents for Christmas?'—because they would get one gift," she says. "That just showed them that the culture was already changing. Kids were more spoiled than they were back then because the parents had a little more money than the parents in the generation before. So they felt that I really had to struggle because I had culture shock myself."

Teresa's eagerness to talk did not endear her to one nun, in particular—a teacher in an active order who had transferred to the cloister. "Quiet!" the nun called out, shushing Teresa when she thought she talked too much or too boisterously. "And that used to make me so mad!" Sister Mary Gemma says. "And sometimes I would get impatient with her at recreation. But I always told her I was sorry afterwards. She was always so kind and forgiving and would say, 'I'm sorry, too.'"

Teresa's visits with her family in the parlor exacerbated her loneliness, her longing for her former life. They talked of their camping trips; Teresa missed the outdoors. Her Novice Mistress advised her to take comfort in her surroundings and to look to the sky because the sky is always changing.

Three years after she entered as a postulant, the twenty-two-year-old who had been renamed Sister Mary Gemma panicked. She made temporary vows, then thought, "Oh, my, what have I done? I can't leave for three years. It was like by then I'll be too old to get married. No one will want me." Sister Mary Gemma outlined her anxiety to a priest; she felt "torn both ways," as if she were "fighting God" because she longed to fall in love, get married, and raise a family. "This priest did settle me," she says. "He said, 'You definitely have a vocation. The very fact that you've been fighting God so long and He got you here anyway is a good sign that you have a vocation.' He said he didn't think I would have ever actually entered if I didn't actually have a vocation. And he set my soul completely at peace. And I've never wanted, I've never wanted, I've never wanted anything but this life since then. I just needed that confirmation."

Sister Mary Gemma believes that her yearning for married life was typical, "a normal way a woman would feel," and not necessarily any indication of a true calling to religious life. She discovered, too, a critical precept for understanding her own personality: Verbalizing the inner, conflicted dialogue to a spiritual advisor could set her secret temptations "to flight" and defuse the power of her worries.

Still she struggled. She remembers on two occasions sitting in the choir chapel with the other sisters for the Divine Office and feeling a huge sob forcing its way to the surface. "And I thought, 'Oh, now, not here, not in front of everyone.' I just started sobbing right there in church." Sister Mary Gemma believed the outbursts pointed to self-esteem issues she needed to overcome. "I would say I was still working through them after I made final vows, but the sisters were able to see I was going to be able to be okay in time," Sister Mary Gemma says.

In the southwest wing of the monastery, perpendicular to the corridor of cells where the professed nuns live, Sister Ann Frances's cell in the infirmary overlooks vegetable gardens and a few flowerbeds. Sister Mary Gemma spends much of the day there, as well as part of the night, when the Alzheimer's disease confuses Sister Ann Frances's circadian rhythm and she stays awake all night, then sleeps during the day. The infirmary is the only place in the monastery where nuns are permitted to talk freely.

Sister Ann Frances smiles when Sister Mary Gemma appears in the doorway. Sister Mary Gemma sings and talks and reads to the aging nun. Sister Ann Frances's dependence on Sister Mary Gemma might be poetic justice. Sister Ann Frances is the former teacher who shushed the teenaged Teresa during recreation. Over time, the two nuns developed a close bond, and Sister Mary Gemma has helped care for Sister Ann Frances for almost a decade.

"It's interesting the way God works," Sister Mary Gemma says. "It's just interesting that sometimes the ones that you struggle with the most end up being the ones you love the most." Sister Mary Gemma says a true friendship formed while she was still in the novitiate because they were able to forgive one another so readily. As the talkative Sister Mary Gemma has cared for Sister Ann Frances around the clock over the past couple of years, watching the elder nun respond positively and gratefully to the stories and attempts at conversation, Sister Mary Gemma says, "I just have grown to love her very, very deeply. She's just as sweet as can be."

Sister Mary Gemma does not relish the rare occasions she must leave the silence of the enclosure. The world outside "kind of encroaches on our recollection," she says. "When you're used to this type of environment, it's kind of a shock. It's so different." Once, the extern sister drove Sister Mary Gemma to a doctor's appointment, and then they stopped at a grocery store. Sister Mary Gemma stayed in the car with the window down and was shocked when a man yelled at a stranger for parking at an angle and blocking what could have been his spot. Sister Mary Gemma remembers the society of her youth as polite; she wanted to close her window but could not without the keys. She was aghast when the woman responded in kind to the man.

Sister Mary Gemma prayed silently for the man and the woman and the woman's children, also witnesses. "It brought home to me how important our life of prayer is because our whole life is centered on God and a life of paying reverence and adoration and respect to God," Sister Mary Gemma says. "And you always know there's a lot of people that are living a com-pletely different life, they're not even paying attention to God, and then when you're exposed to it, it brings it home that much stronger. And it's not necessarily their fault if they don't know God. They're just picking up what they heard. You don't blame them or anything. But it's just—it was just very, very sad to me to see how the world has changed since I was in it."

The back section of the monastery's fourteen-acre property is lined with evergreens and landscaped with fruit trees. Sister Mary Gemma misses nature. She rarely has time to walk to the backyard. She remembers the *Little House* characters saying, like her Novice Mistress, "You're with nature all the time." The stories offer a respite, reinforcing values that run counter to popular culture, and offering a mental pilgrimage for a middle-aged nun who still feels like an unfocused soul with a fanciful mind.

Called

Sister Mary Clara
of Our Lady of Sorrows

I was Sister Eucharista with my other order, the Felicians. I was there for twenty-two years as a teacher—a primary grade teacher for first or second grade, and sometimes both. I loved them very much; I loved the little children.

I was from Buffalo, in western New York near Niagara Falls. I was born August 11, 1937—Saint Clare's Day. I also was called Clara. My name was Clare. That's how it all began. The Lord has a plan for everyone's life. As the Lord says, "I have formed you in your mother's womb. I have a plan, and your name is written on the palm of my hand."

The Felician Sisters were always in the long habit; they were just like I am now. Because of the Felician Sisters and because of their relationship with my mom, it grew on me. It was an attraction. Many times, it's an attraction; it's a drawing. I have a drawing for prayer, but it's the Blessed Sacrament that I have the drawing for.

When I was in fourth grade I had rheumatic fever. After that, I had to be careful, walking upstairs and so on. I was restricted. I had to go to school on a special bus for one year, and after the first year I had to be on the first floor; I couldn't walk upstairs. In sixth grade, I had to go upstairs. We were in an annex building because there wasn't enough room, and I remember my sixth-grade teacher talking about vocations, talking about sisters and different orders, but more about the Felicians than anyone else. That's where I really think the initial calling came. That never left me. I can still see where I sat in the classroom. I can still see the classroom. I can still see the building. I can still see sister.

I really wanted to go into the aspirancy after eighth grade. The girls lived in the aspirancy, like a boarding school, for four years. But my mom and dad said I had to live at home and experience life before I entered the community, the religious life. They said if I'm still sure about joining and I still want to be religious, they would let me go. So they did; they kept their promise. It was close to high school graduation, April or May, and I slowly approached my mom. I said, "You remember the deal we had?" She said, "What deal?" I said, "Well, you said if I still want to become a religious, a Felician, you would let me go." She said, "Oh, I thought you had forgotten about it."

They allowed me to go. But one thing Dad said that I will never forget, he said, "If you ever want to come back, the door is always unlocked." He didn't say "open." He said "unlocked." It made such an impression to me. For a door to be open, it has to be unlocked. I took it as they would welcome me home anytime. It meant a lot to me for him to say that. But I stayed.

I entered in July and my mom died in March of the next year; '56 I entered, and she died in '57. She had a stroke. When I went with my Novice Mistress to my dad on the day of death to organize things or to talk about things, I said, "Dad, I'm coming home. I talked to Sister and she said whatever I want to do." And he says, "No. You stay where you are. You chose your life. The Lord called you. We can get along. We're able to be home alone. You can come home, but you don't need to." And I looked at my Mistress. Tears were coming down my face. We were going to bury Mom. I had two younger brothers: one in eighth grade and one in fifth or sixth grade, a couple years behind. It was hard. Difficult. But I accepted it.

I thought, I guess the Lord wants me to stay. But it was hard, it was very hard. Sometimes I would be crying. In the dormitory, sometimes I would be sniffling. The sister across from me used to pull the curtain and put her hand through. We would hold hands, hold onto one another, because she knew what I was going through. It was tough. That was the only time I thought that I wanted to go home, because I wanted to be of help to my father. But he didn't feel that I was needed. He was very strong about that; whatever I chose to do was meant to be for my life.

I came here in '78. About three years before that, I knew something was troubling me. I knew I didn't belong with the Felicians. I was searching already then. I had a calling. I had had it with the teaching. It wasn't that I was dissatisfied with the teaching or my children or what I was doing; it was that I had a different calling. The Lord was saying, "It's time to switch gears." So I went for this weekend retreat. Father was there. I went to confession. I said, "I really need guidance." I said "I'm a sinner, but still I need to talk,

Father." I said, "I think I'd like to go to the cloister." He said, "Oh? Where?" I said, "I don't know."

I said, "I want to switch, but I don't know where." He said, "Do you have any idea?" I said, "No." He said, "Do you have any friends in any communities?" I said, "Not friends, but I know of sisters at different communities." He said, "Do you think you're being drawn there?" I said, "I have no idea. I don't know." I know he was really drawing this, pulling this out. He said, "I don't have time to spend on this. I have to go to another commitment." I said, "I understand." He said, "I want you for the next month to forget all about your vocation as a cloistered sister. Get it out of your mind. Do what you have to do, but don't think about the cloister." I said, "How am I going to do that?" He said, "Just don't think about it." I said, "I'll try." He said, "Just give it a good try." I said, "What if it doesn't work? Then what?" He said, "It'll work if you work at it." I said, "Okay." I tried. That was April. I knew this was important. I was so busy with the children it wasn't hard to forget, really. In May, on Memorial weekend, I went to Father, the Dominican priest at the monastery, and I told him what the priest said, that I should come back and talk to him about a vocation to contemplative life. So we did. We spent about two hours together. We talked about my life as a Felician, sharing things about what was drawing me. Then he said, "Do you know where you want to go?" I said, "No, I have no idea." He said, "I can give you a little bit of help. Not much." He said, "Go to the extern sister; they have pamphlets about cloistered life. Ask her to find one for you and to give it to you. Tell her I asked her to give it to you." She found it in the drawer. And one was a brown paper pamphlet, and it was written by a Poor Clare, the Abbess in New Mexico. She wrote a pamphlet, *With Light Step on Unstumbling Feet*, that was about the contemplative life. It spoke about the whole entire contemplative life as a Poor Clare. So I took that and I read that and I was happy with it. And that was it. And that's why I'm here.

The back of the pamphlet listed six or seven convents of Poor Clares. I had to choose one of the convents. I went to Sister Michelle and she helped me write a form letter. I said, "How am I going to know where I'm supposed to go?" She said, "You'll know. I don't know how, but it will come about." I said, "I trust you, Michelle. I don't know how this is going to happen." So we wrote this introduction to my life, that I was a Felician sister, that I was still teaching, and that I still had a few months to go—in fact, the whole year to go of teaching. "I'm committed to my apostolate here, so I can't promise anything, but I want information about your order." I wrote to Mother Mary Francis in New Mexico, I wrote to two convents in California, and then I wrote to one in Cleveland, Ohio, because I knew that would make my brother happy, in case I was accepted there. Then I wrote here, to Rockford, Illinois. Well, Mother Mary Francis answered and said, "It is our policy not to accept transfer sisters who have another community, especially the many years you spent as a Felician Sister." She said, "We're sorry, sister." I accepted it. In California, they said the same thing: "It is our policy not to accept transfer sisters." The Cleveland, Ohio, monastery had a number of older sisters that needed care, so they really had to devote themselves to the sisters. They said they would pray for me that I would find a suitable place for my vocation. I wrote all these places just after January. Mother Dorothy answered me in February. She said, "We would be happy to meet you and to talk with you." That was it. She put in a few other nice sentences. She wrote again every two weeks, just a short note. In March, she asked me to send my life story, why I wanted to come all the way to Rockford. I didn't know why I wanted to go to Rockford, but I knew I wanted to be a Poor Clare. In March I told her I couldn't come any time except for during my Easter break because that was the only time I wasn't in school. That was March 25th in '78.

I flew here in March; my superior was kind enough. That was the first and only time I flew. My family was not exactly poor, but we didn't think of flying anywhere. We traveled by train because my father used to work on the railroad, so we had passes. We never flew. It was interesting. It was exciting; especially looking at the clouds, it just took the breath out of me. I loved it, I really did. I was hoping I would fly one other time.

I came here for an overnight visit, made my papers, met the community, and they interviewed me. From all the letters, I guess the Mother Abbess knew me quite well. I entered in July that same year.

I went home, finished school, and then I had to go to my superior and close up things and get my records, my baptismal records, and all the other records I needed—physical and dental, like you have to have. Then I went to my brother and he wasn't too pleased about it. My father already had passed away. I knew that when Dad died, I knew that if I wanted to do something drastic like join the cloister, I was free. I wouldn't have to hurt him, or disappoint him, or leave him here alone. I was free. But John just couldn't understand. He was young yet. His kids were young. The girls were just in eighth grade, sixth grade, and then the two little boys were just small. He couldn't get it in his head. My brother was stubborn like a lot of men are. We knew each other, what we were struggling with. He couldn't understand why I came here, all the way over to Illinois. I could have gone to New Jersey or Cleveland, Ohio. I said, "This is my calling. This is where the Lord wants me. He wants me in Illinois. I don't think I'd make it anywhere else." John accepted it. He brought me over, set me up, put my suitcases up, and that was it. It's not that I appeared heartless or cold, but some people are just like that.

My brother passed away in '97. That was a struggle for me. I knew I couldn't go to the funeral. I couldn't go see him. I could talk to him while he was in the hospital before he died. Mother Dorothy allowed that, because that's just compassion for the family and the sister. She said, "Pick up the phone and see if you can reach your brother John." I did, but he wasn't able to talk that night. He said, "I don't feel like talking." That was it. I said, "I'll call another time." I knew John. I knew he wasn't feeling good. He was sick. He was dying. When you have someone that's very close to you and you know the person and you know the struggles, it's not difficult to accept his "no." So then I called my sister-in-law, and I started crying. She said, "Why don't you call tomorrow night and I'll be there. I'll pick up the phone." We agreed, and I called and she picked up the phone and gave it to John and we had our last talk. About two weeks after that, he died. He died in July, the last day of July. I called sometime in May.

I found it difficult to say goodbye this last time when my family left because it might be the last time. You never know, because it's so hard to get here—ten hours from Buffalo, New York. It's a long trip. They write to me. I don't always answer the letters, but I know that their love is always there for me and if ever anything should happen, if the devil gets in the way too much and I get tempted too much, I could be tempted to go back home. And I know that the door is unlocked. But of course I'd have to find a new place, because they're moving. I know the door will still be unlocked somewhere else. I would still be accepted.

5

Mothers of Souls

He has not only redeemed us, He has raised us up to the divine life itself. And He couldn't have done that without becoming human, Himself, because He came to earth. He's taught us that we can live a divine life, because He has shown us how, by taking on our humanity. And, of course, we have to have His life within us because the divine life itself is out of our reach except through Him.
                          Sister Mary Gemma of Our Lady of the Angels

The phone calls seem to arrive in patterns: requests for prayers for children with brain tumors one week, couples who want babies another week; threats of divorce one day, financial troubles another day.

The cloistered nuns assigned by their superior to answer calls to this prayer hotline of sorts write notes by hand, and then the names and requests are transcribed by typewriter. Sometimes, the Mother Abbess tapes the list to the doorframe outside her office. Each evening before collation, the Mother Abbess reads the day's prayer requests to the members of the community so that together they can "share in their pain a little bit," Mother Miryam says of the callers, and "take it away a little bit by prayer."

Asked if it is burdensome to hear about tragedies day after day, Mother Miryam says, "Sometimes it gets a little heavy." She adds, though, that cloistered nuns consider the callers their wards, in a similar way that nurses and doctors must regard their patients. "That's what we're supposed to do," she says. "You know, if we didn't do that, we wouldn't be faithful. It'd be like if you left your patients in the hospital and didn't bother about them."

And so the nuns intervene on behalf of humanity. They pray for healing, for safe pregnancies and deliveries, for reconciliations, for financial solutions. They are the comforters and caretakers of the world, believing that their own suspended desires and dreams, their directed intentions, their prayers and their penances, can alter the course of history.

Sister Maria Deo Gratias explains that her role as a cloistered contemplative requires that she act as an intermediary, making reparation through prayer or fasting or some other penance for other people's sins. "There's a dimension in the spiritual life; where there is much sin committed, for instance in a city, there has to be reparation from man," she says. "Man committed the sin; man has to make reparation for it. That's a part of our life; we try to balance out the accountability of others living in sin. And so we make reparation and supplication to love God, because they do not love God. That's part of our apostolate: 'They won't stand before you, God, and so we stand before you, God, in their names so that we can praise you in their names.' For the whole city, there's a special spiritual grace that's given because some people have that apostolate to offer up reparation."

The nuns are active agents; each endeavors to call forth God's plan in lives beyond their cloistered grounds. They merely need a prompt—a phone call, a patron's request, news passed through the Mother Abbess of a crisis. "There's a sensitivity that we're kind of the center of the city, trying to supply the spiritual energy that they need along with their own graces, that they receive from God—that extra help to them. They know they have someone backing them up in prayer," says Sister Maria Deo Gratias, the Vicaress.

"I mean, people have so much faith in prayer. It just makes you really humble," Mother Miryam says of those who phone repeatedly to ask for prayers or to report rescues from their troubles. "They say, 'Ever since I asked you to pray for us, everything's been...'" she trails off, explaining the caller says the tide has turned. "And you think, it's their faith," she says. "That's what the Lord said: 'If you have faith, it'll move mountains for you.' It's their faith. They just have wonderful, wonderful faith, and people have so much goodness in them to respond."

"It's just all in God's care," Mother Miryam says of an aging member of the community, though her words could apply to the nuns' outlook in general. "We watch and care, but just wait and see what He has in store, just in case someone would take off for heaven." The cloistered contemplative Saint Therese of Lisieux, a nineteenth-century French Carmelite nun also known as "the Little Flower of Jesus," inspires and directs her spiritual progeny. "She considered our life as contemplatives to be the heart beating, sending out the blood to the other members of the Church," Sister Mary Gemma says. "That was the way she understood our life and I think that's probably the best description that I can think of. We've had so many missionary priests come and tell us how much they appreciate our life, because they know they would not be able to convert souls to Christ if there weren't these contemplative orders. They believe very strongly that the heart of the Church is in these contemplative orders, and that's why the Church has always encouraged this kind of life.

"I've been thinking about these things ever since I was young. I was thinking, 'Gosh, all those people in the world and so many of them don't know God and I would love to help. How can I help people come to know God?'"

Sister Mary Gemma's parents were Catholic. Her family's house in the midwestern countryside was exposed to natural elements, and so Sister Mary Gemma remembers taking shelter, on occasion, from tornados. No one seemed to worry more than she did. She collected the cats and the dogs and made sure that all of her family members found their way to the safety of the basement. "I mostly wanted my family safe, safe in God's arms in heaven, but I used to often think that I have to have that same concern for everyone because everyone is special," she says. "Everyone is special to God. I had to have that same concern not just for my own family, I had to have that for everyone—people I had never heard of. Everyone is special. And there's so much ignorance of God in the world."

Once, as a teenager, Teresa, as she was called then, went to the county fair with a "whole troop of cousins," as she remembers it. The eldest, Teresa, was charged with keeping track of her siblings and cousins. "I was counting everyone all the time," Sister Mary Gemma says. Her mother was unconcerned for the children, Sister Mary Gemma remembers, because Teresa was "taking care." "She knew I was counting. I could not enjoy that fair at all because I was always counting heads making sure we were all together."

In this mayhem, Teresa identified her deepest desire. She remembers thinking, "Dad says prayer is more powerful than anything else. That's what I should do. I should go and pray at the monastery so that I can help all those souls get to heaven. Since I was small, my dad taught us to be concerned about the salvation of souls. He said there's nothing more powerful than prayer. My dad always taught us that, and so it's probably natural that I would kind of be drawn to this kind of life.

"It seemed to me there was no better way to help people find God than to live a life of prayer and just pray for the world continually," she says. "You can touch any soul around the world. And, of course, we don't know who we're praying for actually, but God knows.

"I would guess that's been a big reason to choose this life; it's a love for the world, but in a different way. We don't want anyone to be deprived of the love of God. It was also that I wanted to live an intimate life of prayer with God. But it's not a selfish life since we want to do it to bring as many souls to God as we can." In this life, Sister Mary Gemma feels responsible for all of humanity. "I mean I'm limited, of course," she says, "but I have to do the best I can, at least."

Sister Maria Benedicta acknowledges that prejudices develop in the course of one's upbringing; but a life of prayer can erode an inclination to judge others. "It's called expanding your heart," she says. "The more you allow God to change your heart and open your heart, the more you realize Jesus went to heal sinners and the tax collectors, you know, the people in the world that others would ask, 'Why is He with them?' But you see, God loves everybody. And it does expand your heart to pray. When we hear terrible news stories, we think to pray for the man who did that. I never would have thought of that before. I would have thought, 'How horrible.' But it's like that man really must be suffering to have done that. To realize *that man* has a soul, too. Or woman. And obviously he doesn't know God. But it is a broadening of your heart. I'm not just cleaning the floor; I'm doing it for God. And you think of all the suffering that people endure and I can do this little thing for God. And He can help those who are suffering. I couldn't help people in Africa if I was doing whatever sort of a job. But, here, your heart can expand to the whole world."

Each woman who joins the Poor Clare Colettine Order takes on a new name; embracing anonymity, she performs her duties before the small audience within her community, and for an unseen, immortal God. "The hiddenness is part of our enclosure," Sister Mary Nicolette says, "that we're not to be known to the world, that we are here, we're here for God and it doesn't really matter who we are, you know. There's an anonymity and hiddenness because what matters is what God sees and not necessarily to be known to anyone outside."

The "hiddenness" of the cloistered monastic life empowers others' lives, Sister Sarah Marie says. "It's the little pulled away, hidden, nobody really knows about you, nobody even cares—might not even care to know about you—that does, I think, have tremendous impact."

Before entering the enclosure, Sister Mary Nicolette knew she would be allowed to leave the enclosure's premises only on rare occasions. She had heard the mantra: The metal grille does not keep nuns in an enclosure; it is a sign that keeps the world at bay. Sister Mary Nicolette believed that with this separation she could give herself to God completely, paradoxically. "We leave the world in order to be for the world," Sister Mary Nicolette says. "See, it's like we're removing ourselves from the world so that we can be wholly given over to others."

Residing within these cloistered walls suits Sister Mary Nicolette. "I didn't struggle with that because I understood it so much as part of the vocation and so much a part of what I desired," she says. "So it was something I longed for—to give myself and maybe not be appreciated and maybe known in the world and, like you say, disappear into obscurity. Nature—human nature—obviously loves to be known and seen and appreciated. But as far as the vocation is concerned, it's something that everybody who receives the vocation desires. It's a part of understanding our purpose, that you desire; you're counteracting something that is very natural, that's perhaps not the best to want to be seen and known, and, 'Aren't I great?' You're denying yourself in a certain way. You're counteracting that natural tendency."

"This is where you want the totalness with Him," Sister Sarah Marie says. "I want to be completely with Him, I want to be totally away from anything that would distract me from my life with Him, from my union with Him."

Sister Sarah Marie was introduced to the Rockford Poor Clares when she still answered to the name Tiffany. Her mother, a member of the Third Order of Franciscans, taught her only daughter that no tornado ever touched down within city limits because the Poor Clares' prayers kept the city safe. "My mom, to her dying day, said, 'It's the Poor Clare monastery that's kept Rockford from being hit by a tornado,'" said Sister Sarah Marie. "Now others of more knowledge will say it's the river," she laughs. "So that's debatable, if you want to fight the old Italian lady on that!"

Raised to turn to the Poor Clare nuns for prayers, Sister Sarah Marie says that when one of her brothers was sent to serve in the Vietnam War, the nuns prayed him safely through his military service; when a pregnant sister-in-law nearly miscarried, the nuns prayed her through a safe delivery; and when Tiffany was living in Kansas City and her fiancé broke off their engagement, her mother called the Poor Clares, and the nuns prayed the young woman through that personal devastation. "It was just a constant outlet," Sister Sarah Marie says of her mother's prayer requests of the Poor Clares.

But when Tiffany announced her plans to return from Kansas City to join the Poor Clare Colettine Order in her hometown and become a cloistered contemplative, her mother resisted. It was an assault on her mother's expectations. She knew more than most people what her daughter's choice—what the vows and the enclosure—would cost. "There would be a line that would be drawn," Sister Sarah Marie says. "Jesus would pull me even more. Here, you give it all. You give Jesus everything. Even visiting home. Even going to see Mama when she's sick. Even going to her funeral. Even to go to the wake, just down the street at the cathedral. That's what the enclosure is and that's why we treasure it so much."

Sister Maria Deo Gratias says,

Some people are called to that—to give to a person, and together they give themselves to God, and then they participate in the creation of God in having a family. Others, like ourselves, are asked—or invited, really—to give ourselves to God alone; so chastity, it's a freedom, because we can give ourselves totally to God and we don't have divided responsibilities. It's not a divided love, because you don't have to divide your attention in such a way that a married person has to. In their life, they fall in love with the person and they want to give that love to each other. We fall in love with our Lord and we want to give that love to God, undivided. We can be concerned with the things of the world, where a married person is concerned with their family.

Sister Mary Clara left home at eighteen; she took a religious name, Sister Eucharista, and became a teacher with an active order of religious sisters in upstate New York. The orphanage also housed neglected children and offspring of divorced parents. Sister Eucharista taught first and second graders. She became best friends with another teacher, Sister Michelle, who knew how to drive. The two would ask for permission to take the community's car on drives throughout the countryside, sometimes stopping at a lake to watch the sun set and listening to music on a tape recorder; sometimes they asked along older religious sisters who would not have had the chance to go out otherwise.

After twenty-eight years as a teaching sister, Sister Eucharista sensed she might be called to transfer to an enclosure. She showed Sister Michelle a pamphlet about the Poor Clare Colettines. "Wow," Sister Mary Clara remembers Sister Michelle saying. "That's all she used to say when something struck her as different," Sister Mary Clara says. "She said, 'Wow, that certainly has a lot in it.' I said, 'Isn't it wonderful?' She said, 'Is that what you want?' I said, 'I think so.' She said, 'Really? You won't ever come back.' I said, 'I know.'" Sister Michelle reminded her she might never again see her brother John. At this, Sister Eucharista cried. "She was feeling me out," Sister Mary Clara says. "That's the way we were, the two of us, and so I reread the pamphlet a number of times. Every time I read it, I knew this was where the Lord wanted me."

Since Sister Michelle could not dissuade her friend, she helped her draft an application seeking entry to the Poor Clare community. She was accepted, and Sister Eucharista ferried plants on the cross-country drive. "In class I always had plants in front of the windowsills. We always, I always, enjoyed them, so I came with a planetarium with plants in a little fish tank and I think I brought four plants in a box," she says, remembering the day she arrived more than thirty years ago. "They're floating around in the monastery somewhere. They might be dead already."

"Somehow," Sister Mary Clara says, "it was easy for me to turn my back on the world and just come here." Poor Clare nuns can correspond with loved ones by letter, and Sister Eucharista is always happy to receive updates from her brothers and sisters-in-law. She does not usually reply, though. "That's what they always cry about: 'I'm still waiting for an answer!'" Sister Mary Clara says. "Well, I'm a cloistered sister," she tells them, adding that she's a terrible writer. "They know I pray for them and I think about them. I say, 'You don't need my John Hancock to remind you I'm here.' So we joke around like that."

Her first fall in Rockford, Sister Mary Clara was dispatched to the outdoors to work in the gardens. She remembers picking green beans and tomatoes and strawberries and apples, and then hearing school buses stop, within earshot, to fill with children. "If you spend a quarter of your lifetime in a community, and then the Lord calls you somewhere else, naturally your thoughts will come with you—whatever you were doing there," she says. "That was a special gift I had received from God, to teach the little ones. I just loved them to bits. I really did. Anything I could do for a little child, I would do."

While she was toiling in the green bean patch one day, there seemed to be an unending procession of school buses. "I thought, 'When will they finish?

Why won't they just go somewhere? Just get away!' " Sister Mary Clara says. "And there I was, sitting on the ground, on the grass, and I couldn't hold the tears back. The tears were falling. A sister came behind me and said, 'Are you all right?' " Sister Mary Clara busied herself, pretending she was fine. The other nun persisted. Sister Mary Clara explained that the sound of school buses reminded her of the children she taught. She missed the children, missed teaching them. The other nun told Sister Mary Clara, "By this time next year you'll be so used to us and you'll be so used to your new life that you won't even think of the buses." The prediction was true, Sister Mary Clara says.

Still, Sister Mary Clara says sometimes a group of children from Catholic schools in the diocese visit. Their chatter and laughter provoke her to ask the Mother Abbess if she can peek into the parlor and look at the children on the other side of the metal grille. Sometimes, the Mother Abbess tells her, "Now, now, you have work to do." Sometimes, the Mother Abbess teases, "Aren't you over that yet?" Sister Mary Clara responds, "I'm over it, but I'd still like to see the little kids." Often, Sister Mary Clara is allowed to check in on the children but "not too often," she says, "because it's a distraction for me and it's something that I have given up. I shouldn't be that attached to the children. The Lord wanted me to do that over there, and now He wants me to do this over here. I have an entirely different life now."

Sister Mary Clara thinks the replacement of her work as a teacher with her vocation as a contemplative nun must be similar to the transition from single life to marriage. "It's the same thing with us," Sister Mary Clara says. "There has to be a break for your own peace of mind and love, too, because you can't have two loves. I can love the children, but I can't have my heart over there, wondering what's going on over there—if the kids are still growing up, still good, or whatever—and then be here in the monastery and praying the Divine Office. That doesn't work well."

Sister Maria Deo Gratias explains:

We are spouses of our Lord, and we said "yes" at our profession and then throughout every day of our life we continue to say that "yes" in a practical way because it's one thing to stand at that altar and say "yes," but it's another thing in the daily nitty-gritty of life to continue to say that "yes" with all faithfulness. And we want to be a faithful community because that gives graces. Because our apostolate is prayer, and

God hears the prayer of a holy person, we strive to be holy, to be heard by God, to intercede for all the people of the world, all the diocese, the people of this city and offer reparations for the sins of the world, the sins of the city. So, therefore, in order to be heard by God, we have to be faithful. But it's out of love. It's not like: "I have to do this." It's, "I want to do this because God has called me into that relationship of love with Him." And part of that relationship is taking on the responsibility of the life, in saying "yes" all the time.

Cloistered nuns keep watch while the world sleeps, waking at midnight for the first of seven prayers each day. They pray each day for the worst sinner in the world, believing that the worst sinner cannot desire redemption without supernatural intervention.

Their sacrifices make way for blessings, they believe, and so they welcome hardships because increased suffering can yield greater rewards, submitting to "death for the sake of resurrection," as modeled by Jesus, according to *Verbi Sponsa: Instruction on the Contemplative Life and on the Enclosure of Nuns*.

When her mother died, Sister Sarah Marie was not allowed to leave the monastery. "And it was hard," she says. "I'm not going to sit here and say, 'Oh, no, easy come, easy go. That's the way it goes.' No, of course, it was hard. But I was closer to my mom and the family spiritually than they were physically present at the wake, at the funeral. I was much closer because I was in our chapel while they were at the funeral. The funeral was at 10:30. I was before the Blessed Sacrament. I was before Jesus, physically present there. I was looking at Him. You see, there was a uniting there. Physically, I wasn't there, of course, but spiritually I was there."

She says her family and friends sensed her presence—perhaps a testament to the fervency of her prayers, the faith of her loved ones, and their shared belief that the most trying aspects of her life can be reclaimed. One friend said she felt that if she turned around at the funeral, she would see Sister Sarah Marie sitting behind her.

Sister Sarah Marie's mother had asked the Mother Abbess if her casket could be carried into the monastery's parlor after she died so that her daughter could say one final goodbye. In a departure from the cloistered community's standard protocols, the request was granted. As in life, the two were separated by the metal grille. Sister Sarah Marie could not reach far enough to touch her mother, or to lay the roses that the Mother Abbess gave her in the casket. Sister Sarah Marie cried. She cried in mourning; she cried because of the distance still between them. The priest walked into the parlor then. Silently, he touched Sister Sarah Marie's hand. With his other hand, he held the hand of Sister Sarah Marie's mother. "She was touched by me," Sister Sarah Marie says. "Our Lord works. You give Him all and He gives it all back to you. He's outdone in all His generosity."

When Sister Mary Nicolette prepared herself to enter the enclosure, she believed that she had just enlisted in a lifetime of boredom. In two decades, though, she says she has never once been bored. "I was talking to my family when they just came to visit this summer. They were asking me, 'Have you ever been bored yet?' That's a joke because I've never been bored since I've been here. When I was out in the world, sometimes I was bored to death. But since I've been here, I've never once been bored. It's like you're going from one thing to the next and it's like a peaceful pace and you always know what you're going to need to be doing next and there's never a time when it's like, 'Oh gee, what should I do?'"

Sister Mary Nicolette says,

When you're listening all day long, you're listening for God's voice and every day is new. He'll ask something new of you. He'll put some new situation in your life or ask something different of you. Every day is different. One of the things that I always thought was, "Lord, I'm offering up the great sacrifice of a very monotonous life and I don't know how I'm going to do it, but I'll make the sacrifice, Lord!" But there's no monotony. No monotony. There's a regularity.

Monastic life has presented other challenges. When her family visited for the first time, Sister Mary Nicolette had not seen them for a year. Her first reaction was to hug everyone. "But the grille was there," she says. "And it was just striking. And it made me realize there is a definite, a real separation." The last time she hugged her parents was in 1999, when she made solemn vows. "My mother didn't want to let me go. But they were very good about it. It's always very moving—not just for the sister herself and for the parents, but for all the sisters. You know, everyone starts crying. It's just very moving."

"When it is a sacrifice that costs, you can offer that for someone who's maybe struggling with something," she says, like a mother who cannot hug a child serving in Iraq. "That makes it all worthwhile and bearable, really, and something that you feel this is something that I can offer this for someone," she says. "It's a very heavy burden on them, and so if I say by my offering I can help alleviate that heart of that other person. It's just the idea of helping carry one another's burdens."

In her effort to become a spiritual intermediary, living on behalf of humanity, her novice Sister Maria Benedicta finds herself lacking. "That's the hardest thing—you want to love God," she says. "That's why I'm here. You want to love God with all your heart, all your soul, with all my mind, with all my strength. But I don't always do it. Because when you see how much He loves us, how much He's done for us, to die on the cross for us, to give us the Eucharist, to be in the Tabernacle with us constantly, to forgive all our sins, you just want to give Him everything. But sometimes you just fall into your own selfishness. And you think how could I do that? And He's been so good. It just crushes you."

Not long after Sister Mary Clara arrived at the Corpus Christi Monastery, the three aged extern sisters passed away. Sister Mary Clara offered herself as the next extern sister, to operate as a conduit between the world and the enclosure, communicating with visitors to the gift shop and running errands by car. The Mother Abbess turned her down. "No," Sister Mary Clara remembers being told. "You joined the cloistered sisters, so you will remain cloistered. Your original calling wasn't to be an extern sister, out there. You're supposed to be in the cloister, in here."

Sister Mary Clara's innate social temperament found an outlet at the monastery as one of the few nuns assigned to answer the phone calls for prayers. Every morning, Sister Mary Clara expects to hear from one woman who recites the names of her immediate and extended family; she asks that the nuns pray for their safety and well-being and for her own health, that the cancer remain in remission. Sister Mary Clare does not often speak to the woman directly; her caller prefers leaving a message on the answering machine and will hang up the phone gently if Sister Mary Clare picks up.

Typically, Poor Clare nuns do not reveal to the callers their religious names, even if pressed; the nuns are instructed to say, if asked, that they are just one of the sisters, in keeping with their aspiration for anonymity and separation from the world. This also helps prevent callers from becoming too attached to a particular nun and asking to speak with her. But Sister Mary Clara cannot help but bond with some of the callers.

One elderly woman tells Sister Mary Clara she is nearly blind and lives alone. "I don't know what I would do without you sisters," Sister Mary Clara says the woman tells her. "I know that you're there and I know that you'll pray for me." Sister Mary Clara says she replies, "Keep calling and we'll keep answering. And if we're not here, you just leave it on the answering service. You talk to the answering service and we'll listen." Sister Mary Clara describes the answering machine as the monastery's "salvation" because it allows the nuns assigned to phone duty to participate in the Divine Office.

At times, when Sister Mary Clara answers the phone, a caller reminds her of a previous call and asks if she remembers the conversation. "You have to think, 'Who was it who called?'" she says. "You wrack your brain, 'Who is it that's calling?' But in order to keep peace, you say, 'Of course I remember.'"

Other callers are cautious, reluctant to disclose their names. Sister Mary Clara tells them they do not have to disclose the information. If the person asks how the nuns' prayers will be directed to the appropriate individual, Sister Mary Clara says, "All I know is that God knows. God knows who you are, and He knows your petition, and He'll take care of you. All I'm going to do is pray—pray for all the people that called today and then leave it to Him. That's all we do."

Although Sister Mary Clara revels in her assignment for her delight in interacting with people, the phone calls are a disheartening glimpse into the state of the world. "They're desperate," she says of the callers. "They're very desperate."

One woman phoned after her husband died and asked if the nuns would pray for her daughter, who had turned to drugs and tried to take her own life. The widow still calls, at times after long intervals; she always sounds rushed and always requests prayers for her daughter and herself. "That's one that I feel very close to," Sister Mary Clara says. If she hasn't heard from the woman in a while, Sister Mary Clara asks permission from the Mother Abbess to write the woman a note. "She needs me now and she knows who I am because of the telephone calls," Sister Mary Clara says. "I can write to her and console her, and let her know that I'm praying for her."

Sister Mary Clara ends each phone call with a promise that the nuns will pray and make penances on their behalf. "What kind of sacrifice are you going to make, sister?" Sister Mary Clara remembers one caller asking. "Your life is a sacrifice already." Sister Mary Clara concedes that she cannot give up food, if the nuns are already fasting. "I cannot drink some water, just not take a glass of water when I'm thirsty. That doesn't break my fast, so I can say I will offer that up," Sister Mary Clara says. "The Lord knows who needs something, so He'll take that sacrifice. He'll take that glass of water and give it to somebody who needs water."

As Sister Mary Clara ended one phone call, the woman told her that she would also do something for her. "Alright, you do that," Sister Mary Clara said. "We'll help each other out." Many express their plans to pay back the nuns for their supernatural efforts, offering to buy presents for the nuns during pilgrimages, but Sister Mary Clara tells them the nuns do not need anything; they have enough. "What would we do with all the things they want to bring us anyway?" she asks. She tells the callers that the Poor Clares would welcome prayers or the lighting of candles at shrines or sacred sites. "Everybody tries to remember us because we remember them to the Lord," Sister Mary Clara says. "That's the exchange we make."

Sister Mary Clara says there are days "that you get moods." "I miss going out. I miss going out with a friend like Sister Michelle," she says. "I guess there are days that you just wish you could go out and go for a walk. Well, we can go for a walk because we have the back filled with trees and we can walk around back there. But it's different. The devil's out here saying, 'Aha, I've got her wanting to go out.' If I allow myself to dwell, to think about it, he can win over and he can get me out there. But I think I'm stronger than I was before. I wasn't as strong before, but I'm stronger now. When my family left I found it a little difficult, but now it's okay because I know if I live longer they'll come to visit me again."

In becoming a cloistered contemplative nun, Sister Mary Clara's charges are no longer her students, but the public at large. "I can listen and I can feel for people. I can understand their needs," she says. Answering phone calls connects her with humanity.

"We're a little bit different than anyone imagines," Sister Mary Joseph admits. She recalls her first exposure to manual labor in the novitiate: Performing garden duty, she and another novice, the current Mother Abbess, spent the day plucking strawberries from the patches; nearly sixty years later, they recount their exhaustion and their lighthearted response. Feeling sorry for themselves, they agreed to sing to keep their spirits up; with a hint of irony they borrowed the tune of a Jewish lament. "When we were feeling down we would go, 'Woe, woe, oh woe, is me. Oh woe, oh woe, oh woe, is me,'" Sister Mary Joseph says. "We'd do that for the fun of it."

"People think, 'Oh, you're going to do all this, and you're going to be all disciplined and you're going to accept sufferings, and voluntary mortifications—you're going to be miserable,'" Sister Mary Monica says, citing a stereotype of what she calls the "prune-faced" nun—women in the past who found themselves in cloistered monasteries even if they weren't truly called, or who became teaching sisters even if they did not want to work with youth. "But, no, if you do it right, you're not going to be miserable. You're going to be joyful and nobody's going to know the difference."

Their whimsical outlook appears to have physical benefits. Sister Mary Nicolette was surprised when she first began to learn the ages of the nuns in her religious community. "I remember thinking, 'Oh my goodness, I thought she was like twenty years younger than that,'" Sister Mary Nicolette says. She articulates the phenomenon of extended youthfulness: "Cloistered nuns are removed from the pressures, the fast-paced, go, go, go modern culture that is otherwise a source of twenty-four-hour stress. When you're removed from that, there's a certain peace that your soul is steeped in. It doesn't mean that our lives are stress-free, you know; I don't mean that. Everyone has a certain amount of personal stress that you work through and whatnot. But what I mean is the stress from the outer environment is closed off. This is a very peaceful and like a controlled environment, almost. We cut out the outside noise and all the worldly news and concerns. So I think that has a big, big impact, on our lives in general."

Sister Mary Nicolette, whose family teases that the decades of observing monastic silence have eroded her skills at small talk, jokes that there could be another explanation: "But also there is a secret. The habit covers a lot. It covers the double chin and the gray hair!" Sister Mary Nicolette laughs and says she knows she has just blown "the mystical illusion."

"The whole purpose of sacrifice and penance, " says Sister Maria Benedicta, "is to strengthen your body against wanting all these comforts that aren't good for you, strengthening your mind against all these thoughts that aren't godly thoughts. But if you go beyond that and say, 'I'm going to not sleep, not going to give myself that luxury,' well, then you're going to be so down. When you don't sleep, you don't have any defenses against temptations. It's not strengthening you; it's making it worse. There has to be a balance. There's a saying, 'Virtue is in the middle.'"

In a spiral-bound booklet handmade by the nuns to mark the Golden Jubilee—the Corpus Christi Monastery's 1916 founding—the caption under a photograph of five tombstones in the cemetery states, "Fifty years have passed and only in the annals of eternity can the true record be found of the joys and sorrows, the hard work and many sacrifices of this half century. Five times death came to the monastery forming a closer tie between heaven and earth as God called cloistered and extern sisters to enjoy eternal life and the hundredfold promised to those who leave all to follow Him."[1]

Cloistered nuns serve as intermediaries between the physical world and the unseen, eternal realm. Sister Mary Nicolette enacts her deepest beliefs in an invisible, all-powerful God, laboring on behalf of people she will never meet. This vocation delivers an unknown, intangible harvest. She will not learn in this lifetime the results of her life of devotion and sacrifice. "Sometimes we just have to go by faith that what we're doing really makes a difference," Sister Mary Nicolette says. "Because we don't see the fruits of our lives. I think one of the trials that every cloistered nun goes through at some time is just clinging to that faith to know that, 'Yes, what we're doing makes a difference.' Because you don't see the fruits, and so that's all you have sometimes—to go by that faith, that you believe little sacrifices are going to do something, that your prayers that you don't feel are worthy—your whole life given over, and you don't see the fruits of it."

"She'll never see how many hundreds, thousands of souls receive the fruits of her prayers," says Sister Maria Benedicta of her Novice Mistress.

The nuns assigned to field phone calls share repeat calls that credit the nuns' prayers for keeping a marriage intact or a disease at bay. "Sometimes we get calls like that and it helps us to continue," Sister Mary Nicolette says. "But many times we just go by faith that there is a purpose, that there is a reason, and that it's good."

The Mother Abbess reads the newspaper each day. She chooses which stories to share with the nuns. She always tells them if there has been a murder in Rockford. On occasion, she clips an article to be placed on a table in the library. Sister Mary Clara answers the phone, taking note of personal tragedies and global catastrophes. And then the community takes action: They pray, and then they "wait and see," Mother Miryam says, what God "has in store."

Sister Joan Marie
of the Child Jesus

My mother was home all the time. She was always home. When I was born she got sick. A nurse kept a heating pad on her too long. First her arm got stiff, and then her leg got stiff so they called up my grandmother who lived in Parsons, Kansas—that's where my mother came from—and so she took care of me when I was little, when I was just a baby. I don't remember it, but that's what they tell me. My mother couldn't walk very well because she had that stiff knee. My father took her to a specialist, and he said, "Walk to me. Walk." She said, "I can't." "Walk," he kept saying. "Walk." And so she walked. Evidently, she could walk after that, but with a stiff knee. My brother used to blame me because before that, Mother used to take him on the sled, but when I came along she couldn't do that anymore.

My sister's the oldest, five years older than me. My brother was two and a half years older. The older two would talk for me; I didn't have to say much. I had to have speech therapy because others couldn't understand me. I had a tutor, and I learned the vowels and to pronounce better so they could understand me.

There was a gas station across a big street, but I was kind of little so I took my brother and sister with me. The Overhands owned the gas station—just a little gas station—and they had caramels and things. They would give me penny candy, and so I went there as often as I could. My brother and sister liked to come, too, because they got to share. I used to keep a jar of money—pennies and things I got. Anyway, I would shake that jar, and when it shook like there was enough, I would take them over; they would go with me—my brother and sister and cousin, too. I treated them. I wanted their company because I wanted to go over there, and I couldn't go alone! I was only five or six. The Overhands took the money and said it was enough, and they asked each of us what we wanted; they got Pepsi-Colas and stuff.

The Overhands were wonderful people. They took an interest in me. One Easter, the bell rang and I went to the door. Mother went to the door and I went along. They had a clothesbasket and inside were two bunnies—white bunnies—and they were so cute. They were for me. That's what I mean; they just took an interest in me because I was the baby, I guess, the youngest. That was really something. We kept those bunnies. There was one that lived longer. Mother said when he got to be the size of a milk bottle, we had to get him out of the house. She thought he would give me pink eye, or maybe he did give me pink eye. I don't remember. Anyway, we would have to get him out of the house then, so I would measure him. The bunny would come to the breakfast table and it was so funny. Finally, my father said he would make a fence so we could still keep him outdoors. He made him a fence, but the next morning, the bunny had dug under the fence. We never got him back. I guess they never looked for him.

What really got me as a child was Christmas. I didn't know what Easter was because I didn't know anybody that died, but I knew what Christmas was and I knew that God became a child like me. That just went over and over in my head—that God would become a child. Because what was I? Insignificant as a child.

My mother and father never went to church, but my mother always had good books. I remember this one book she had—the Old Testament story about the little girl that was sold into slavery. They had a picture of the little girl and I always wanted to be that little girl who said, "There is a prophet in Israel!" That influenced me a lot, that book about the leprosy and the girl. She was a slave girl from Israel. It's an interesting story, in Nehemiah or something, I forget where it is in the Bible. We hear it in Mass sometimes. I've read it since, many times. I remember the pictures, too. It's a child's book and the picture of the little girl looked like she was my age.

It always did impact me—that story—that the slave's master would get cured, and the way he got cured. The slave girl said, "There is a prophet in Israel that will cure you." He was her master and she wanted him to go to Israel. He did. He got cured, but it was a roundabout way. The prophet said, "Go plunge in the Jordan seven times." And he said, "What, are not the rivers in Egypt good enough?" He didn't like that. He was mad. He said, "I thought he would come out and lay his hand on me." But the prophet didn't; he just said, "Go." The slaves tried to argue with him, "Now, if he had said something great big, you would have done it. So why not this?" So he plunged seven times in the Jordan and came out clean like a baby's skin.

Ma had a lot of good books she used to read to us because my brother couldn't read. She would read not religious books, but books that boys would like—*The Count of Monte Cristo.* I liked them, too—books about Doctor Dolittle and by Frank Buck, things like that. Because my brother had trouble reading, my parents were supposed to let him stay back; the teacher wanted to keep him back in first grade or kindergarten, but my father wouldn't let him; he wouldn't hear of it. My sister was so smart and he thought that the next one should be that smart, too, so he wouldn't let them. So my brother moved on, but he couldn't pick up the reading; he had trouble with the reading.

I remember staying home from school when I got sick. I mean, I pretended I was sick in order to stay home. A big tree was cut down in our yard and we wanted to have fun in that tree. Mother knew I was just pretending, but she let me stay, so all day we played on that tree. That was fun.

We had to rent a house so we could go to school, but I don't remember school much. I didn't like it. My sister liked school and she was an "A-plus" student in everything. She had to be top in everything, and she was. She studied. She studied hard to get those grades. It wasn't like it came easy, although she was like a genius, I guess. My father was a genius because he could take any job. He could seem to.

My sister had a boy that would come over; he liked her. She played the teacher; she liked to teach, and she would keep him in the corner. He was always in the corner. My mother didn't like that. She didn't think that was right. I don't remember standing in the corner, just him. But he would come back for more. He liked it. Mother thought that was awful. Isn't that funny?

They always expected me to be like my sister. I couldn't match that. I was lucky if I made a "C." My mother always said, "Well, don't worry if you don't get better grades. You can understand others better when you're just normal, average." She tried to console me. But anyway, I guess I just wanted to play all the time.

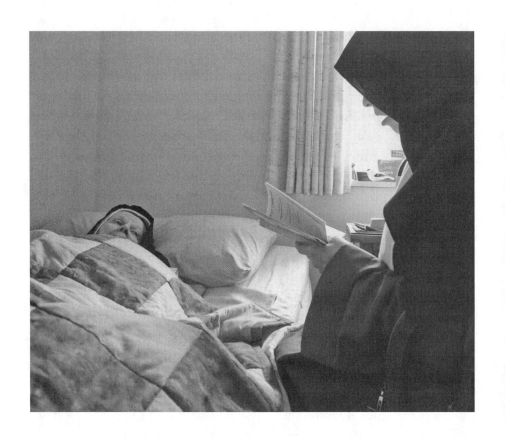

6

The Suffering Servants

In a sense, I think that's what God asks of us—it's that trust element. He's saying, "Are you willing to risk everything for me? Do you really love me? Do you really love me enough to risk everything for me and trust that I will take care of you?" And it has to come out of a personal relationship, and a deep personal relationship with our Lord, knowing that, yes, I can trust Him and He will take care of me and He won't let me down. He won't just drop me, leave me in the lurch, or just dump me. But we can really, really trust that He loves us and wants to give us the best.

Sister Mary Nicolette of the Father of Mercies

When Sister Mary Gemma entered the Corpus Christi Monastery, she left behind a younger sister poor in health. When her family visited, Mary was wheeled into the parlor. Sister Mary Gemma says her mother "kept her father real" and both parents helped Mary learn to contend with her disease: colitis, an ulcerated colon. "She was only in seventh grade when she started to suffer," Sister Mary Gemma says.

Since the onset of Mary's disease, their father had scoured health journals and medical books on Mary's behalf, always hopeful of finding new treatments. The pattern continued through Sister Mary Gemma's tenure in the Corpus Christi Monastery. Her family still lives near the monastery, and so together they would drive there to see Sister Mary Gemma for each of her four allotted family visits each year. "I still remember Mary sitting in the wheelchair and Dad all excited because he was giving her *this* now, and Mom sitting in the back now going like *this*," Sister Mary Gemma says, shaking her head.

Mary prayed for her own healing; she wanted to be made well. Still, she ended each prayer asking that God's will be done in her life. Sister Mary

Gemma says, "Because of the guidance she received from my parents, she learned how to use the suffering, how to offer it to God, how to accept it, and how to unite her suffering with the suffering of Christ. She grew in love with God through all that."

Over the years, Mary's condition changed as the disease advanced, led to joint and spine problems, to open-heart surgery and a full colostomy, but not before an infection poisoned her colon and breached other organs. Mary was an avid needleworker until a rheumatic disease ate away the bones in her hands. Sister Mary Gemma says children gravitated to Mary; she allowed them to play with her deformed fingers, to push them backward and watch the fingers twist and flatten. This did not hurt Mary because her joints and cartilage had completely deteriorated, Sister Mary Gemma says.

As her body self-destructed, Mary appeared to grow lovelier in spirit. "She was one of the happiest persons I ever met," Sister Mary Gemma says. "She always had a smile on her face. She was always joking."

Mother Miryam witnessed the same transformation in Mary—a "lovely little thing" who initially grappled with her "crippled" state until doctors said they had done everything possible and Mary understood she would not recover. Eventually, she believed it was her vocation in life to suffer.

Self-deprecating, Mary joked that a cousin selected her as a wedding attendant, along with two friends who were seven months pregnant, because there was "nothing like two pregnant women and a cripple in a wheelchair to make you look tall and thin." Referring to her electric wheelchair, she called herself the "remote-control cousin."

Mary survived and suffered until a medication thinned her blood, and she had a stroke. She died within twenty-four hours. "I think she was ready for heaven," Sister Mary Gemma says. "I was so happy for her to be with God, where she wanted to be, that I couldn't even cry for her after she died. I think it was harder for my family who were with her all the time, but I only saw her four times a year. And we were very close but I just felt nothing but joy for her. Not that I don't miss her, but I just still feel real happy for her. That's what my parents always taught us—we're living for heaven. We're here on earth to get ready for heaven and that's what we all want, for us all to be together in heaven someday."

After Mary died, Sister Mary Gemma learned about Mary's brush with death a year earlier. Mary told a cousin about the experience and asked her not to share the story with anyone yet. After Mary died, the family read

Mary's own account of the events in an essay she titled "My Journey toward Heaven." "I have had a lot of pain in my life, but this was the worst," Mary wrote at the age of forty-two. "How could a bladder infection cause so much pain?" A tentative diagnosis of a tumor, abscess, or a blood clot was followed by hallucinations—a side effect of the medications and the barium tests. Told she would need to undergo an operation, Mary scheduled a confession with her priest. "I have felt for a long time now that I would never survive another major surgery," she wrote. "My feeling was that I would not be coming back." Friends visited Mary in her hospital room; she told them that if she died she "wouldn't mind." "I felt my life fading away," she wrote.

Four days after she was admitted to the hospital, doctors scheduled a CT scan of her lungs and abdomen to determine the cause of her breathing difficulties. "Before I was taken away for the scan I had an urgency to tell Mom and Dad where my will was. I felt death was very near, but I didn't want to alarm them," she wrote. She told her mom, "I don't want to be kept alive by extraordinary means."

During a CT scan that should have been somewhat routine, Mary could not catch her breath. The technician thought she was hyperventilating and advised slower, deeper breaths, before she realized Mary's system was shutting down. Mary remembered her pushing emergency buttons, remembered the technician screaming for help. "It became extremely painful. With every gasp after gasp I could only think, 'God how long can this go on? God, please take me now, this is torture!' Then it was over. I must have finally passed out."

Later, when Mary described what happened next, she said the pain left her body at that instant. She felt surrounded by a "golden kaleidoscope of a yellow bright light." She believed she had started her journey to heaven. She was ready. But then she heard voices of confusion and panic. A doctor repeated her wishes: She did not want extraordinary measures taken to save her life. She heard a men's choir and she felt soothed. She thought she was about to end her journey. Then Mary saw "black and gray." Her throat hurt. She realized she was alive but worried that the nurses would not know she was. An emergency tracheotomy revived her. "I was not able to finish my journey to heaven," she wrote. "I knew my trials and struggles were not over after all."

"They worked on her for quite a long time and she came back to life again," Sister Mary Gemma says.

After Mary died, her cousin e-mailed family, writing that Mary told her she heard, "not through her ears, just in her heart," a voice asking, "Will you still suffer for the poor souls that have no one to pray for them?" Her cousin replied, "Yes, if you want me to." The emergency tracheotomy that saved Mary was a "cruel twist," the cousin wrote, because it stole her ability to sing—her only remaining creative outlet.

Her family believes that her spiritual encounter consoled Mary for her decades of chronic debilitating diseases. Mary died at forty-three years old. Looking back now, Sister Mary Gemma says of her younger sister's descriptions of approaching heaven, "I honestly can't say what she experienced. Certainly, it was a mystical gift that she received, to hear the angels singing. And you could tell—she always already was a beautiful person to me—but after that, there was so much peace in her. Before that, she always had a certain fear of dying, I think. And that's natural to the human condition—to fear death. In God's original plan, the soul was not meant to be separated from the body."

Sister Mary Gemma believes that suffering can bring good, purifying a person's soul of selfishness and uniting her with the suffering of Christ. Although the reasons for this suffering remain a mystery, Sister Mary Gemma believes that God is an all-powerful being, an "infinite genius."

Daily, Poor Clare nuns pray for those who call the monastery seeking relief from their circumstances. The nuns seek treatment for their own ailments as well. Mother Miryam underwent knee replacement surgery after postponing it several times, insisting she was too busy overseeing the monastery's operations to take a break for the operation and a period of recovery.

"Suffering gives us empathy for others because you're understanding more the suffering of Christ in a certain sense; there's no way He loved us more than suffering on the cross for us," Sister Mary Gemma says. "That kind of gives you an appreciation of what He suffered for you....It really does have an effect on your love of Christ, if you don't become bitter about suffering, and use it to draw closer to our Lord on the cross. And then you can't help loving Him more. Of course, some people don't have to suffer to have empathy for others....Actually, what really purifies us for God is love; loving God and loving our neighbors is what really purifies us. But sometimes we have to suffer....It's how God purges away our selfishness, is through suffering. He can use our suffering for souls, for the salvation of souls. And I know from my experience that your union with Christ deepens through suffering. He allows suffering for a reason. There's two ways that you can handle suffering in your life—either trusting God, or you can turn to bitterness. But your spiritual life deepens when you suffer and you learn how to suffer graciously."

Sister Mary Gemma is not speaking abstractly. Not only did she suffer and empathize as witness to her sister's struggles, but Sister Mary Gemma has also endured her own physical trials. She, along with another member of the Corpus Christi Monastery, are both victims of serious diseases. One of the two nuns is now healed; any sign of the disease has vanished. The other nun continues to wrestle not only with her condition but also with the degree of self-care required to accommodate the affliction. Both reconcile their illnesses, and their present states, through the looking glass of faith.

Sister Mary Nicolette was diagnosed with dermatopolymyositis, a rare autoimmune disease, in childhood; the illness, which causes muscle weakness, flared twice. "I had recovered both times, but it's a hereditary disease that you don't usually ever get over," she says. "You just live with it the rest of your life." A daily regimen of expensive medication stabilized her condition, and Sister Mary Nicolette learned to deal with the symptoms, limiting her physical activity and monitoring her health.

When Sister Mary Nicolette applied to enter a cloistered monastery in Ohio, she mentioned the disease in her application, not expecting it would bar her entry since her condition was stable; she was turned away. In 1993, Sister Mary Nicolette was twenty years old when she was invited to join the Corpus Christi Monastery as a postulant. She brought a year's worth of medication, not wanting her illness to present a financial burden to her new religious community.

She fulfilled her duties, including the sometimes demanding manual labor required of all novitiates, under close medical surveillance; regular blood tests tracked her enzyme levels. Tests revealed that she was stable, but she felt weak, with limited mobility in her muscles and tendons. "If you didn't know that I had this, most people wouldn't notice, but there were some things, like bending, that took a lot of effort to do," Sister Mary Nicolette says.

But the more she worked outdoors, the stronger she felt. Several times during regular consultations with the doctor who makes house calls to the monastery, she said she did not think she needed the medicine anymore. The physician suggested reducing the dosage. "So it was gradual," Sister Mary

Nicolette says. "Very gradual, very gradual, very gradual." Eventually, she was no longer on any medication, "which is very unexpected and very out of the ordinary for this illness because it's not something you're ever cured of."

Today, she has no sign of the illness. She does not take any medicine. She no longer undergoes blood tests. "And I'm as strong as an ox!" she says. Sister Mary Nicolette knows why she was healed. "God," she says. "I just feel like if there's a need in the community, especially with the outdoor work and everything, the older sisters can't do that and I'm here and I can do it," Sister Mary Nicolette says. "And I think God strengthened me to serve community in that way, and do some of the manual work that maybe some of the older sisters can't do."

Asked if she thinks she would have been cured if she had not entered the monastery and assumed the trying duties of a cloistered contemplative nun, Sister Mary Nicolette says, "That's an interesting question I don't know the answer to." She pauses, then adds, "Yeah, I don't know. I don't know. It's something very mysterious to me and perhaps only God knows. But I do feel like there was a purpose at the time when I became sick—to draw me closer to God—and there was a purpose why I was healed, so I that I could help community and be a strong sister in the community."

Sister Mary Gemma grew up in a nearby farming community. In 1975, she entered the monastery. She was nineteen. Assigned the manual tasks of a novitiate, Sister Mary Gemma began experiencing chronic back pain. Seven years after entering the monastery, she experienced a type of pain she had never felt before: a burning sensation that seemed to jump from one area to another, traveling up and down her arms and legs.

The pain began to spread. She did not understand what was happening within her; she had trouble finding words to accurately depict the sensation. Changes in the temperature seemed to trigger discomfort, as did any sort of emotional strain.

After years of pain, punctuated by more tests and a trip to a pain clinic in Chicago, doctors eventually diagnosed her with fibromyalgia. Her condition did not improve with treatment, however, and so doctors conducted more tests. Almost two decades after the pain started, Sister Mary Gemma's hand swelled up and turned blue; this helped the physicians deduce the underlying cause: reflex sympathetic dystrophy (RSD), known also as complex regional pain syndrome. Her doctors believed the previous diagnosis was correct, too, and that she also has fibromyalgia. Possibly the result of a previous injury, RSD had operated with free reign, advancing unchecked for so long before Sister Mary Gemma was diagnosed and treatment started that in spite of potent doses of daily medication, small changes in temperature and minor injuries provoked major flare-ups.

Once, her hands began to ache while she was playing the organ but she kept practicing; it took her a year and a half for the pain to subside. "RSD just takes a long time to quiet down," she says. "It's not a nice disease. I actually have a mild form of it, but the doctor said the problem with me is it's gone into my legs and my arms, and since I've had it so long, it's harder to cure."

Sister Mary Gemma's treatment has included nerve blocks—temporary fixes that limited the pain for less than a year. Through trial and error, Sister Mary Gemma tries to accept her chronic condition and manage it with rest and medication (covered by Social Security disability payments). Even too much excitement or laughing too hard seems to awaken pain signals from hibernation. "Clearly a weird thing," she says.

Doctors have told Sister Mary Gemma that her symptoms will improve if she can avoid cold temperatures as well as heat, which makes her sweat; they suggested she move from Illinois to a more temperate climate. "I just feel this is where God wants me," she says, "and I feel so much that the community here understands my disease. They're so understanding of it. I felt like it would be a burden to put on another community just like that, although I'm sure other communities would be willing to take me. But the sisters have grown with me. They've been with me through the whole thing. They've been supporting me through the whole thing. And I just...this is my home. They provide heat for me and they do everything they can for me to help me."

Sister Mary Gemma believes she would not have been accepted into this religious community if her diagnoses had been made before she asked to join. She does not regret her decision to become a Poor Clare, in spite of the fact that her condition might have been detected and stabilized sooner if she had been living a more "normal life" out in the world, she says. "I think it's a blessing for me that I'm in the monastery because I have a community who—they're all very understanding. There are times where I cannot work at all and I have to rest a lot. I don't know how I would survive if I wasn't in the monastery."

Sister Mary Gemma does not fully comprehend her affliction. She knows her body has failed her. God never intended suffering or death, Sister Mary Gemma says. "Our body and our soul are a unit. He did not make us to be spirit only, like the angels, and He did not make us to be body only, like the animals; He gave us a body and soul and He did not intend, in the original plan, for the body and the soul to be separated."

Like her younger sister, Sister Mary Gemma prays for her own healing. She closes her prayers just as Mary did—that God's will be done. She has not experienced substantial healing, physically. But she believes that suffering can serve a redemptive purpose. And she believes that God has answered her prayers. "I think God has helped me, not with an actual miracle, but He has helped me get the doctors that can help me," she says. Since childhood, Sister Mary Gemma grappled with issues relating to her self-esteem. Once, a few years ago, when she received the Sacrament of the Sick, she says, "I can remember that I was asking our Lord to heal me in whatever way He wanted to, and I felt a great strength emotionally after that." Another time, as Sister Mary Gemma observed her hour of prayer before the exposed Blessed Sacrament, she knelt down and said, "Jesus, I failed you again. And I felt His voice coming from the Blessed Sacrament going right to my heart: 'I love you still.' I was so surprised, I said, 'Jesus did you just talk to me?'" Sister Mary Gemma says. "I didn't hear it again. But I felt it so strong. It felt like an echo in my heart and it was one of those things that kept me going through this tough time of low self-esteem. He loved me anyway. And He loves me anyway."

An assistant in the infirmary, helping watch over Sister Ann Frances as she contended with Alzheimer's, Sister Mary Gemma is thankful that Sister Ann Frances can remain in the monastery and has not been sent to a nursing home, where Sister Mary Gemma thinks she would be even more confused. Working in the infirmary allows her a more flexible schedule. Not wanting to "spoil herself," she has had to learn, repeatedly, not to try to soldier through the early warning signs of RSD; otherwise she will need to be admitted to the hospital to receive intravenous pain medication. A necessary regimen—frequent rest—feels like punishment for the sociable Sister Mary Gemma.

Mother Miryam says it is hard for any of the nuns when they cannot take part in community because they are sick and bedridden, but it has been especially hard for Sister Mary Gemma when she is forced to remove herself to her cell. Mother Miryam says Sister Mary Gemma questions, "Am I giving in to myself?" Mother Miryam describes Sister Mary Gemma as phlegmatic by nature and not prone to push herself; she says Sister Mary Gemma has made great strides in the steep learning curve to know how much she can handle once she feels pain and when she should stop working.

Sister Mary Gemma does not walk barefoot—unlike the fictional Ingalls family, unlike the other Poor Clares. RSD forbids her feet from greeting the cold floor. "That's part of my suffering, too, because I came here to live a life of penance and to live a hard life, and I'm not able to do that because of my health situation," she says. "And yet I am living a hard life within my situation. It's hard for me not to live the life as I thought I was going to. Through spiritual direction, I've learned to accept it; this is how God wants me to suffer. He wants me to suffer by not being what I would call a *Colettine* Poor Clare. We have a very strict penitential life and that is what I came for, but it's God's plan that I'm not able to do that. I suffer in a different way."

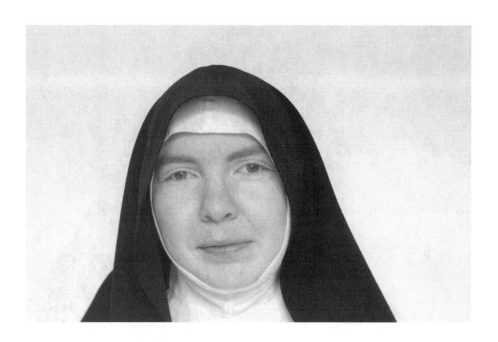

A nun works in the monastery's woodshop, equipped with tools of every type after one woman joined the Poor Clares and, in keeping with her vow of poverty, gave up all belongings, donating them to the community.

To honor their vow of enclosure and separation from the world, Poor Clares try to maintain themselves as much of the property as possible. Here, a nun cleans the boiler.

A nun and a novice garden together. The Poor Clare day comprises regular alterations between prayer and manual labor.

A John Deere tractor—a rare concession by the Poor Clares to technological advancements—is operated only so that the nuns can mow the acreage more quickly in order to return to prayers. Rather than relying on the tractor for hauling, the nuns use a wheelbarrow and pitchforks in keeping with their life of manual labor. Here, a nun passes the gardens and a storage shed.

A nun has passed away. Her coffin, seen through the grille, is placed on the enclosure side of the parlor before the funeral.

Part III

The Threats

7

Idealism and Reality

It's in self-giving that people find their truest fulfillment. And it's a paradox; it's one of those paradoxes that seem to be a contradiction. Now if you look at something as beautiful as marriage, you see how, when two people sacrifice themselves for one another and give themselves to each other wholly and completely, there is a true fulfillment there. It's the same in religious life and on a supernatural level; when people are able to sacrifice themselves—give themselves up—that's when we can find the deepest fulfillment, not in seeking selfish ends and selfish motives. When we're seeking ourselves, or seeking ourselves in creatures or in creation, it's so finite; we're seeking what it can't give. Only God can fill infinite desire.

Sister Mary Nicolette of the Father of Mercies

After Sister Mary Michael's forty-fifth birthday, her family witnessed a quick transformation, somewhat miraculous, totally disruptive. "It all just happened so fast, out of the sky. I compare it with Paul being knocked off his horse," Sister Mary Michael says.

Her journey from an insurance firm to transcendence took shape in the utterly mundane. When family members borrowed her red car and turned on the engine, they knew to anticipate blaring country tunes; now they were baffled, instead, to find cassette tapes playing spiritual lessons, and her radio tuned to church music. Her young nieces and nephews, who had looked forward to her visits and the spoiling that inevitably ensued, became the objects of her evangelism. Poolside in her backyard and during hikes in the woods near her family's cabin in Wisconsin, the children tired of her efforts to impress on them religious teachings and stories. She taught them the sobering story of the holy children of Fatima, who saw visions of the Virgin Mary in Portugal; two of those youngsters had learned they would not live long, and so they dedicated themselves for the remainder of their days to only what mattered for eternity—prostrating themselves for hours in prayer and practicing acts of self-mortification.

Sister Mary Michael, known then to her relatives as Jenny, told the children that in the story of the Fatima children, an actual modern-day morality play, she could identify with the little boy who quit dancing and stopped singing to contemplate quietly behind a bush. She wanted to spend her life praying, growing closer to God. "Just to be nice to me, they would, but they weren't interested," Sister Mary Michael says. "Of course, they weren't going to understand. They were going to lose me. We were real close." As Jenny's interests and attention tunneled in a religious fervor, her nieces and nephews complained that she was changing; they distanced themselves from her. "It was like I went overboard and they couldn't understand," she says. "I feel sorry for them because I was so excited and I was trying to push this onto them."

At her niece's confirmation party, Jenny stood in the hall with the other celebrants. She felt ignored by the guest of honor, but she was not sure the slight was intentional until her niece apologized. "Later, she told me she was sorry she didn't introduce me to her friends because she was upset," Sister Mary Michael says. "They were just so hurt because what they had was going to be lost. But they were getting older and they were going to have their own lives pretty soon. But at that time they were still quite young, so this was quite hard for them to let go."

On weekends, Jenny typically brought her mother to her nieces' and nephews' basketball games. She remembers that when she first started desiring the cloistered life, she went to one of the games. "You know how it is in the gyms, with those bands playing and the crowd?" she asks. "I had never noticed how loud and how awful the noise was before. It just seemed so horrendous and I didn't want to be there with all that noise. When my mother and I were going home, my brother called my sister and wanted to know what was happening. It went on like that; I went up there again a couple of times, and they'd get upset, and I'd try to talk to them, and they'd try to understand."

Jenny's family was bewildered by the middle-aged woman they once knew as a tomboy who stole cigarettes from her parents' gas station store and swiped the complimentary maps to roll cigars stuffed with weeds.

As a medical student in college, Jenny was impervious to dissecting cadavers and remembers, matter-of-factly, trying to scrub her fingernails free of the fatty tissues that accumulated there before she and her lab partner went to dinner. Jenny dreamed of becoming a missionary doctor, but, fearing interactions with patients and the pressure to diagnose and cure their ailments, she quit medical school after her third year. She says now she might have enjoyed clinical research if she had thought to consider that as an option. Her parents, who had claimed her desire to become a doctor, were distressed by word that she was about to drop out, and they sent her older brother as an emissary on a fruitless mission to dissuade her. An advisor, who mistakenly believed that her parents held too much sway in suggesting that she quit, badgered her to reconsider abandoning the program.

Jenny enrolled in computer classes at a technical school and then began working as a programmer analyst for an insurance firm that overlooked Lake Michigan. For eighteen years, Jenny worked in Chicago, commuting from her home in Indiana to her job. She saved money, bought a house, drove a convertible. "I was fortunate to have such a good job and to have something I enjoyed to do so well," she says.

In her mid-forties, living with her sister and brother-in-law in northwest Indiana, just down the street from her mother, Jenny had a reputation as easygoing and averse to conflict. For the second time in her life, Jenny charted a course in direct opposition to her family's wishes.

The changes in Jenny began with meager gestures—her reading material now consisted of biographies of the saints—that shifted her path completely. "What drew me was just a desire that God put there inside of me," Sister Mary Michael says. "It wasn't anything that I did. It wasn't anything I was searching for. It just happened. I mean I had this desire to love God. It's like I fell in love with God and nothing else mattered anymore. It's like from His side because the desire was put there. I didn't have anything to do with it, and so it just became stronger."

Jenny's family members became bystanders, shocked by her changing values, priorities, and temperament, uncomfortable with the new dynamic in their relationships and their passive status. Jenny's stamina in the face of her family's opposition to her fortified spirituality surprised her. "I was really close to my family and it was grace that I could stand up to my family because normally I would say, 'Well, forget it. They don't want me to do it, I won't.' That was really hard," she says.

Jenny told her sister of her impending first visit to the monastery only "because I lived with her, so she and her husband had to know," she says.

"They weren't real happy about it. It was really hard because they didn't understand. I can understand because it's such a switch, such a shock to say you're going to leave and live a contemplative life. So we didn't tell my mother. I was gone a whole day or so. We just didn't tell her."

Her visit was disappointing: "It seemed like everything was so dark and dingy." She learned from the Mother Abbess for the first time that there are "even priests that don't believe in cloistered life. That was a shock. It got late and I was planning on going home that night, but I stayed overnight. I woke up at midnight for the Mass choir to listen. Then I got up in the morning, they gave me breakfast, and I went home. When I got home, I was just kind of confused. I wasn't impressed," she says. "But there was still that feeling that I wanted this life." Sister Mary Michael remembers that her sister tartly—perhaps hopefully—said of her visit: "You expected to see saints flying around."

Still, she had not thought about home while she was visiting the monastery, and she attributes that to God's grace. "I know it was," she says. "I wasn't wishing I was back there. I was here and I was supposed to be here and that was it. It was like I was real strong inside, I guess, like you're doing the right thing, whatever had to be done."

After Jenny returned home, she informed her mother she planned to enter the Corpus Christi Monastery. "No, you're not," she remembers her mother saying. But Jenny told her mother, who was terminally ill, "I have to."

Jenny was drawn to the radical and idealistic roots of the Poor Clare Colettine Order, and she identified with the original mission; she wanted to live as Jesus lived. Sister Mary Nicolette draws strength today from the simplicity and poverty of Saint Francis, who was initially met with disapproval by the approving body in Rome for his community of contemplative friars. "They said, 'This is just not livable,'" Sister Mary Nicolette says. "'It's just phooft,'" she sweeps her hand over her head, signaling the lofty standards set forth by Saint Francis of Assisi. "And they were saying idealistic is not realistic." Sister Mary Nicolette summarizes the historical account of the exchange that followed and led to the founding of the Poor Clares, the second order of Saint Francis: One wise cardinal stood up and warned the others, "Brethren, beware of saying that we cannot approve this, that it's not livable, because if you say that, you say the gospel is not livable." "And no one could argue with that," Sister Mary Nicolette says, "because Christ gave us the ideal in the gospel. And if you say we can't live that, you're saying that

Christ asked us to live something that's impossible, and that's not true. So it's something that's very on my heart."

Sister Mary Nicolette matured in a breathtaking scene—the rim of the earth's crust that is the Alps. She developed, spiritually, during solo hikes in the Italian mountains. A self-professed woman of high ideals, she says, "It was like nature spoke to me of God and I realized that there was something deeper in life than I had ever experienced." An heir to the eight-hundred-year-old order who still marvels at finding herself free of an incurable disease, Sister Mary Nicolette comes by her romantic outlook rightly.

Sister Mary Nicolette, a visionary, is within prayer's reach of eternity. She, like all cloistered nuns, is "entirely dedicated to God," according to the book *Verbi Sponsa: Instruction on the Contemplative Life and on the Enclosure of Nuns*, which is given to each new postulant at the Corpus Christi Monastery to assist in her formation and training. Called to renounce not only "things" but also "space" and "contacts" and the other "benefits of creation" in a "ceaseless straining towards the heavenly Jerusalem," the cloistered contemplative yearns for fulfillment in God, alone, "in an uninterrupted nostalgia of the heart" toward "the realization of this sublime contemplative ideal."[1]

Those who abide by Franciscan virtues submit themselves to a radical way of life. Sister Maria Deo Gratias explains her aim in elementary, yet incredible, terms: "The challenge is to become a saint in the life. That's the challenge—to give 100 percent each moment of the day no matter how I feel—100 percent in the virtue of charity, 100 percent response in the virtue of my own prayer life, and giving God totally all the facets of our life. If I can just give 100 percent, that's the challenge that I see."

Sister Mary Nicolette believes the same hands that struggle against nature's restrictions should reach for perfection. Sister Mary Nicolette says the gospels give readers the example of Jesus' flawlessness; the saints proved that it is possible for men and women—nondeities, who are not God incarnate—to attain this: "They made it. They got there. Now it doesn't mean that they didn't struggle, but we know with certainty that they reached the goal that they were striving for. And we have their example and that's why the Church raises them up as examples. That's all the Church is saying, is that they lived heroic virtue and it's possible, and that you can arrive at this. And it's going to be a struggle; it's going to take your whole life, but it's not impossible and it's not in conflict with reality."

Not everyone—not even all of the monastic nuns at the Corpus Christi Monastery—believes that idealism and a full acceptance of reality can be reconciled. Sister Mary Nicolette describes a recent theological exchange. "We were talking about reality versus ideals," she says. Sister Mary Nicolette does not place the two concepts on opposite ends of a spectrum or regard them as mutually exclusive, "because I really believe that the reality is the vehicle that leads us to the ideal. I don't believe that being idealistic is being unrealistic. I wed them together. I believe that the reality that we live should be such that we're growing toward the ideal and that the ideal is something that can be reached. We're going to be short; most of the time we're going to be living short of the ideal because we have a lot of growth to go through before we get there, but I personally reject the idea that being idealistic is being unrealistic. I think the two go together. I think you're on your way if you're idealistic."

The reality of the cloister can conspire to subvert the spiritual pursuit of ideals. Some women are simply not equipped for cloistered monastic life. The principled—and arduous—quest is for those who can cope with reality, who can reconcile the impossible standards and their own limitations with the rigors of the cloister. "When you enter the monastery, the life is structured," Sister Maria Deo Gratias says. "And so I don't just say, okay, I'm just going to 'x' it out and I'm going off to spend the time walking in the woods. It's a total giving of yourself. And that time is not yours to 'x' off. That's part of your poverty—that we don't own anything. And we don't own the time that we have either."

Interrupting one's sleep at midnight for the Divine Office, never again hugging one's family—all of this is "not natural," Sister Maria Benedicta says. "God chooses the weak to make them strong. He gives them His power to be able to do it. And it's like, okay, I can do it. And you realize your utter weakness because He has to come in and He has to do it, because we can't. It's beyond our own capacity."

When she was a postulant, in training and learning about the ancient customs, Sister Mary Gemma was nonplussed by her fellow spiritual travelers. "You are very idealistic and you want to keep that idealism, but you're not quite realistic when you first come because you see the beauty of the monastic life and you expect that everyone's going to be a saint," Sister Mary Gemma says. "And then you find out more about yourself. As time goes on, you find out that you have a lot to work on, too. You understand when you notice faults in others, as you grow in the spiritual life and you grow with your own struggles with your faults, it makes you more compassionate with your sisters. You realize this life is hard; striving for a life of perfection is going to be hard, even though there's so much joy—so much joy living in community. But it's hard, too. The religious life is a life of perfection. But you're striving for perfection. You don't come perfect; you're striving for perfection. That's what you promise when you make your vows. You're promising to strive to follow Christ, and to become perfect, like He said: 'Be perfect as your heavenly father is perfect.' So our life is a striving for that. But we fail and we get up and we keep trying because we're human and we have that tendency to fail. That's just the way life is. The important thing is to get up and to keep trying."

Sister Maria Deo Gratias believes that the monastic island within a crime-ridden urban area is "a suburb of heaven." "Our destination is heaven," Sister Maria Deo Gratias says. "We're not camping out forever. We're passing through. Even in this suburb of heaven, it's not heaven yet. So, therefore, I'm traveling. We're all pilgrims and coming to that perfect union, which is heaven."

Disarming in her frankness, Sister Maria Deo Gratias personifies two competing interests: a compulsive industriousness to embody her ideals, and an acceptance of her present circumstances. She sacrifices daily for her beliefs; she also detaches from that which she believes she cannot or should not control or change. Sister Maria Deo Gratias's last assignment in an active order—working in the psychiatric unit of a Chicago hospital—illustrates her willingness to bend herself, but not her beliefs, to each situation. When this former teacher was asked to work in the psychiatric unit, another religious sister offered to lend Sister Maria Deo Gratias "civilian" clothes, because she thought the modified habit of her active order, which did not cover her ankles, would create conflict with the patients. Sister Maria Deo Gratias dismissed the suggestion; she felt the other nun was already "putting the expectations on" that she could not come into the unit as she was. When Sister Maria Deo Gratias was interviewed by the director of the psychiatric unit, he, too, raised the topic of her hospital uniform. She said she would wear her habit. "I said, 'If you want me to come into the unit, I'm wearing the habit. If you don't want me to wear the habit, then I don't come in.' I just said it like that because that's how I felt," Sister Maria Deo Gratias says. She remembers the director replying, "No, I want you to come in. I'll give you space." Sister

Maria Deo Gratias, who says the uniform issue was "rigamarole," told the other religious sister in the unit that she would just try the post and leave if it did not work.

Sister Maria Deo Gratias recalls that once, possibly on her first day in the psychiatric ward, she was told that a woman, accompanied by police officers into the emergency room, had been found "running around on a billboard, hardly any clothes on, just really drugged up." "They brought her into the unit and then, like dummies, they took the cuffs off. She ran all over and I'm trying to calm her down." When the woman was finally subdued, the woman asked Sister Maria Deo Gratias, "Why aren't you wearing a long habit like the sisters used to wear?" Sister Maria Deo Gratias laughs. "I said, 'See! See! Now I'm getting into trouble because I don't have a habit long enough!'"

Raised in a Catholic family that built their own cottage together, stone by stone, Sister Maria Deo Gratias was an independent child who defied her mother when she announced in the sixth grade that she intended to become a nun. Today, she appears to be a well-adjusted cloistered monastic nun, casually indifferent to whatever might fall in her path. "When I enter a new experience, I guess I don't expect anything," she says. "I just say, 'What is there? I'll find out what is there when I get there and I'll go with the punches, go with the flow.'" Sister Maria Deo Gratias might be a spiritual pragmatist in her efforts to participate in the redemptive work of Jesus on behalf of humanity. "I just fell in love with God, and said, 'Whatever you want, I do,'" Sister Maria Deo Gratias says. "That's just the way I came about it." She says that since she didn't have any expectations when she came to the monastery, no hopes were ever dashed. "There was nothing to get disappointed about," she says, "because I didn't know what the life is. But I just know that I'm called to be a cloistered contemplative in this particular community. And so I entered and whatever unfolds in my training as to what it means to be a cloistered contemplative nun, I'm learning that."

More than two decades after entering the Corpus Christi Monastery, Sister Maria Deo Gratias says she still catches herself walking too fast in the corridors at the alert pace she kept in the psychiatric unit. She reminds herself to slow down, to enter into the silence that is the presence of God: "Wait. Where I have to go isn't an emergency."

In Sister Maria Deo Gratias's life devoted to prayer, she asks God to "give the special graces and the nudges you need to think things out. And I think it's a very important role that I can't take for granted. I'm only an instrument, as each of us sisters are; but we have the responsibility to be good instruments in our apostolate of prayer. And God does give extra graces when you ask, but a lot of people don't think about asking. So even those who don't call us and don't contact us in any way, that don't believe in us, we can touch their hearts. It's really a privilege to live this life and I think we get more than we give. That's definitely true. He didn't have to call me, but He did, and I wouldn't want anything other, so I'm really grateful God called me! You know, I would not choose another life."

Aware that she is subject to "the human condition," a fragile and imperfect state, Sister Maria Deo Gratias does not cling to anything too tightly, including her own perceptions of life, others, and herself. She readily accepts that she will not see the full, or completely clear, picture this side of heaven. "You stand in the truth. And the truth sets you free," Sister Maria Deo Gratias says. "I am who I am regardless of whether you think I am that way, or not that way. I am who I am. And I may even come to realize I am not who I think I am, and that's where my growth comes in—you know, I'm fooling myself, and I've got deeper growth to go because I'm seeing the truth that isn't the truth. So I have to be humble enough to say, you know, I don't have it all together here. I have to go back to the drawing board and say, 'Lord, help me to know myself so that I can know you more.' There's that sense of openness that even though we stand in the truth, I still may not be seeing the whole truth. We should always, until maybe ten minutes after we die, always see ourselves with that possibility—that we may not have the whole truth, that we still have things to learn. And be open to life, whatever comes your way—to be open and respond in a charitable way, in a virtuous way, in response, no matter what it is. I think that's where true poverty lies.

"So we always live like on the pilgrimage to heaven. Then, in heaven, I'll say, 'I've arrived.' But until that, I haven't arrived yet. I still have growing to do."

Sister Mary Nicolette says,

Like we always say, the Church is composed of human beings who have faults and are sinful, so naturally there's going to be a little bit of that in religion. We're all fallen, so to speak. But I think looking at the life as we strive to live it, our rule of life is really living the gospel so if you look at Christ in the gospel, there's nothing narrow-minded about Him. That's the ideal. That's what we're trying to live and what we're trying to imitate and take on. And it's very simple—the gospel life. That's our Rule. Our rule of life is to live the gospel for our Lord Jesus Christ, of our Lord Jesus Christ, and plain and simple without any alterations, without any adaptations. And what it comes down to is that—there won't be a narrow-mindedness the more and more converted and the more and more changed deep in our heart we become, because, naturally, we all come like that. But the more we grow in Christ the more we shed that off and become more embracing and more loving.

The maximum age for women entering the Corpus Christi Monastery is forty years old. This criterion was raised in recent years on account of the dwindling population. After she first visited the Corpus Christi Monastery, Jenny called one other monastery in the hope of scheduling a visit, but she was turned off by what sounded like a standoffish tone when the nun learned her age. She was welcomed into the fold at Corpus Christi, which made an exception in accepting her when she was forty-seven.

Believing quite fervently that she belonged in this foreign subculture, Jenny gave her family everything, including her Oldsmobile and control of her checking account and retirement savings. "When I came I didn't have any questions. I didn't have any doubts: 'Did I do the right thing?'" Sister Mary Michael says. "It was really funny. I didn't understand it. I didn't have any doubts—from the day I came. And it was awkward. I had to learn to chant the Office. I didn't know how to chant the Office and I had to learn to do all that. I stuck it out. I just knew I was supposed to be here so whatever happened, happened. I never had any doubts. I felt so much inside of me that God wanted me here. I knew this. I don't know why, I just knew this. So everything that came along, I just accepted this was the way of life. This must be what God wants because He asked me to come here. I just didn't question things. However they lived it, that was fine. It didn't bother me. But I do know some that come and they want to know, do we do this, do we do that, and it makes a difference to them. Well, I didn't. I just knew I was supposed to be here and so I accepted things. I know for some it was harder, but for me that was an advantage because I didn't question everything: 'Why do they do things that way?'"

In adjusting to the pace and purpose of the monastery, Sister Mary Michael exhibited the same easygoing temperament her family expected from her. She admits, "If God didn't really call us here we couldn't live this life. You can't live it unless you're really being called. Because it's so different—countercultural—especially today when so many people are so self-centered. You give up everything, really."

The transition was excruciating for her family and her colleagues. Sister Mary Michael remembers them asking her, "Why do you want to throw your life away? What will you do all day?" "It was just like somebody died when I came here. It was that hard," she says. "And I can see it because if it was the other way around I would feel the same way, I'm sure, because it's hard to understand. You're cut off. You don't go home anymore. It's very hard to understand. It's all faith."

Her colleagues did not want her to leave and phoned her sister for updates. Still, they celebrated with her at a going-away party, eating a cake decorated with a depiction of a nun.

Sister Mary Michael's younger brother, whose children struggled to comprehend her metaphysical changes, yielded eventually when she insisted that she belonged in the monastery. "They thought they should let me go and try, that I'd probably come back home, I knew I wanted to come here," she says. For years, every time they visited, Sister Mary Michael remembers their tears. "They depended on me in some ways, financially—not totally, but I did help them a lot because they had three kids. They missed me, too, but financially it was hard for them." "You can come live with us," she remembers her brother telling her. "Why don't you come and live with us?" Eventually, her brother, sister-in-law, and their children seemed to understand; they yielded their resistance to her choices. "They know that I am real happy here and they even said, 'We know that you belong here,'" Sister Mary Michael says. Her brother's family, although scattered geographically, with families of their own now, visit once a year. "I marvel at it," she says. "They're real faithful. They write all the time."

Her sister still writes in every letter, almost twenty years after she joined the monastery, that she misses her little sister a lot. "I feel sorry for her," she says.

Her older brother and sister-in-law visit the monastery but Sister Mary Michael does not think he has made peace with her religious vocation, although his opinion has improved; she remembers that during an early visit he said, "You're living in the Dark Ages."

Sister Mary Michael's mother visited her several times after she became a postulant. "It was hard," she says, "because she would come and sit here and say, 'Are you happy?' And she looked miserable. Of course, she was sick. And

I was content. But it was hard for her." The two did not talk much during those visits, just sat awkwardly, she says. She learned from her older sister that her mother became "gloomy and grumpy" back home, upset over Sister Mary Michael's absence. When her sister informed their mother that the situation was not going to change, she says her mother "snapped out of it." Her health digressed, though, and she moved in with her other daughter. "It wasn't like I was leaving her uncared for," Sister Mary Michael says, "because that you wouldn't do." Her mother died four months after she joined the monastery. "And again, the grace was there because I didn't fall apart or anything," she says.

Sister Mary Michael remembers, as a child, overhearing a conversation between her parents: a neighbor's daughter had joined a Carmelite order of cloistered nuns. When family brought food to the girl at the monastery, they could not even see her because a curtain covered the metal grille. "That's the only time I ever heard of contemplative life and it was this kind of on the negative side," Sister Mary Michael says. "They couldn't understand it, how she could do that." Asked if this influenced her mother's ability to accept her new life, she admits, "It could be." Asked if this life feels natural to her, she says, "Oh, yes."

Today, Sister Mary Michael reflects on what she perceives to be the few negative aspects of her life. "What makes a bad day? Let's see," she says. "I think it's mostly community living. You live with the same people in a small area and I think it's marvelous how we are able to get along that well. You have normal problems and sometimes they seem like mountains, but they're not—I mean, different personalities. We're all not the same. So I mean, sometimes you might get on each other's nerves, little things that are annoying. A lot of that is just living in community and normal problems of community life and struggling with that."

Sister Mary Michael has considered that she might have wanted to leave the monastery after her whirlwind arrival. "Just think—if I went back, if I went back soon enough, I probably could have gotten the same job I had, but I don't know that for sure, either," she says. "At that time, I was forty-seven. That isn't that ancient. That isn't *that* ancient, but the longer you stay here, that gets to be scary because what are you going to do, especially with computers where everything keeps advancing and if you don't keep up with it you're going to be lost? It keeps changing. So that would be a real problem. It would be scary. What would I be doing if I was in the world? I would be retired, I'm sure. You retire early. I'm sure I wouldn't be working. I'm glad I'm here because what would I be doing?"

Sister Ann Marie
of His Holy Wounds

God never tells you, "I want you to go here, go to Rockford" or "This is where I want you." It's an inner feeling. And the call is there. You can feel it. You can feel like you can hear it, and yet if it's true, why can't I see?

I just liked to know if God is really calling me or not. That's the thing. It's in me, and yet is it? Is it? You don't see any calling to join this community. You want to see a tangible answer. But God is playing hide-and-seek, you know; it's kind of like that.

I was born in the Philippines, and I was born in my mother's hometown, where my father and mother met. And then we moved to Manila, and that's where my family still is.

I'm the oldest. I have three brothers and one sister. I remember my three brothers were super-active. They loved to play. As soon as we'd get home from school, they'd just throw their things out and go out and play. And my sister used to stay home and the two of us would play with dolls.

When we were young, my father had to go to Vietnam, to work there to help support our family. He's a civil engineer. He was hired by part of the US government to work in Vietnam. He worked there for eight years, and so my mother was the one who took care of us. One time, my father got sick; they found that he's diabetic. He was hospitalized there, and so my mother had to be with him; she brought my two youngest siblings with her to Vietnam, and I was left with my brother, the next younger one, because we were both school age. He was in kindergarten and I was in first grade, so we stayed with my grandmother—my father's mother—in my father's hometown. It was only a year or so, I think, and then my mother came back, and we were back together. My father continued to work in Vietnam. He came home once in a while, once a year, or every three years. I can't remember how many times he came home; I was so small then.

192 | THE THREATS

I can't even remember when he left. All I remember is I was seven when my brother and I had to stay with my grandmother and my aunt. You miss your parents and younger siblings. My grandmother was kind of strict; she was kind of sickly then, but she was kind of strict, but I guess she had to be because we were super-active kids then. She was older then and could not take too much.

I was thinking of religious life even when I was little but I never had a calling. You have to know where God wants you. So when I was in the Philippines, I never really felt any calling to any communities there. We had a Poor Clare monastery in the Philippines, only fifteen minutes away from us, and my mother used to take me there. We always went there for prayers, but I never felt I was called there.

I told all my classmates I wanted to be a sister. Everyone else would get a crush or like "this person," but I never really got involved with anybody— just like a movie star, whom you like because he's handsome or because you like her hairstyle. I admire beauty in people so I feel like I'm quite normal, but still in me it's not something that's satisfying. It fades away. It doesn't give me peace; it's more a passing joy, you know what I mean?

Since I was little, I felt that God was calling me but since I don't know where, I didn't know if what I was feeling was really real. I had this constant seeking: What does God want of me? It was an interior struggle, if God is really calling me, or not. If yes, why doesn't He show me where I should go?

I was a nurse. There was an agency in the Philippines that contacts hospitals here that need nurses. At that time there were a lot of hospitals that needed nurses, so the hospitals hired this agency and then the agency put an advertisement in the newspaper and then we went there for an interview, and they sent our papers to the hospital here. I went to work in New York.

Before I left the Philippines I talked to our parish priest, and I said, "You know, my desire to serve God is, like, bursting in me, or bubbling in me. But I really don't know where to go, and I've already committed to go to the States. I really would rather stay in the Philippines and serve God wherever He wants me. I really would answer God, if He just tells me where He wants me to go." But our parish priest told me, "Since you have all the papers done, since you've already committed yourself, just go. That's God's will."

I also talked to a nun in the Philippines, a Poor Clare nun; she's dead now—Mother Rosa. I had talked to her before; I didn't plan to enter the Poor Clares, I just went there because when I was little and my mother had problems, she went to talk to the sisters. She gave the same advice. "You go." She didn't invite me to join the monastery. I didn't really feel called to their monastery. They saw that my papers and everything was settled. They just said, "Maybe it's God's will that you go."

I never thought it was bad advice. I felt kind of nervous going to a foreign country away from my family. I guess my thinking was, "I'll serve God close to my family." My own premonition, inner desire, is that if I'm going to serve God, I really want to be close to my family. God had another kind of way of putting it. He wanted me to be away from my family. I never thought that I would enter here in the States. I thought after I finish work here, then I would go back to the Philippines and find and see where God wants me, that kind of mentality. I never thought God would call me here.

I worked in a nursing home in New York, with the Carmelite Sisters of the Eucharist. They petitioned me, and I worked there for one year and a half before I entered here.

The Carmelites wear a full habit. I always went to church. They have a chapel in their nursing home, and I always went there before work and after work to pray. One of their sisters—she was the youngest in the community— one time stopped me after I prayed and said, "Do you want to be a sister?" It just struck me because the other Filipino nurses would do the same thing, you know, and they were also religious, but some of them were married. So when she asked me, I said, "Yes, but I don't know where God wants me." So she said, "Oh, I'll pray for you." Even the superior thought that I would like to join them. Well, I really didn't feel called to join them. You have to feel a call. I never felt really called here, too—I mean to a monastic life. In the Philippines, a monastic life means you'll never see your family again. Well, I knew that would be quite hard for me and I knew it would be quite hard for my family.

We had a mission in New York at the parish church. They call it a mission because it's a calling back of lax Catholics to their faith, or strengthening their faith. I think it was laypeople proclaiming, sharing how God touched their lives. I went to Mass that day; I decided to stay and listen, and then that stirred me up and I went to confession and for spiritual direction. After that

194 | THE THREATS

I became restless. That surfaced the call within me. I felt that God was calling me, but I still didn't know where. I said to the parish priest, "You know, Father, I feel like I'm being called to religious life, but I really don't know where I should go, it's just strong in me. I don't know where to go." And he said, "Well, where are you from?" I said, "I'm working at Saint Teresa's Nursing Home under the Carmelites."

The parish priest I talked to said, "Why don't you join them?" I said, "I don't feel called to join them," because I was a nurse and working there with the sisters, but most of them are administrative, not nurses like me.

I have an aunt—my father's sister—and she and her husband are kind of rich; they support some religious organizations, including a retired home for sisters in the Philippines. One time my aunt and uncle visited our family, and they took us to visit their friends, these sisters who are retired in their motherhouse. One of the retired sisters, when she learned that I was here in the States, she wrote to me. She would send me letters and inside her letters were letters that I should mail here in the States. One of the letters was for the Poor Clares here in Rockford. She was asking them questions—how to make rosaries, I think. I copied the address because I wanted to ask for prayers because I was taking my nursing board exam. I asked the Poor Clares for prayers, and then they wrote back and said they would pray for me to pass my board exam.

I still felt uneasy. Like I told you, when my mother was low, she always brought me to the Poor Clares in the Philippines to ask prayers when she had problems. So I told myself, "I'll try to call them." Well, there was no telephone number in the letter, so I called the operator and she tried to find their number. Finally, I got it and I called the sister and asked for prayers. I said, "Sister, can you pray for me? I feel like I have a vocation, but I really don't know where God is calling me." The sister immediately said she was going to get Mother Dorothy to talk to me. Mother Dorothy was the Abbess then. I said, "I wonder what Sister's doing? I just asked her to pray for me. I didn't tell them I want to come, you know. I'm not inquiring about their life, you know."

I really just called the monastery to ask them to pray for me. I had already taken my board and I was asking for prayers that I passed it. Passing the board was the only way that my visa would be extended because I was on a working visa. That's the main thing—to pass the board so that I can stay here longer so that I can work; that was just a means for me to keep working here.

But that was not my life's goal. My life's goal, which I was more interested in, was to find out if my real vocation was to enter the monastery because that would answer the questions within me: Am I called, or not?

I talked to Mother Dorothy, and she said, "Well, I think you have a vocation, but would you like to come and visit?" I said, "I really don't have time to visit because my friend is going to the Philippines and I'm doing her shift, I'm going to work overtime. I really can't." She said, "Well, just take your time. When you have time, just give us a call."

That made me speechless. I felt like I really wouldn't have time because my friend was going to stay there for a month or longer; I knew it would be a long time before I could visit. Still bugging my mind was why she was asking me to visit. But I became restless again. I felt like I had to do something. My friend was leaving the next week, so I only had one weekend free. Anyway, I finally arranged it; I came here on a Sunday, I left on Wednesday.

It's amazing. When I came here, everything was perfect. Everything fell into place. I called the airline. The plane flight was so cheap then—just $89 back and forth—the first time when I came for my visit. I was surprised because the next time I came here, it was double. And the bus—as soon as I got out of O'Hare, there was the bus going to Rockford. And then when I was here, I felt God. I felt so much peace. I felt that God was calling me here. Before I left, I committed myself already. I had my entrance day. The place felt like a presence.

I always carried with me a picture of the Sacred Heart of Jesus. It's a picture of Jesus with the Sacred Heart exposed. When I left, I left that picture here where I slept downstairs. Mother Dorothy called me and said, "You know you left your picture?" I said, "Yes, I left it intentionally because I told Him I'll be back." When I was here, I just had that peace, that searching, that I finally found it. I didn't hear Jesus, like the saints said, "This is where I want you," but I just feel like that inner call, that calling in you, finally: "This is it."

I think that other girls feel that same way—applicants that come here and didn't feel that when they came here. They feel it in another monastery. After they visit another monastery, they write back, "When I went to that monastery, I just felt at home."

When I came back from my visit, as soon as I got to our house, my friend said, "Oh, wow! Congratulations! You passed your board!"

As soon as I came back to New York, I settled everything quick. I told the nursing home, and they said I could have two weeks." The Mother Abbess gave me all the requirements—towels and things—so I bought everything.

Then I called my family. I said, "I think I have good news and bad news for you. The good news is I passed my board. My bad news is I think I'm going to enter the monastery." My mother said, "Oh, no. Don't enter yet." I said, "I think I have to, Ma, because God's calling me now and I want to know. I don't want to wait. If God is calling me now, I really want to answer now." I was just afraid. I was twenty-five then and I felt like I was really old. In the Philippines, they enter at sixteen. They entered young—sixteen, seventeen, eighteen, and sometimes after college. So at twenty-five, I felt like I was ancient.

It was hard for my parents. Well, it was hard for my whole family, but especially my mother. My father said, "If that's what you want..." But my mother said, "No." But I said, "Ma, I'm twenty-five." I had to decide, you know. And like I said, this longing to serve God has been with me since I was a child; I just don't know where to go. Once I knew, I said, "Ma, I really have to know if this is God's will. I'd rather know it now than later." My father said, "Oh, your mother cries every night." She wanted to see me.

I visited here May 26 and I entered July 16. I entered that quickly. The second time was hard because the plane ticket went up and different things. But it was fine. I felt like when I had come here before; I felt so much peace that God was calling me here. It's where He wants me.

My father died a year after my profession. I was solemnly professed in 1991 and he died in 1992. But I'm glad, though, because I always wanted to see him, and I saw him before he died. I hadn't seen him since I came to the States. I came here in 1983. From 1983 to 1991 I hadn't seen him; I hadn't gone home to the Philippines. That was the first and last time I saw him after I left the Philippines.

He had worked for the Americans, so he spoke English well. It was funny because when he came here for my Solemn Profession, he was interviewed by the US Immigration in the Philippines, and the interviewer said, "Is that all you're going to do there?"—you know, to see my profession? He said, "No, we're going to see the whole country, your beautiful country." They were so impressed when my father said that. The thing is, my father was diabetic then, and he really couldn't travel that much. Even when they were here for two weeks, or a week, I could tell he was kind of tired. He loved to travel before, when I was young. But when he was here, he didn't travel, really. But they did go to California because my mother has lots of relatives there.

When I entered everything was fine with me. I didn't have a hard time, except the cheese. I can't eat cheese. I am lactose-intolerant. I didn't know that then, because in the Philippines we don't eat that much cheese. When I came here, we had cheese every night for supper—two pieces of bread, cheese, and an apple—and I was just getting sicker and sicker from it, I could hardly sleep. Well, I got through it. I knew they wouldn't change the whole diet just for me! I knew that. So I tried everything. I put jelly in it. I put margarine in it. I mean I tried. I was willing to do as much as I could do because I felt if it was God's will that I stay here, He will give me everything I need to endure it.

I didn't think I was lactose-intolerant. I knew milk bothered me, but I just keep going. After a few years, it got real bad. I had really bad diarrhea. My doctor then told me I might be lactose-intolerant. I said, "No, I can't be, I'm eating all this milky food." And then she said, "I'll put you on the test." So she put me on the test, and then I found that I'm really lactose-intolerant. Since then, I ask permission not to take any milk at night, because I learned my lesson; I just have trouble with digestion and it keeps me awake at night. Sometimes I take a little bit and then I have to deal with the result. But I still take some. I still drink milk. I eat everything. I'm pretty good. In the morning and in the afternoon for lunch, I can take it; I take a little.

For the night vigils, it can be hard to get up, but it's something that I want to do and I have to do it. It's for the Lord. You know what I mean? I just have to think that what I'm doing is for the Lord; it's not for me, it's His will. I think that's the main thing; if you're doing things for the Lord, He gives you the grace. I still have that peace. I still miss my family, but I just have to keep trusting that God will see me through. Although I had peace within me, I mean, I still was kind of unstable, like a temptation: 'This life is hard for you, you can't do it, your family is suffering.' All these kinds of things. I didn't think I could live it. But it's all in God's grace. I just kept praying, I only want to do God's will. That's all I prayed every day was to do God's will. And that's what I think kept me going is that it's His will.

You know, to tell you the truth, I really didn't know what to expect. I was just trusting that this is where God wants me. There was a mixed feeling: It's kind of exciting because this is all I wanted all my life and I feel I've been called since I was little, and then still there's kind of pain because I hurt my family and still felt the uncertainty—is this really for me?

I struggle being away from family and the culture. Even when I was working in New York, we ate Filipino food, but here I have to eat regular food—mashed potatoes and other things, which we never had there. We always ate rice. They won't eat the fish with the head here; the way we cooked fish is different than the way we cook here. That's the way I grew up. We fried the fish with the head and tail and everything. We cleaned the insides but left the skin on. And the language—it was hard for the sisters to understand me, at first, but I got slang, I got adapted to the way they speak. I'm not saying my English is perfect. I'm just saying I had to adjust so that they can understand me better.

You have different traditions here. Our Christmas is very simple, and here you have lots of decorations. And the climate—we don't have snow in the Philippines. It's always hot. It's different, not to be able to talk to a Filipino. My Tagalog is kind of broken, and even now when I pray, I pray in English. I don't pray in Tagalog anymore. It's kind of hard to remember all of my Tagalog words.

I'm in charge of getting the applicants their books. I have felt so many of them were called, but they have to do this, they had to do that, and then they lost their call. They end up in different things. I mean, if she's not called here, that's fine; she could be called to another community, but what I mean is answering God's call. All I know is sometimes I feel, I wish that young women would really open their hearts because I know that there are a lot of young women that are called to our life. It's just they have to really trust in God, really trust in God's call to them.

Some of the women I've talked to have told me, "Oh, yes, when I was a little girl I also wanted to be a nun. I felt like I was called." But they got married. And they're happily married. But it's like, is it a real call for them, or not? Or is it like, "The nuns are so pretty, aren't they, in their habit"? Maybe God was calling them, I don't know what. But they mostly said, "Even when I was a little girl, I felt called, too." Some are benefactors. They're older now. They said that when they were younger, they thought that they were called to the religious life, but they got married. They found out it's not really a call; they were called to get married.

Some women are called. I'm not saying that everybody is, but a lot of women, I think, are called to the religious life, but it's kind of a struggle between themselves and God's call. There's so many things that influence them in choosing whether they want to follow God's call, or they want to do what the world thinks they should be. The only thing I could advise them is to have a deep prayer life because whatever they choose in life depends so much on the salvation of their souls. I think if they could have a deeper prayer life, go on retreat, have prayer before the Blessed Sacrament, or go to Mass more often, to listen—because I think therein lies their strength in choosing what they should be. If they're really for marriage life or single life, then that's something that will give them health and strength; they will be light if it's God's will. Whatever is God's will, that's our salvation because that's what God created us for, to do His will.

My main thing is I feel like God is calling me. My main thing is, I was thinking of myself being called here as a Poor Clare to a more deeper life of prayer, intimate prayer with our Lord, though with all my duties and all my distractions sometimes.... But that's my main thing, I feel like an inner call within me, to deeper prayer life, communion with Jesus. You know, it's like to enter that prayer life to draw people to it. Do you know what I mean by grateful prayer? Grateful for all that God has done for us and grateful for all the people that have supported our life. We owe so much for our friends and benefactors; they support our life and so I feel so much gratefulness for them. I feel like I really have to pray for them, remember them every day in my prayers for their needs, but also so they know God and grow closer to Him.

I can't remember her words, but Saint Clare was so close to God, her heart was full of joy being close to God, and she wanted others to feel that, too. She wanted everybody to feel that joy and closeness to God. I feel like that's kind of something that God wants me to do. Each sister is different. Some pray more for priests and religious; that's more of their calling. Everybody's different, you know.

We are all called to be holy, to holiness. Jesus said, "Be holy as my father is holy." I think a lot of women thirst for that intimate union with God, but it seems that the world offers them more options to be happy. But real happiness really doesn't consist of what you have, or what you do, if it's not God's will and it's not for the sanctification of souls.

It isn't a perfect life. We still have struggles like everybody else with temptations, personal difficulties—challenges that we should really continuously change our attitudes toward being a better person, being a better Christian, relationships with each other. We don't have many temptations like in the world—cars to fight with, or dresses. We have the same habit. We don't have to wear earrings. We don't have all these things—temptations that the world could offer; we don't have that here.

The spirit of our founder, the Holy Father Saint Francis and Saint Clare, is poverty, which is living in simplicity. I guess in here I just have more time for prayer and to reflect, to meditate, and in everything I do, in everything that happens, God is more present, more close.

I can feel the difference. When I was still with my family and during the part of my life before I entered, I could feel God taking care of me and He was with me. But now my entering is like a fulfillment. It's closer now. Before, it was like a calling, a calling to be more intimate with Him. Now that I have answered the call, it's more close with Him now. I still struggle with all my human weaknesses, you know, but God in our life provides me all the things. In this environment, we all strive for the same goal, closer union with God, and to answer His call for more closer intimacy. All our works—our prayer, everything we do—should grow us more closely to Him.

I think that before I used to do things just for the sake of doing, but now I'm doing everything for God and I always offer up everything I do for God. And when you do things for God and you love God, you do it with joy. There are things that are hard to do, but if you accept it as God's will, then you know God transforms that and He gives you peace to carry it out.

It's not just cloistered nuns who are called to holiness. Everybody is. You are. Your family. Your friends. All our benefactors' families. All are called to holiness, whatever the vocation. It's Monsignor's homily, too, that whatever state of life we are in, we are all called to holiness; if all people of whatever religion only answer that call to live a holy life, to purify our hearts from all the hatred and revenge—the evil that's in our heart—if we could only purify that and put God's love in it, this world would be a better place. Everybody has their own perception of God, but one thing that's true is God is a holy God. He is a pure God.

I still sometimes doubt. I still doubt sometimes. I guess it's more of my human nature and my human weaknesses, that maybe this is hard and not for me. But always God's grace triumphs. I always have to end prayer, whatever God wants. Sometimes I say, "This is hard," but then, "Whatever you want," because I only want what His will is. That gives me strength.

Sometimes, you can feel it's from the devil when you have trials, when you have a misunderstanding with a sister, or when you feel sick and all these things come up to you.

8

Erased from the Landscape

I think every vocation story is a love story of how God has really shown that soul His infinite love for her. He's invited her to live in that love in a very special and intimate way. Just like all young girls who dream of love, you know, of a husband or something, some of us are blessed, through nothing that we've done on our own. But somehow God has given this divine invitation, this special look of love, and invited us to live with Him. And it's beyond what we dream of, of finding the perfect husband or whatever in life—perfect happiness. It's so much beyond what you can dream of when God shows you how much He loves you. It's no question, "Absolutely, of course I'll do it, God," because He shows that love, and it's just beyond anything.

Sister Maria Benedicta of Saint Joseph

The youngest nun in the Corpus Christi Monastery, Sister Maria Benedicta grew up—in her words—in "Secular, USA." This assessment of her upbringing in a Catholic family that prayed daily together and never neglected Sunday Mass might be influenced by the stories she has collected in brief discussions with her new family members. Compared to her Novice Mistress, whose adolescence brought her into the company of the Pope, Sister Maria Benedicta's experiences seem more conventional, if not secular. Her family did not say the rosary together, and because there was no Catholic school in the vicinity of her rural town, she attended a public school. Sister Maria Benedicta, still called Maria at that time, did not see a nun—in person, or on television—until the fourth grade.

When Maria finally did see a nun for the first time, the impression was indelible. Her youth group stayed overnight at a Benedictine abbey, a prelude to their trip to an amusement park, and each child was paired to sit with a nun for the Divine Office; Sister Maria Benedicta says she was matched with "the cutest little old thing." She did not understand what the sister was praying, or grasp the symbolism of what she was witnessing, but she thought the incense-stained atmosphere exotic and appealing. Sister Maria Benedicta says, "I remember looking at her and thinking, 'She prays with God all day. She has the perfect life. Oh, I could really do that.' And then it was reality: 'That was the weirdest thing I've ever thought in my life. Forget it.' And I really did forget about it. It wasn't always in the back of my mind, 'Oh, she has the perfect life. I should do that.' No. I completely forgot about it until years later."

Sister Maria Benedicta's first contact with a nun could be described as a signpost. "God puts it in your heart," Sister Maria Benedicta says. "Somehow He showed me the beauty of it, even though I was like, 'What are we praying? Where are we going?' But I remember thinking, 'This is the house of God and this is the perfect life, living for the perfect God.'" Today, Sister Maria Benedicta enters, seven times a day for the Divine Office, a chapel similar to the one that awed her as a child. The prayer stall that seemed, to her grade-school eyes, straight out of a movie set, is now characteristic of her daily routine. From fourth grade through college, Sister Maria Benedicta says she did not reflect again on her first encounter with a nun; she did not see any other religious sisters. "How we can just push that out of our mind and not think about it? What's real life about? That's the true reality that lasts forever. But I forgot about it for years. It's terrible. But God works, here and there; you can see how he's planting the seeds."

While some of the cloistered nuns struggle to recall memories during oral history interviews, sifting the decades to frame and share their experiences after a lifetime of anonymity and perpetual silence, Sister Maria Benedicta considers such retrospection a gift. A recent arrival to the monastery, her memories are still at attention; it is easy to pull emotionally charged strings to each phase of her former life, find the corresponding anecdotes and conversations, and connect themes to the events. "It's a good principle in the spiritual, religious life, you know, when prayer is difficult or there are hard times or suffering in your life, to look back and see what God has done, look how He's loved me, look how He's shown me His love," she says.

Calling memories to the surface of her consciousness reinforces the lessons of her life, and it reminds Sister Maria Benedicta how God has provided for her. With hindsight, she sees now what she did not always discern at the time—the ways that God was directing her to a cloistered contemplative life. Looking back, Sister Maria Benedicta is surprised she did not recognize sooner that she was intended for this otherworldly realm, although she can pinpoint the moments when God opened up before her the path He wanted her to take, showing it to her step by step, at her own pace. "It's not coincidences. He's guiding everyone," she says, "but we have to listen to Him to experience Him."

Sister Maria Benedicta was a softball pitcher, coached through high school by her father and admitted to a Catholic college on a full softball scholarship, when she detected her life would evolve in a dramatically different way than she had dreamed about. There was a turning point: Before she signed away her only means of paying for college, before she accepted her religious calling, she was working at Wal-Mart. One ordinary day, Sister Maria Benedicta remembers, she was working the first of forty-five cash registers; the line to her register was backed up. An hour into a very busy, very trying day, it occurred to Sister Maria Benedicta for the first time ever to introduce her prayer life into her workplace. "I said, 'Lord, help me. Just help me. I can't do this,'" she says. "The next customer handed me this wooden cross. He said, 'I want you to have this, and remember Jesus loves you.' And I thought, 'Oh my! God just answered my prayer.' He could have handed that to anyone and it could have meant nothing." Naturally attuned to serendipity, Sister Maria Benedicta became increasingly aware of the spiritual mysteries in her life. She believed that God was telling her, through the cross the stranger handed her, "I love you. I'm going to help you. I'm answering your prayer. I know you're crying out for me. I'm going to help you through this day." "That's true mysticism," she says, "seeing that God is there, even in Wal-Mart."

The youngest member of the Corpus Christi Monastery, Sister Maria Benedicta swam upstream to reach this place. "It's amazing that God can, in these days, break through all the noise to get to the heart," she says, "which is so crowded with so many things. But He's all-powerful so I guess He can do it. But you have to allow Him."

As a child, Sister Maria Benedicta's faith was relegated to church life on Sunday, not integrated into her daily life with her family or school. She did not know then, she says, that saints were in her midst, that angels were praying for her, and that "God is everywhere." The idea that a spiritual realm eclipses any physical reality dawned on her in college. Her dorm room was above the chapel, and she could hear the Mass below. One day, she attended chapel. She still remembers a visiting priest's homily about the Eucharist: "Jesus Christ comes down into this chapel every day. What is more important than that?" "Wow," Sister Maria Benedicta thought. "He's right. I was thinking, in college you're searching for answers about your life, and the purpose of your life. The purpose of life is to love and to get to heaven, you know? When he said that—'what is more important than God coming down to be with you?'—I said, 'Yeah, there's nothing more important than that.' It was so clear this is the purpose of life. This is why we're here. Everything else is to lead us to God and to heaven."

She contemplated the Blessed Sacrament and realized, "That is God. That is almighty God right there in the form of bread. That is so unbelievable. Why would He make himself so small in this little host? It's unfathomable. The only reason why He would do that is because of His immense deep love for humanity. I kept thinking how much He loves us, to do this."

Despite the unanswerable questions, Sister Maria Benedicta had received the gift of faith. She thought about God descending to earth every day into what she describes as an "obscure chapel" in a dormitory building because He loved her completely. "Everything changed," she says. Her perspective and priorities shifted. She began to think, "Now what's more important, God coming down to earth, or this phone conversation, or this math assignment? My friends told me I was falling in love," Sister Maria Benedicta says. "I was. I was falling in love with Jesus! They laughed. And I said, 'I'm sorry. I just can't get enough!' I was a fanatic, falling in love with Jesus."

Soon afterward, the dorm director invited her on a group outing to a convent; the trip conflicted with her softball practice schedule, though, and so Sister Maria Benedicta said she could not make it. "It was true, but I was glad I had an excuse," Sister Maria Benedicta says. "I thought, 'She's crazy. I'm not a nun.' I didn't know anything about the religious life. You have in your mind it really is not fun." A week later, the dormitory director told her she had signed Sister Maria Benedicta up for the road trip. "It was terrible," Sister Maria Benedicta says. She thought, "I can't tell my coach I'm going to visit a convent. Good grief! 'Where are your priorities?'" Although the softball team practiced every weekend, the coach happened to cancel practice, and so Sister Maria Benedicta rode with a van full of girls for an "eye-opening" weekend. The nuns laughed. They played tennis. Their convent rested on beautiful grounds. "Oh," Sister Maria Benedicta says she thought, "these are real people." Sister Maria Benedicta remembers the superior singling her out to ask what she thought and if Sister Maria Benedicta might be called to religious life. Sister Maria Benedicta said she did not think so. The Mother Superior replied, "If God calls, He will turn your heart to only want that." On the drive back to her college campus, Sister Maria Benedicta thought, "My heart does not want that, so I'm off the hook." She prayed that if she did desire more than anything to live as a nun, she would know that desire was from God, "and I would do it because I knew it wasn't coming from me."

After the visit to the convent, the dormitory director offered Sister Maria Benedicta a ticket to hear Pope John Paul II speak in St. Louis. "Absolutely!" Sister Maria Benedicta said. "It was no longer, 'I have softball practice.' It was, 'Absolutely, I'm going.'" Once in St. Louis, every conversation, every occurrence seemed a message sent directly from God. "It's the way God turns your heart," she says. Standing in line for the restroom, a nun handing out literature bypassed dozens of women to give Sister Maria Benedicta a pamphlet about the religious life. "It's a sign," her friend told her. Then, emerging from the masses, Sister Maria Benedicta saw a nun from the convent she had recently visited. Inside the bag of freebies, which included a flag to wave when the Pope appeared, she found a prayer for discerning one's vocation. Sister Maria Benedicta dropped the prayer back in the bag. She was startled to pull out yet another prayer to discern her vocation. Then Pope John Paul II, stricken with Parkinson's disease at the time, took the stage. "He was on fire. We saw the Church was alive and young," Sister Maria Benedicta says. She remembers listening to the Vicar of Christ—the voice of Christ on earth—say, "'Go now, don't wait, God needs you.' He was so emphatic that God uses human beings. God could do it Himself, but He has chosen to use human beings. I just knew that what I was called for was to love God in a special way in a religious life. That's a special grace, too," she says, "because everyone else heard it, too."

Sister Maria Benedicta was convinced that God was giving her the confirmation she needed. "God knows every soul and what's going to get them—what one person can say to you to turn your heart," she says. "He inspires that person. It's really amazing." When a friend asked Sister Maria Benedicta to travel with her to another convent, an active religious order of Marian Sisters in Lincoln, Nebraska, Sister Maria Benedicta intended to decline. She had procrastinated on an assignment to read a three-hundred-page book, and she planned to cram that weekend. But when she opened her mouth to say "no," she heard herself instead agreeing to go. "It was the weirdest thing," Sister Maria Benedicta says. "I've never experienced that before. I don't know what happened." When she visited the Marian Sisters, she was smitten. "Everything about the life was so beautiful," Sister Maria Benedicta says. "Everything was for God—the sacrifices they make. It was all so beautiful." In the convent's chapel, Sister Maria Benedicta prayed, "I don't know what you want, but this is what I want more than anything." She remembered then her prayer following her first visit to a convent—that if she desired the life of a nun, she would know it came from God and not herself. "And so I knew this was what God wanted," she says.

When Sister Maria Benedicta returned to college, her best friend told her she seemed like a different person. Sister Maria Benedicta confided that she wanted to become a Marian sister. Her best friend told her that she was going to miss her at college and on the softball team, but Sister Maria Benedicta explained she wanted to complete her two final years of college. In the days that followed, Sister Maria Benedicta fished out her notes from the St. Louis speech by Pope John Paul II. She read, "Don't wait, God needs you now."

"I said, 'Lord, let me know,'" she says. "'I will do what you want, but you better let me know, because I'm not going to do something crazy, quit school, leave everything, scholarship, my whole livelihood. But if you let me know, I will do it.' Boy! Ask and you shall receive!"

Like an allegory, Sister Maria Benedicta faced three obstacles in quick succession. First, she felt pain in her pitching shoulder. She asked her father, her lifelong coach, to watch while she pitched to see what she was doing wrong to trigger the pain; he could not see a problem. "I thought, I've been doing it for fifteen years," she says. "Maybe it's wearing out. But if I can't play, I don't have my scholarship, I can't come here." Next, when Sister Maria Benedicta tried to sign up for a full load of classes for the following semester, she was not able to schedule more than nine hours—which would be part-time status. "I couldn't graduate with this type of a schedule," she says. And then, when two sets of friends were sorting out lodging, separately, both groups assumed she was planning to live with the other group, and Sister Maria Benedicta realized she did not have anyone to live with. "God was showing me through the very ordinary circumstances what His will was. It was not to be there," she says.

Her thoughts were starting to anchor beyond the physical sphere. She remembers standing on the pitcher's mound in the last inning of one game, a high-pressure situation that should have prompted her to focus and perform well, she says. Instead, her mind drifted: "This really isn't important compared to eternity." "I'm thinking about this at the strangest times!" she says. Hearing her astronomy professor lecture on the expanding universe, Sister Maria Benedicta thought that although "billions and trillions and gazillions" of years had passed since the earth began, "compared to eternity that is just a drop. I mean, eternity is so far beyond what we can imagine and this life is so small compared to that eternity, which a gazillion years is just a fraction; it's just a second compared to that. This life is just so short we have to do all we can to get all these people to heaven."

Sister Maria Benedicta adopted the philosophy of a college friend who said that she lived thinking about her deathbed. "I realized I have one life— one life—and you're not reincarnated," Sister Maria Benedicta says. "We live this one life, and we either go to heaven, or we go to hell. We have one life. I remember thinking, 'If I'm laying on my deathbed, if I'm eighty or ninety, what will I wish I had done in life? Will I wish I had that car? Probably not. Will I wish I had a better house? Probably not. You know, when you're dying, you want to know you're going to heaven. That's the purpose of your life." At twenty, Sister Maria Benedicta asked herself, "Would I rather have said, 'I finished my two years of school and had fun and was on the softball team,' or would I rather say, 'I did the will of God'? It was, what is more important? What is the most important thing in my life? It's doing God's will."

When Sister Maria Benedicta received an invitation from the Marian Sisters to attend a retreat, she told her best friend it conflicted with the upcoming softball tournament. "I made a commitment to the team," Sister Maria Benedicta said. Her friend replied, "Don't you dare miss that retreat. You know you're supposed to go." "She was so good in helping me keep perspective," Sister Maria Benedicta says. "She was a very good friend because we truly were striving to be holy. We had our priorities: It was God, family, friends, school. There's a hierarchy of what's important, and if you obscure that, if I put softball above God, that's wrong," she says.

Her coach agreed, reluctantly, that she could skip the tournament. "I knew that was God because I had prayed, 'God just show me,' and it was the answer. He had closed the door to the next year of school. But He showed me right there, 'This is what I want,' " Sister Maria Benedicta says. She prepared to inform her parents, who attended all of her softball games, that she would not be at the tournament because she would be on a retreat at a convent. This first shock would be a mere segue to another revelation: She planned to ask the Marian Sisters if she could return and join their community.

In Sister Maria Benedicta's master plan, she would tell her parents after the final game before the softball tournament. "I was so nervous the whole game, I didn't think a bit about the game," she says. "Afterwards I was so nervous; I was stalling. Usually, we would just jump in the car and go to Sonic or McDonald's. I said, 'Oh, just let me jump in the shower real quick first.' So I was really stalling and taking my time. Usually, I would throw my hair up; I was blow-drying my hair—really stalling. My parents were thinking, 'What has gotten into her?' It was just so countercultural and I knew it was going to be a shock. We were in my dorm room. My parents were very patiently waiting. At my dad's work, they had old computers on sale and he said, 'I bought you a computer.' I was thinking, 'Oh, boy, I don't need it.' I said, 'Oh, Dad, that's really nice.' I didn't ask anything about it; I didn't care. I'm sure he thought that was kind of rude. I was just so focused. So we get in the car and it was a Sunday and the school was in a small town and everything was closed. I was panicking, 'Oh, no, what if we don't find anything open?' So finally we walk into the one place still open and all the softball team is there with their parents. I thought, 'What a disaster! I can't tell them with all these people here.' But I had stalled so long they were almost finished eating and they were leaving. So finally I said, 'I've got to tell them.' My dad said, 'For that game before Easter, can we just take you home, or do you have to come back to school?' I said, 'I'm not actually going to go to that game.' I said, 'I'm going to go on this retreat and ask these sisters if I can join them.' Dead silence. You want to kill a conversation, that's the way to do it! Oh. Oh. Shocked!"

While Sister Maria Benedicta was agonizing about the retreat—"I was just in knots," she says; "how do you ask someone to join their family?"—her family asked if dropping out of college to enter a convent seemed like the hallmark of a stable and secure life. They asked if she would have health insurance at the convent. She did not know. She remembers telling her family, "I just love Him and I'm going to live for Him and that's it. That's all I know about it, really." It was as if, for the first time, Sister Maria Benedicta and her family were speaking different languages. "We have the highest security—in God, who's all powerful, all loving, all knowing," she says. "But it's looking beyond the visible to the true reality." In retrospect, Sister Maria

Benedicta understands her parents' concern and bewilderment. They wanted her to explain her logic and the rationale for her livelihood. Maybe, she says, it also felt like she was rejecting her family's values. "They want you to be happy and they can't imagine you being happy living a life of poverty, obedience, and chastity, because they found happiness in marriage and through children and they think you're giving that up," she says. "That's where they found happiness and they think you're not going to be happy. It's just a different way that God leads you to find your true happiness and fulfillment, and once they realize that, then gradually they're okay because you've found what they wanted you to find, which is happiness and your purpose in life."

Word spread that Sister Maria Benedicta wanted to join a convent, which came as no surprise to friends and teammates, even though she says she only shared her interest with her best friend. "They said, 'We knew that,'" Sister Maria Benedicta says. "I said, 'Why didn't you tell me? It would've been a lot easier!'"

The day she signed away her softball scholarship, Sister Maria Benedicta walked outside and thought, "What have I done? Honestly!" She knew she would never be able to afford college without a scholarship, and she had the nagging suspicion that her plan was not only contrary to what she thought she wanted for her life, it simply was not the way she thought "life is done."

"I realized, Lord, I'm giving you everything. I'm putting my trust in you. I'm going to take a leap of faith because I don't know. Give me a sign, a word, anything," she says. Sister Maria Benedicta opened her Bible to Psalm 119. She read the word "nun," which gave her the assurance she wanted that she was making the right move. Later, she learned she had merely stumbled upon a man's name in a biblical genealogy, as in Joshua, son of Nun. "I thought, 'Oh, isn't God funny? Some man's name, and I'm like, 'I'm supposed to be a nun!' I just needed a direct answer. That gave me the courage to leave everything for Him." Upon reflection, Sister Maria Benedicta is not put off by the message she accepted as divine direction for her life from that one word; despite her ignorance of the proper context, she does not believe she was mistaken in interpreting the meaning. Sister Maria Benedicta believes her naïveté reflects the gospel message: Jesus told His disciples they must become like children in order to enter the kingdom of heaven. "In so many ways, He was just saying, 'You're such a child," she says, "and I think I was in the hands of the Father saying, 'Okay, here you go. I don't know anything.'"

Sister Maria Benedicta became a Marian Sister, and the community became her family. Almost six years later, when she appeared to her parents to be at home in the order of active sisters, with the stable and secure life they desired for her, Sister Maria Benedicta informed her family that she planned to transfer to the even stricter, more removed world of a cloistered monastery. The notion began to percolate when, as a twenty-one-year-old pilgrim with the Marian Sisters to Assisi, Italy, the spiritual birthplace of Saint Francis's Friars Minor and Saint Clare's Poor Ladies, she toured the Poor Clares' motherhouse, San Damiano. When she saw the abject poverty of their lodgings, that they "had nothing," it reminded her of Jesus, who was so poor He had no place to lay His head. "I just fell in love with Saint Clare. But I just loved where I was, and so it didn't enter my mind to do something crazy like enter the Poor Clares."

Several years passed. Less than a year remained before she was to make final vows as a Marian sister. "It was a sense of this isn't fitting," she says of the other religious community. "Saint Augustine says, 'Our hearts are restless until they rest in you, my God.' And it's that way; once you finally discover what God is asking, there's a peace and, yes, there are struggles, but it's okay. 'This is what God wants and he's going to help me.' There's a peace. If you join any community, everything is not going to be perfect all the time. That's a given. There are going to be sacrifices. But there should also be a peace. You fit; it's just like a peacefulness, you are at home, you fit with the apostolate."

Sister Maria Benedicta had tried various jobs with the active religious order. She taught catechism. She studied nursing. "Nothing ever really fit," she says. "So that kind of added to the unsettling, the searching. It was just like He wasn't asking me to make this sacrifice. It was, like, that's not the sacrifice He was asking me to make.

"Looking back, I can see God was asking something of me that I couldn't quite put my finger on," Sister Maria Benedicta says. "I thought, 'I think I can just do more by praying.' "

It became increasingly clear to Sister Maria Benedicta that she was meant to take a path away from the Marian Sisters. She felt unsettled, thinking that God was asking something of her that she did not yet know, and so she went on a retreat and met with a priest to seek spiritual direction. She said she could not fathom leaving her community. Then she said, "I just love Saint Clare and I want to live like her." "I just threw that in there," she says. The priest asked if Sister Maria Benedicta was considering the contemplative life.

The question surprised Sister Maria Benedicta, although she says now that if someone wants to live like Saint Clare, it is likely she would choose to withdraw from the world and contemplate God in a cloister. "When he said it, it was like, 'Oh, oh,' like a light bulb."

Still, Sister Maria Benedicta struggled to reconcile her calling. She did not want to leave her close-knit community in Nebraska. "I couldn't believe it because I was so happy," she says. Plus, when she was called to the Marian Sisters, she says "it was so obvious that God was calling me there. It was tangible almost. 'This is what God wants.' Being in a community is different. You can't just go visit these Poor Clare convents whenever you want. It took me a couple of years to come to terms with it and to discover what God was showing. I prayed about it a lot; really, it has to be through prayer."

Sister Maria Benedicta learned of the Corpus Christi Monastery through a search on the Internet. She prayed for guidance from the Holy Spirit before she went online. "Oh, this is it," she thought when she read about the Rockford Poor Clares. "This is it. I can't even describe it, but I just knew. God was speaking to my heart, I guess, 'This is how I want you to love me. This is the way it should be.'" Every day for several months, she heard one of three words: Illinois, Clare, contemplative. "You can hear those words a lot, but something jabbed in my heart like, 'Are you listening? There it is. There it is.' Day after day after day after day, it was God showing me. He was asking me every time, 'Are you going to go? Are you going to wait? Are you going to serve me? Are you going to love me?' It was always, 'I should do this.'

"When God asks that of you, you kind of really make sure that's what He's really asking," Sister Maria Benedicta says. "It's a commitment and you really have to believe with all your heart that this is what God wants. It's for life—not five years down the line, 'Whoops!'" After the novitiate, the Marian Sisters renew their temporary vows every year for five years until they make final, permanent vows. "I knew I had to find out before making that commitment," she says. "I think that's a human thing, 'Are you sure, God?' I think He really did show me." Halfway through the year before she was to make final vows as a Marian Sister, before she even visited the Rockford monastery, Sister Maria Benedicta determined she would leave when her yearlong commitment ended in order to embrace the Rule of Saint Clare.

During her visit to the Corpus Christi Monastery, she heard the same Scripture reading that "flipped everything upside down" in college, when she made her first retreat with the Marian Sisters. Sister Maria Benedicta paraphrases: "Jesus said to Saint Peter, 'Put out for the deep for a catch of fish.' And then he said, 'From now on, you will be catching men, souls.' That really struck me. Put out into the deep; go out, go to where you've never experienced the deep, deep things of God. Go deeper." When she returned to Nebraska, another biblical passage, read in Mass, cut to the core of her decision. Two sisters, Martha and Mary, were friends of Jesus and hosted Him at their home. While Martha served Jesus and His disciples, Mary sat at Jesus' feet and listened. Martha complained to Jesus, "Tell her to help me," but Jesus replied, "Mary has chosen the better part and it will not be taken from her." "The better part was to sit at the feet of Jesus, to love Him, to contemplate Him, and I just knew that was what He was asking of me," Sister Maria Benedicta says.

"Yes, it was so difficult to leave my family the first time to join the convent," Sister Maria Benedicta says, "but that's what we're made to do; we're made to leave our home and our family and pursue our vocation, whether it's marriage or the religious life. But once you're in the religious life, you think, 'This is where I am.' It's difficult to leave." Sister Maria Benedicta knew that if she left the Marian Sisters, her decision would hurt her religious sisters. "When you're on the deeper and the spiritual level and you share things that are very important to you, it's very hard to break those ties," she says. The decision would also affect her family, who had grown to love the Marian Sisters when they saw how happy she was there.

Her parents insisted on traveling with Sister Maria Benedicta on her first visit to the Corpus Christi Monastery; they hoped to participate in her decision-making process. After the trip, her father was disappointed. "It seems you already made up your mind before you visited," she remembers him saying. "That was hard," Sister Maria Benedicta says, "but God had already given me that assurance, through prayer, that this was what He wanted."

Her parents tried to dissuade her, knowing that the cloistered monastery would erase any last vestige of normalcy they had managed to retain: She would never be granted another home visit; they could not hug her; she would never hold her niece again. "They didn't understand why," Sister Maria Benedicta says. "They said, 'You have so much. Why would you give it up?' I said, 'I would only give it up for one thing, and that's for God.' I told them, 'I've already given my life to God. I'm going to do what He wants. When I made my vows, that's what I meant: I give my life to God completely for whatever He wants. I had no idea He would ask that, but He did.' I said, 'I'm sorry. I've already given my life to God. He asks, I say, 'Yes' because I've already given it. He asks something else and I give it in a different way.' That was difficult for them, very, very difficult."

Other voices—of reason, skepticism, and antagonism—weighed in, unsolicited. Sister Maria Benedicta remembers feeling as if her college softball coach was grilling her: "What are you thinking? Have you lost your mind? Wasting your life? What are you doing?"

The decision-making process—refuting the outside world, a world her loved ones would remain part of—was not without temptations. At a family reunion several months before she planned to join the Poor Clares, Sister Maria Benedicta looked around at her relatives. "In my mind, it went over and over, 'Can you give this up forever?' And it was like ugh, ugh," she sighs. "I love my family. But it just kept going in my mind, 'Can you.... ?' And I was like ugh. It was like, 'I can't, but God can.' You know, God can do it because I cannot."

Another scene tested her resolve. She was completing her training to be a nurse; she felt constant pressure, always worried she was about to make a mistake. Tending to a newborn in the maternity ward, she considered a sacrifice she had not thought of before. When she first made her vows to the Marian Sisters, she says, "I was just so swept away with Jesus." Six years later, while carrying an infant to his first-time parents, Sister Maria Benedicta says, "I just saw their love, and it was like God was saying to me, 'Look what you're giving up. Will you give this up for me?' "

She says she believed she was being called, "But it's like He does require that leap of faith, too. It's not like you're 100 percent sure all the time. He does give it, but He also asks for the leap of faith, 'Do you trust me enough to do it?' It's such a hard time, particularly, because everything is bombarding you. You're giving stuff up in your heart, but you're still there. It can be hard."

Sister Maria Benedicta's college volleyball coach cried when she learned of her impending move to a cloistered contemplative order, which she thought conveyed a rare act of selflessness. "If you realize that the giving of yourself is the ultimate fulfillment, it really does strike something," Sister Maria Benedicta says. "It's really something that people see, that God is the fulfillment, but we can let everything get in the way and say, 'That's what's most important,' and forget about Him."

On April 6, 2006, the day Sister Maria Benedicta graduated from nursing school, her parents drove from Kansas for her pinning ceremony. They picked her up in Lincoln, Nebraska, and with her two sisters, drove her to Rockford, Illinois, so that she could join the Poor Clare Colettine Order.

"Now I have this wonderful family here. Now I have two wonderful religious families," Sister Maria Benedicta says. The Marian Sisters in her first religious community still write to her. "There were no hard feelings. It was beautiful how they prayed for me."

In the six years before a nun makes permanent vows as a Poor Clare, several events indicate her progress, a sequence that ends when she dons a ring during her solemn profession of final vows. At the Clothing Ceremony one year after she arrived, Sister Maria Benedicta put on a habit for the first time. Her hair was cut short. "It really struck me that I'm a new person," she says. "You turn away from the things of the world. A woman's hair, I think Saint Paul says, it's her adornment, and we just chop it off. We just offer everything. It's not important to us. We come to be holy, and so we give everything. It's really, really something—that you're just a new person." For the second time, Sister Maria Benedicta was given a new religious name.

Forty-year-old Sister Mary Nicolette, the second youngest nun in the Corpus Christi Monastery, instructs Sister Maria Benedicta as her Novice Mistress. Although there is just seven years' difference in age between the two, Sister Mary Nicolette knows that she was exposed to an America that changed radically while Sister Maria Benedicta was still experiencing it. When Sister Mary Nicolette entered the monastery in 1993, she had heard rumors of the Internet, but she had never used it, and she has never sent or received e-mail. "I have a very basic understanding of how that functions, how that works," she says. "And even, like, cell phones, most of the women who come to visit bring their cell phones with them; that's something that I never experienced." Only a few years after Sister Maria Benedicta departed popular culture, Sister Mary Nicolette thinks that elements of America might be unrecognizable to her pupil today. Sister Maria Benedicta agrees. She has heard family members discuss iPods and texting, devices and modes of communication she cannot picture. "It's changing so fast," Sister Maria Benedicta says. "I mean, we can't even keep up with it. And we do choose, thankfully, to give it up."

Sister Maria Benedicta thinks the technological upgrades, intended to save time, instead are "filling, filling, filling the time, filling the silence with noise, filling all these things with the things that really distract from what's really important." She shares an anecdote depicting the unnecessary technologies: A friend, after buying a cell phone, told Sister Maria Benedicta, "I thought a lot more people would call me!" Sister Maria Benedicta laughs. "You really don't need it! You know what I mean? It's really not a need; it's superfluous and it's not leading to God.

"The world sees freedom as, 'I can do what I want, when I want, how I want.' That's not freedom," she says. "True freedom is to give yourself to God, to be taken in by His love and His truth. I think it was Saint Augustine who said, 'Love, and do what you will.' He doesn't mean do what you want. It means if you truly love God, everything you do is for God and you're not going to do what He doesn't want you to do. The world sees freedom as doing whatever you want, but how many of those things are not what God wants, and they're not what God wants because they're not for our good? If you're in line with that, it's just a free existence. It's authentic. It kind of is a lightheartedness, an authenticity, like we don't have to worry about so many things, either about the world or about what's going on, or what others think of us, or how others see us."

The technological regression and the slower pace of the monastery agree with Sister Maria Benedicta. She associates "technology" now with the monastery's John Deere tractor, a convenience the nuns only operate to mow the yard, enabling the nuns' pursuit of union with God. "If we're able to get the mowing done more quickly, then we can go in and pray," Sister Maria Benedicta says. Rather than motoring the tractor to transport mulch for the gardens, the nuns instead push the mulch in wheelbarrows and heft it with pitchforks. "I mean, no one would think to do that, you know," Sister Maria Benedicta says. "You have a tractor sitting in the garage, and we're out there with wheelbarrows and shovels. People would think we're crazy, but the manual labor is such a good balance for our life. A lot of our day we're sitting and praying. We need exercise and work and to get our mind off things."

As the distance grows between Sister Maria Benedicta and the culture that she once identified with, the values of her adopted home have created—or perhaps revealed—fissures between Sister Maria Benedicta and her loved ones. A sports fanatic from cradle to college, Sister Maria Benedicta has lost interest in college and professional athletics, once hallmarks of her quality of life. Loved ones, meanwhile, scarcely recognize her for who she once was.

During visits, they ask, "You don't care that *this* team beat *this* team? Or that *they're* going to the Super Bowl?" "But it's like, oh!" Sister Maria Benedicta says. "There's so much more, you know what I mean? There is a huge difference in what you realize is important." She shares these impressions from the enclosure side of the parlor, where she sits with her Novice Mistress. Their sparse environment—and lack of televisions—reinforces a disregard for her former hobbies, she says. "You think about it and you're like, 'Oh, they're still doing that?' "

"What a quaint tradition!" I tease. Both laugh.

"I know!" Sister Maria Benedicta says. "They're still doing that? The world still goes on without me? Are you sure? If I'm not watching it, they're still going to put it on TV? They still have TV? I'm kidding. You realize that's still going on, but you're immersed in a higher reality, not because of anything we've done. It's not because of anything we've done. It's purely the grace of God. But the reality is, you realize what is important."

Sister Maria Benedicta recognizes her calling is contrary to the way that the rest of the world lives, and it is at times contrary to the beliefs of fellow Catholics. Just before Sister Maria Benedicta transferred from the active order of nuns to the Corpus Christi Monastery, a woman at her parents' church asked Sister Maria Benedicta about the cloister. "Girls still do that these days?" Sister Maria Benedicta says she responded, "Yes, they do! This one does."

Sister Mary Nicolette can appreciate the woman's disbelief. When she visited a cloistered monastery for the first time with two college friends, intent on a relaxing weekend holiday, Sister Mary Nicolette was awestruck; she did not realize anyone still lived like that, but she was thrilled to find a place that epitomized the life she wanted. Still, she had mixed emotions. "Is this reality?" Sister Mary Nicolette asked herself. "I must be crazy. Nobody does this anymore." "All of that floods through your head, even if God's calling you," she says. Quiet time in prayer moved her through the discernment process into acceptance.

Sister Maria Benedicta reflects on the differences between life outside and inside the monastery. "There is a retreat when you go away and you just focus on God. That's our whole life. We're not always on retreat. We have work to do, but in a sense we are separated so that we can focus our whole lives on God. If I had a job or was in the world, I wouldn't be able to think of these things. But here, it's all focused on God, and we do it all for Him. We're made body and soul, and we're called to sanctify both. So even the physical things we do—eating, sweeping the floor, everything—we bring that mystical dimension into it. God. We do it all for God. I'm not going out like the missionaries and converting the world, but I put my faith in God that everything I do, I do because it's His will. I have a set schedule, so I'm constantly doing the will of God at every moment, if I'm doing what I'm supposed to do. And He will use that obedience for something that I don't even know and that we can sanctify, even the normal bodily things. 'Lord, I'm going to eat this meal so that I have strength so that I can serve you. I'm going to sleep so that I can be awake and pray to you.' You can do even that for God. It's really amazing to think that even in the normal things, that you can experience God in every aspect."

When Sister Maria Benedicta played the hand she believed she had been dealt, and dropped out of college to become a religious sister, she says, "Everything you've ever believed in, you're giving up; or everything you've dreamed of, it's not important anymore.

"It is a sacrifice," she says. "The Church says it's such a gift—these lives that God has given grace—that these people are for God alone. It's so precious to the Church, because the prayers and the sacrifices are what keep the Church going; it's prayer. And we've chosen this and we know that these are going to be the sacrifices."

Sister Maria Benedicta says families should not wonder what they have done wrong when daughters heed the religious vocation, rather than marrying and starting their own families. She thinks families should ask, "What did we do right?" The answer, she submits, is that "we showed them God, that somehow in the family it was fostered that God is important." "It is very hard for them," she says. "When we first enter, we receive the grace of the vocation, we are in love with God, we're wrapped in Him. We have our new life, all these wonderful things that happen to us, all these experiences behind these walls. They just see the empty table, the empty chair at the dinner table, or Christmas without us. It's harder for them to see how missing a family Christmas brings you happiness, but there's more to it than that. We find our love. They find God through their love of husband and wife and family. We find our love directly to Him in the religious life. There's just that difference. And it is hard. They haven't experienced it to know it is real. It's real."

Sister Maria Benedicta prays daily for her parents. "I owe them my life," she says. "They gave me my life and they gave me, taught me God—taught me who God is. I owe them so much; and I repay them with my prayers. I think that through prayer we're a lot closer, because we're on that spiritual relationship."

As her relationship with her family settles on a spiritual plane, she notes that God relates to her differently. "Before, God was showing me these signs and what I needed," she says. "I hope now our relationship is deeper. When He called me to the Poor Clares it was more prayer and the silence of the heart. There was that growth, where He didn't have to show me 'nun' in the Bible, or all these little signs. You hope there's growth when you look back. But look how God takes you where you are. He knew what I needed when I needed it. I needed that little cross at Wal-Mart that day. Now, He might just let me receive His consolation in prayer and let that be enough. I know that that is true. I may have sufferings now, but I know He's faithful and this is for my good. Maybe it's for my purification or maybe it's so I will offer it with Him on the cross for some other souls, but I know there's a reason for it."

Once, a friend told Sister Maria Benedicta that she has it so good; her spouse is always perfect. Sister Maria Benedicta agreed: "I said, 'You're right. He can never let me down. He's all good, all loving, all powerful. He will always do what's best for me.' I said, 'You're absolutely right. But if there's ever a problem with our relationship, it's me. I can't blame it on anybody else. It's my fault.'"

Monastic life demands constant assessment and an awareness that there will always be room for improvement. Sister Maria Benedicta says, "Perseverance in the religious life isn't just, 'I will stay here until I die.' It is, 'I will strive to live perfect charity and to become holy.' That's what perseverance is; it's not just staying here and 'I made final vows, smooth sailing until I die.' Or a comfortable life. No. It is striving to perfection and to live charity and to give of yourself. That's hard. To dedicate your life to that, it's serious. It's a life commitment. I know that to not let it die—your love for God—does take work. You can't just come and live a luxurious life and grow in the love of God. It takes work, like any human relationship. If you get married, you wouldn't say on your marriage day, 'We're done.' Relationships are work. But to believe that God is really alive, He's living, He's alive and present here—it's not an abstract idea. He's personal and He's living and in the sacraments, and especially in the Eucharist, I receive Him into my body.

Those are the ways that we, with God, foster that relationship and grow. We have to continually work at prayer. We have to fight distractions. We have to fight our imagination wandering. Like any relationship, it takes work. It is a commitment. I will do this for the rest of my life."

Days before making temporary vows, Sister Maria Benedicta sits with Sister Mary Nicolette at the metal grille and attempts to express during an interview with me the significance of her impending ceremony. After a few years of observing monastic silence, albeit with more opportunities for dialogue because she has been in training in the novitiate, she verbalizes her thoughts tentatively. "God wants little me," she says. "And it's not like any...it's just really...I don't even know what to say about it. It's incredible, really."

Her Novice Mistress shares her own reflections from the same experience seventeen years prior. "I just remember the overwhelming feeling was the condescension of God—the condescension of God, that He would take a broken and fallen human creature to be His spouse," Sister Mary Nicolette says. "And like, 'Who am I?' The fact that He would do something like that was just very overwhelming and moving and overpowering."

Sister Maria Benedicta chimes in then: "When you first come, you have to get over your normal, big things. But then God shows you all the little things, and you see how much you're corrupted. You see how poor and weak you really are because the mentality in the world is, 'I can do it,' but when you're face to face with God and you see what you really are, you say, 'Does God really want this?' Humbling. But my goodness, He shows you what you are."

"He still loves you," Sister Mary Nicolette says.

"Yeah, you think, 'Is He crazy or what?' I don't know. It's hard to even describe. You see how much work there is to be done. Every bride wants to give her love something, but then you see, 'Here I am, Lord. Sorry! This is all I can give. It's everything, but boy is it little, you know what I mean? But anyway, I'm excited, but it's very humbling."

A few weeks later, on April 19, 2009, her family reunites for Sister Maria Benedicta's ceremony of profession, to watch her make temporary vows. Relatives fly in from Kansas. Members of her second family, the Marian Sisters, drive from Nebraska to Rockford. After a somber ceremony, Sister Maria Benedicta's loved ones gather on the other side of the grille, talking, laughing, crying.

Sister Maria Benedicta's purpose in life is clear: "I just have to live like Saint Clare. That's my way to God—just to live like this. He creates you for a purpose and He'll direct you there." She prays and she makes sacrifices and she asks God to deliver graces to those in need. In her hidden life in the enclosure, Sister Maria Benedicta is a silent witness to the world.

As one of the few people to whom God has broken through, Sister Maria Benedicta explains simply, "His love was so compelling I couldn't resist." "I think a lot of people have the notion this life is dying out or that girls don't do this anymore. It's very sad that people don't realize God is calling young women to the religious life, to join these religious communities." The culture beyond the monastery's premises is so loud, with radios and television and cell phones—"all these things I don't know about anymore," she says. "They can't hear God calling them anymore. God whispers in the heart; if there's no silence, they don't hear Him speak."

When passersby see the monastery or learn about the cloistered nuns, Sister Mary Nicolette hopes people pause to wonder, "Why would someone do this in our day and age?" Sister Maria Benedicta, who almost majored in Spanish so that she could become a missionary "because I wanted to go out and help people," believes she would have reached a limited number of people that way. "But here, I can reach the whole world through prayer and offering everything to God and Him using it as He wants," she says. "I don't say now, 'Only use this penance for my mom, or for my sister,' but I let Him use it as He wants and He can reach the whole world that way because He knows who needs it the most. He's not going to abandon my mother and my sister. He's going to give them graces, too, because it's united with Jesus' infinite merits.

"No one ever sees us go to pray. They don't see us because we're behind the wall, but they know we live our life just for God, that we pray, and it's to be a witness that God is worth giving everything for. God must exist if people are willing to give their whole life for this through a sustained effort. Some people give their lives for things that are not right, like the terrorists; it wasn't right. But a sustained effort—he has kept the Poor Clares going eight hundred years since Saint Clare lived. God has sustained that. It's from the grace of God. People must think there's something there that's worth it, that's worth giving up everything for. It's a sign of the world to come. We hope when people think of us, see us, or experience something of us, 'They're living for heaven,' to think, to grasp, to pull themselves out of the secular world they're living, and ask, 'Why am I living? What's important?'

That's what we hope to be a witness of. Through our prayers and sacrifices, God is going to use those to give those graces to people."

When Sister Maria Benedicta makes her final vows as a Poor Clare Colettine, she will then wear the silver ring of a solemnly professed nun. The community will have accepted her as a permanent member. And on the rare occasion that she must leave the enclosure, for an appointment or to vote, Sister Maria Benedicta will find herself a stranger in her homeland.

Sister Mary Veronica

You're a postulant for the first year, and you keep your original name at that time; at that time, you're not really a nun, you're hoping. Not until you take vows would you really be considered a nun, properly speaking. And then you become a novice when you're clothed. You become a novice, a sister, and from then on you are *Sister So-and-So*. When you take the vows—when the Church accepts you, and then you are representing the Church—it's ratification, and it's spousal at that point.

Mother Abbess chooses both parts of your name—your title and your name. Before you receive the habit, after your postulancy and you've been accepted, you present three choices, if you want, of possible names. And you might get those, or you might get one completely different. Or some people say to Mother Abbess, "Just pick."

I had had it inside me to tell her just pick, but I didn't go along with it, so I wrote down three names. It was really interesting because I said, "Holy Spirit, you're letting me know I should have trusted," because when she gave me the name, she said, "I knew what I was going to call you for months." She knew what she was going to give me before I ever gave her the names. It was actually one of the names I gave to her—Veronica. It's very interesting because Mother Abbess is very intuitive, but the Holy Spirit works through her, so we both had that name. But I should have just trusted and I think God would have given me more grace if I had.

I don't think it would make any difference in the name, but I think I would have more grace to be more faithful to interior inspirations and have more confidence—just trust God and have confidence, and be open and trust in other people, too. And the more you trust, the more you will receive from God. The more faithful you are, grace builds upon grace. And the more faithful you are to graces, the more God gives you. Saint Peter said to our Lord, "Ask me to walk on the water." His immediate reaction was that he stepped out of the boat and he was walking on the water, but then he started doubting and wondering, and he sank. Our Lord still saved him and pulled him up. But what would the graces have been if he had the faith not to look at the waves and to really trust Jesus? He could have walked all the way to Jesus on the water. Not only would he have done that physical thing, which is a miracle, how would God have blessed his faith? That is what God really wants; it's not really the outside, it's the inside, and how would He have strengthened Peter's faith?

In secular things, let's say you're learning how to do something. If you do it halfway, you're not going to make as much progress as when you put your whole effort into it, your whole heart into it. I think God works in those things, too, in the secular things. He wants to give us graces, but how much effort am I going to put into it? The measure of the effort I put into it, I will receive—I will be capable of receiving. I can't receive what I don't embrace or what I won't accept.

I think it would have given me more grace to be more faithful. I think that people lack the confidence to follow what they really believe is right. They end up doubting, like Peter, and they sink. It's not like it's anything that would hurt. And it's really a thing of trust in God. If I say, "I'll leave it to Mother Abbess to pick and I'll know it's God's will," then I should trust God. And if it doesn't come out that way, that's not what He wanted.

I would probably have more of a tendency now to say, "No, let's trust and do it," rather than doubt, doubt. I think a lot of us could do much more if we didn't doubt and waver over what we really feel inside. I think we get stopped a lot. I know I have. And I've met other people, too, that have said that kind of thing. I mean if you don't try, you'll never know! You'll never know. I don't know if a person can see that many results in themselves; maybe other people can see the results better than you can. I know if I just keep trying to be faithful, God will help me to trust more and more and more. I trust in that.

Veronica means "true image." She was the one who, when our Lord was carrying His cross, and His face was so bloody and He couldn't see from all the sweat and blood in His eyes, she was brave enough to break through the guards and she gave her veil to Him to wipe His face on. After she did this, He wiped His face and His face came onto the veil. They have, in Rome, the actual veil. I have always been fascinated by that Station of the Cross. Of course, I am to pray to and imitate Veronica—Saint Veronica and her boldness. It took a lot for her to do that, so hopefully I, too, can make reparation to our Lord and wipe His face for all the harms and all the bad things done by all of us. I do many bad things, too, but at the same time, our Lord accepts from sinners. You know, He accepts beautiful gifts from sinners. He imprinted His image on her veil for her act. And not only did He imprint His image on her veil, at the same time He imprints His image on her soul. So each time I or someone else does an act of love or reparation to our Lord, then His image gets imprinted on our soul, and then if we're doing this on behalf of not only ourselves but for everyone, then His image gets imprinted on everybody.

A novice has a white veil and traditionally, like in the old times, a white veil was for a woman who was a fiancée; she changed to a black veil when she got married. When you take your vows, you are truly becoming Christ's spouse and becoming married to Him. You are completely set aside and dedicated to Him at that time, and then you wear the black veil. There are other responsibilities that come with that, because I am supposed to live for Him and on behalf of His people, and that's supposed to be my entire life. If I'm faithful, and do well, then God will bless the world more.

It is a big responsibility. It's a very serious responsibility. And that's why it would usually take you three years before you could take your vows, and then I have three years of temporary vows. So I have at least three years of temporary vows, and then in three years I could take the solemn vows, which is permanent. That will be wonderful.

Epilogue

When I first approached the Mother Abbess with my request to engage with the community, she told me the nuns would need to pray and get back to me.

In reflecting on the contours of this project, I see that it has unfolded at a peculiar pace. That I adopted to a rate more akin to the monastery than to the fast-paced culture beyond the enclosure was key. About a year after the nuns agreed to let me work with them on this oral history and photography project, I moved a little farther away from the monastery. (Before that, I had lived an hour's drive from the Poor Clares.) There were longer lulls between my visits and phone calls. There were lulls between my visits and phone calls to the monastery, and I received more handwritten letters from the Mother Abbess, who informed me that I was welcome when I had the time. In retrospect, I believe my absence prompted the nuns' greater commitment to this project. The dynamics shifted; the Mother Abbess solicited my visits.

This was not a conscious strategy to withdraw so that they would solicit me, but I believe that it established a tenor that the community was comfortable with. A few years later, my engagement again waned. I think that this pace suited the slower pace of the monastery, and it led to greater buy-in and engagement from both parties. The project unfolded at a deliberate pace, on terms that were mutually agreeable.

Just as I choose potential subjects, they choose me. After multiple visits, Mother Miryam elaborated on the community's prayers regarding this project; they believed that God had sent me.

I rarely repeated any details conveyed to me in the one-on-one interviews in subsequent interviews with other nuns. Once, though, I asked Mother Miryam about a comment made by one of the nuns; Sister Sarah Marie said that if a young woman thinks she has a calling, she should visit the monastery to see if she belongs and if, after a couple of days, she starts to miss Wal-Mart, "well, we aren't going to keep them if they're missing Wal-Mart!"

I asked Mother Miryam about this comment and was surprised to hear strong dissent. Mother Miryam stated that she missed certain activities, including drives, when she first joined the community. Working outdoors in the monastery's gardens, she heard the traffic beyond the enclosure's wall and she wanted out; she wanted to go somewhere, anywhere. "You can miss all those things," Mother Miryam said. Until that moment, the two nuns did not know that they embraced such divergent views on Wal-Mart—of all things—or on the mega-chain's impact on a religious vocation. In the nuns' lives, they would not find occasion or opportunity to discuss philosophical differences of a cloistered calling.

In general, in keeping with their values of anonymity and hiddenness, I believe it was prudent to repeat little of what was shared during those interviews. Yet it revealed a complex perspective of the monastery's population to learn about these spectrums of opinions.

Early on, I learned that when a member of the community passes away, a biography is written of that nun's life for the monastery's records. Mother Miryam told me that it is challenging to draft a nun's biography, given that they rarely have occasion to tell one another their life stories. I told her that I would give the nuns transcripts of the interviews for their archives, as well as for the nuns to review their own interviews with the option of scheduling an additional oral history session if a nun wanted to clarify anything in her own transcript. The Mother Abbess stated the transcripts would be included in the monastery's archives and she was grateful for this exchange. I delivered heaps of transcripts in 2009 and 2010. Later, one nun gave me a scrap of paper with the correct spellings of several pronouns she had mentioned in her interview. Another handwrote six pages of clarifications on scrap paper (the blank side of a handout for a capital campaign).

In the spring of 2011, one of the aged nuns died. A World War II veteran, Sister Ann Frances had been bedridden in the infirmary for years; her health declined as her Alzheimer's disease advanced. I interviewed Sister Maria Deo Gratias, who entered the monastery at the same time as Sister Ann Frances; they went through the novitiate together, and Sister Maria Deo Gratias knew her life story better than the other members because they experienced the training, the transition into monastic silence, together. The Mother Abbess asked if I would like to make photographs of the funeral procession from the rooftop. I did. I think it was critical that I made myself available when they made these offers and suggestions and requests.

Looking back, I wish that I attended more of the events they invited me to—the ceremonies for those who were progressing from postulants to novices to making temporary vows to final vows, and the Jubilee celebrations for those who had made their vows fifty years prior. In retrospect, I think it would have been beneficial if I had been a quicker study of the liturgical calendar, and more cognizant of the impact of my requests and visits on their schedule. All of the nuns knew from experience, though, that it takes time to be socialized into a cloistered community, where communication is abbreviated and silence is observed, and they were patient and gracious. Because of their indirect style of communication, it took a while to realize that they would not ask me if they could take a break in the interviews for a glass of water. I regret that I did not think to bring water for them and that I did not ask permission from the Mother Abbess to bring a special drink for the sometimes-lengthy interviews. (When it occurred to me that although the nuns lead lives of sacrifice, they are allowed to accept donations, I brought them homemade cookies and muffins. One evening, I stopped at the monastery with a delivery of baked goods; my nephew met the Mother Abbess, who greeted us outside, at a side door.)

A few months after photographing the procession from the rooftop, I met with Sister Maria Deo Gratias and told her that I was still realizing their trust in me. I explained that when others learned of this project, I was often asked if I wanted to become a nun. Not missing a beat, Sister Maria Deo Gratias exclaimed, "You would have to become Catholic first!" I said that I had felt no such pressures from the nuns. Then I asked why the community decided to let me in. Sister Maria Deo Gratias told me what others in her community had said before—that it was a major exception. A few months later, the community held elections. Mother Miryam had served her term limit as Mother Abbess, and she needed to take a break from her position. The Vicaress, Sister Maria Deo Gratias, was elected Mother Abbess. She mailed me a card with a drawing of Saint Francis on the front. Inside, she articulated the answer to the question that so many had posed: Why did they allow me in? Mother Deo Gratias says,

You have a beautiful way of making people feel "at home" with you. Being a good listener, you are able to pick up and perceive what is being said in a true way and are not afraid to ask about what you might not understand. You have a genuine sensitivity to handle precious things shared with you in a respectful and reverent way. In interviewing you have a good way of drawing out what may be of interest for your project without doing it in a prying manner. If the person hesitates in sharing something, you are very good about leaving it go, even if you would have wished otherwise. You are so careful not to intrude—so sensitive to the situation at the time. We were so impressed with you when you came into the enclosure—our sacred space—in keeping the atmosphere of silence. In choir and in the refectory you took the pictures in such a wonderful way, wishing not to disturb what was going on in there. In all the places you had a way of going about it that did not draw attention to yourself.

Sister Maria Deo Gratias has mentioned that a true friendship formed in the aftermath of my car accident en route to the monastery in 2009. While driving on icy roads to the monastery early one foggy winter morning, I was in a head-on collision; I broke my back, sustaining a compression fracture to my vertebrae. The nuns could offer support through prayers, she told me; this was their mission.

In my first visit to the monastery several weeks after that car accident, it dawned on me the concessions the nuns had made to allow me to undertake this project. In the hallway of the cloister, Sister Sarah Marie told me the nuns were praying for me. (A young woman I knew during the six years that she considered joining this monastic community told me that she never entered the cloistered monastery until the day she became a postulant.) "I know," I told Sister Sarah Marie. "You're wonderful. Thank you." I repeated what I had told a friend: If I'm going to be in an accident, I'm glad it happened en route to the monastery because the nuns would suspect something amiss, and pray. Or, I told Sister Sarah Marie, maybe you just assumed I was running late, as usual. Sister Sarah Marie smiled, tears in her eyes. She told me that the morning of my accident she had prayed to the Archangel Raphael, patron of travelers. She said that she always prayed to the Archangel Raphael when she knew I was traveling. In fact, she said, she and the other nuns prayed for me every day since my first visit to the monastery. I was stunned.

Mother Miryam found me in the hall a moment later. She underwent knee replacement surgery the same day as my car accident; she phoned me several times from her hospital room as we both recuperated. Mother Miryam told me by phone that she was eager to start physical therapy, eager to progress, eager to return to the monastery, eager to see the community's cat, which she admitted she spoiled. She shared all this, and then she told me we would learn patience together as we contended with our limitations.

In the monastery that day, the Mother Abbess and I walked slowly down the dark corridor together. If she noticed my tears, she did not mention them. "Two cripples," she said. We laughed.

Acknowledgments

At times as I have worked on this project, my life has begun to mirror aspects of the cloistered nuns' lives. I appreciate silence, find myself withdrawing from aspects of popular culture, and realize that I have adopted the nuns' dedication and devotion.

A constellation of individuals—mentors, friends, and family—and organizations have been instrumental in the development of this work as I ride these phases of retreat and engagement with the outside world.

I am incredibly grateful to Steve Rowland, who not only is technically astute but also has an empathetic spirit that is a source of inspiration and guidance. He values the nuns' ideals. I trust his counsel.

Peter Maguire availed himself to inquiries throughout the process of interviews, writing, and the book contract. His input was precise and substantial.

Anthony Bannon enabled me to articulate my vision for the images and to refine my photographic approach.

In the early stages of the manuscript, Carlee Tressel Alson was reliable and tenacious; her gracious feedback improved the work and her friendship is invaluable.

Friar Benet Fonck OFM and Sister Joan Mueller, both authors with busy schedules, made time to explain the intricacies of the Franciscan lineage and the Poor Clare Colettine order, Mueller having entered the Rockford Poor Clares' Corpus Christi Monastery and experienced cloistered monastic life.

I am very thankful for all project support, including from the Illinois Arts Council, the Foundation for Contemporary Arts, the Puffin Foundation, and SHURE, Inc.

Anna Belle Nimmo has been like a fairy godmother.

After the car accident en route to the monastery, a number of foundations that assist visual artists and writers intervened, creating a very welcome safety net.

Months after that accident, the women I met on a writers' retreat at Ghost Ranch became my lovely and supportive community.

With the manuscript complete, Cynthia Read rallied forces. Donald A. Ritchie opened doors. And Nancy Toff blazed the final trail to bring this book into being, moving the manuscript from acceptance through production, and correcting, with mild amusement, my penchant for malapropisms.

It seems now that a clear line can be drawn between this book and my high school teacher, Pat Toth, who fed my interest in writing and other cultures, supplying me with reading material such as folklore from around the world.

Throughout adolescence, my sister Fairlight was like a highly specialized film librarian; she screened—and sometimes even let me join her in viewing—Jean-Claude Van Damme flicks, musicals, and classics. *The Nun's Story*, with Audrey Hepburn, made a lasting impact on me, and probably ignited my desire to understand the religious vocation and the women who heed that calling. Fairlight's perspective helped shape the way I processed and produced this book.

I have also been aided by the expertise of Eric J. Palmer; the generosity of my newest sister, Angela Angelovska Wilson; and the presence of Julie Swanson, Kimberly Lamm, Laura Turner, Megan Coleman, Alicia Eisenbise, and Clare Rosean.

My parents introduced me to religion—sharing their childhood encounters with Judaism and Catholicism, and the Protestant faith they chose to embrace. Because of them, I learned moxie and humility, qualities integral to my approach to ethnography, art, and life.

I am especially appreciative of my two creative younger brothers, Isaac and Aaron, for their unrelenting assistance and support.

Finally, this ongoing eight-year endeavor is only possible because the Poor Clare Colettine nuns in Rockford, Illinois, allowed me to enter their world on occasion. Because of them I have been "changed for good" and "for the better."

Appendix: Interviewees

The nuns selected pseudonyms to be used in place of their actual religious names. The nuns also chose pseudonyms for their childhood names, which are used instead of their actual birth names.

Interview Date	Religious Pseudonym	Childhood Pseudonym
March 18, 2005	Mother Miryam	Catherine
August 25, 2005	Mother Miryam	Catherine
September 15, 2005	Sister Mary Clara	Klarka
September 15, 2005	Sister Mary Joseph	Josephine
September 15, 2005	Sister Sarah Marie	Tiffany
September 18, 2005	Sisters Mary Nicolette	Monica
	Maria Benedicta	Maria
September 18, 2005	Sister Mary Monica	Mary
October 29, 2005	Mother Miryam	Catherine
July 25, 2008	Sister Mary Joseph	Josephine
November 14, 2008	Mother Miryam	Catherine
November 14, 2008	Sister Maria Deo Gratias	Clare
November 14, 2008	Sister Mary Michael	Jenny
November 29, 2008	Sister Mary Gemma	Teresa
December 5, 2008	Sister Mary Gemma	Teresa
January 2, 2009	Mother Miryam	Catherine
February 6, 2009	Sister Joan Marie	Virginia
February 19, 2009	Sister Joan Marie	Virginia
February 19, 2009	Sister Sarah Marie	Tiffany
February 25, 2009	Sister Maria Deo Gratias	Clare
April 1, 2009	Sisters Mary Nicolette	Monica
	Maria Benedicta	Maria
August 4, 2009	Sister Maria Benedicta	Maria
August 4, 2009	Sister Mary Nicolette	Monica

(Continued)

Continued

Interview Date	Religious Pseudonym	Childhood Pseudonym
	Mother Miryam	Catherine
September 24, 2009	Mother Miryam	Catherine
September 24, 2009	Sister Ann Marie	Lisa
September 24, 2009	Sister Mary Michael	Jenny
December 16, 2009	Sister Ann Marie	Lisa
January 26, 2010	Mother Miryam	Catherine
January 26, 2010	Sisters Mary Nicolette	Monica
	Maria Benedicta	Maria
March 12, 2011	Mother Miryam	Catherine
March 21, 2011	Funeral for Sister Ann Frances	
April 5, 2011	Mother Miryam	Catherine
May 26, 2011	Sister Maria Deo Gratias, on the life of Sister Ann Frances	
July 30, 2011	Mother Miryam	Catherine

Notes

Preface

1. Michael Frisch, *A Shared Authority: Essays on the Craft and Meaning of Oral and Public History* (Albany: State University of New York Press, 1990).

2. "Displacement and Community," Oral History in the Mid-Atlantic Region annual conference, April 20, 2011.

3. Antjie Krog, *Country of My Skull: Guilt, Sorrow, and the Limits of Forgiveness in the New South Africa* (New York: Three Rivers Press, 1998), 64.

Introduction

1. *Verbi Sponsa: Instruction on the Contemplative Life and on the Enclosure of the Nun* (Libreria Editrice Vaticana, Vatican City, Congregation for Institutes of Consecrated Life and for Societies of Apostolic Life; May 13, 1999), 13.

2. *Post-Synodal Apostolic Exhortation Vita Consecrata of the Holy Father John Paul II to the Bishops and Clergy Religious Orders and Congregations Societies of Apostolic Life Secular Institutes and All the Faithful on the Consecrated Life and its Mission in the Church and in the World*, Rome, March 25, 1996, http://www.vatican.va/holy_father/john_paul_ii/apost_exhortations/documents/hf_jp-ii_exh_25031996_vita-consecrata_en.html.

3. *Verbi Sponsa*, 10.

4. Ibid., 27.

5. Pope Benedict XVI, *Biographical Sketch of St. Clare of Assisi*, September 15, 2010, http://www.vatican.va/holy_father/benedict_xvi/audiences/2010/documents/hf_ben-xvi_aud_20100915_en.html.

6. Ibid.

7. Colettine Poor Clare Nuns, *Golden Jubilee: 1916–1966* (Rockford, Ill.: Corpus Christi Monastery, June 29, 1966), 6.

8. Ibid., 5.

9. Ibid., 10.

10. *Come Follow Me*, a brochure written and published by the Poor Clare Colettine nuns at the Corpus Christi Monastery.

11. Ibid.

12. Friar Benet Fonck, e-mail message to author, September 3, 2011.

13. Ibid.

14. "Frequently Requested Church Statistics," Center for Applied Research in the Apostolate, a Georgetown University affiliated national not-for-profit research center on Catholic data, Catholic statistics, and Catholic research, accessed on June 19, 2013, http://cara.georgetown.edu/CARAServices/requestedchurchstats.html.

Chapter 3

1. Editors Regis J. Armstrong, J. A. Wayne Hellmann, and William J. Short. *Francis of Assisi—The Saint: Early Documents, Volume 1*. New York: New City Press, 1999. Page 103.

2. Bullarium Franciscanum I:771. Translation in Joan Mueller. *Clare's Letters to Agnes: Texts and Sources*. St. Bonaventure, NY: The Franciscan Institute, 2001. Page 208. Also, Joan Mueller, e-mail message to author, July 31, 2013.

Chapter 5

1. Poor Clare Colettine Nuns, *Golden Jubilee: 1916–1966* (Rockford, Ill.: Corpus Christi Monastery, June 29, 1966), 25.

Chapter 7

1. *Verbi Sponsa: Instruction on the Contemplative Life and the Enclosure of the Nun* (Libreria Editrice Vaticana, Vatican City, Congregation for Institutes of Consecrated Life and for Societies of Apostolic Life, May 13, 1999).

Further Reading

Fonck, Benet A. *To Cling With All Her Heart to Him: The Spirituality of St. Clare of Assisi.* Cincinnati, OH: St. Anthony Messenger Press, 1996.

Fonck, Benet A. *Ritual of the Secular Franciscan Order.* Cincinnati, OH: St. Anthony Messenger Press, 1995.

Fonck, Benet A. *Called to Make Present the Charism: Ongoing Formation for Secular Franciscans Based on the Footnotes of the Sfo Rule.* Cincinnati, OH: St. Anthony Messenger Press, 2001.

Fonck, Benet A. *Called to Build a More Fraternal and Evangelical World: Commentary on the Rule of the Secular Franciscan Order.* Cincinnati, OH: St. Anthony Messenger Press, 2002.

Mueller, Joan. *Clare of Assisi: The Letters to Agnes.* Collegeville, MN: Liturgical Press, 2003.

Mueller, Joan. *Clare's Letters to Agnes: Texts and Sources (Clare resources series).* St. Bonaventure, NY: Franciscan Institute Publications, 2012.

Mueller, Joan. *The Privilege of Poverty: Clare of Assisi, Agnes of Prague, and the Struggle for a Franciscan Rule for Women.* Philadelphia: Pennsylvania State University Press, 2008.

Norris, Kathleen. *The Cloister Walk.* New York: Riverhead Books, 1997.

Rogers, Carole Garibaldi. *Habits of Change: An Oral History of American Nuns.* New York: Oxford University Press, 2011.

Index

THE OXFORD ORAL HISTORY SERIES

J. Todd Moye (University of North Texas)
Kathryn Nasstrom (University of San Francisco)
Robert Perks (The British Library Sound Archive)
Series Editors

Donald A. Ritchie
Senior Advisor

Doing Oral History, Second Edition *Donald A. Ritchie*

Approaching an Auschwitz Survivor: Holocaust Testimony and Its
  Transformations *Edited by Jürgen Matthäus*

A Guide to Oral History and the Law *John A. Neuenschwander*

Singing Out: An Oral History of America's Folk Music Revivals *David
  K. Dunaway and Molly Beer*

Freedom Flyers: The Tuskegee Airmen of World War II *J. Todd Moye*

Launching the War on Poverty: An Oral History, Second Edition *Michael L.
  Gillette*

The Firm: The Inside Story of the Stasi *Gary Bruce*

The Wonder of Their Voices: The 1946 Holocaust Interviews of David
  Boder *Alan Rosen*

They Say in Harlan County: An Oral History *Alessandro Portelli*

The Oxford Handbook of Oral History *Edited by Donald A. Ritchie*

Habits of Change: An Oral History of American Nuns *Carole Garibaldi Rogers*

Soviet Baby Boomers: An Oral History of Russia's Cold War
  Generation *Donald J. Raleigh*

Bodies of Evidence: The Practice of Queer Oral History *Edited by Nan Alamilla
  Boyd and Horacio N. Roque Ramírez*

Lady Bird Johnson: An Oral History *Michael L. Gillette*